First World War
and Army of Occupation
War Diary
France, Belgium and Germany

5 DIVISION
14 Infantry Brigade
Devonshire Regiment 1st Battalion
and Cheshire Regiment 5th (Reserve) Battalion
21 August 1914 - 31 December 1915

WO95/1565

The Naval & Military Press Ltd
www.nmarchive.com
Published in association with The National Archives

Published by

The Naval & Military Press Ltd

Unit 10 Ridgewood Industrial Park,

Uckfield, East Sussex,

TN22 5QE England

Tel: +44 (0) 1825 749494

www.naval-military-press.com

www.nmarchive.com

This diary has been reprinted in facsimile from the original. Any imperfections are inevitably reproduced and the quality may fall short of modern type and cartographic standards.

© Crown Copyright
Images reproduced by permission of The National Archives, London, England, 2015.

Contents

Document type	Place/Title	Date From	Date To
Heading	14 Infantry Brigade. 1 Bn Devonshire Regt. 1914 Aug To 1915 Dec. 5 Bn Ceshire Regiment. 1915 Feb To 1915 Dec.		
Heading	WO95/1565/1		
Heading	WO95/1565-1 5th Division 14th Infantry Bde 1st Devon. Regt 1914-Aug-1915 June		
Heading	8th Brigade. 3rd Division. Battalion disembarked Havre 21.8.14 1st Battalion The Devonshire Regiment August 1914		
War Diary	Jersey	21/08/1914	21/08/1914
War Diary	Havre	22/08/1914	24/08/1914
War Diary	Amiens	25/08/1914	27/08/1914
War Diary	Rouen	28/08/1914	31/08/1914
Miscellaneous	Instructions for The Inspector-General of Communications. Appendix K 10.		
Miscellaneous	Contents		
Miscellaneous	Instructions for The Inspector-General of Communications		
Miscellaneous	Part II-Preliminary and General		
Miscellaneous	Part III-Embarkation and Disembarkation		
Miscellaneous	Part IV-Movement To The area of Concentration, Detrainment and Billeting		
Miscellaneous	Part V-Organization of The line of Communications		
Heading	8th Brigade. 3rd Division. 1st Battalion The Devonshire Regiment September 1914		
War Diary		01/09/1914	30/09/1914
Heading	14th Brigade. 5th Division. 1st Battalion The Devonshire Regiment October 1914.		
War Diary		01/10/1914	30/10/1914
Heading	14th Brigade. 5th Division. 1st Battalion Devonshire Regiment November 1914		
War Diary	Festubert	01/11/1914	01/11/1914
War Diary	Lestrem	02/11/1914	03/11/1914
War Diary	Vieille Chapelle	04/11/1914	04/11/1914
War Diary	La Couture	05/11/1914	05/11/1914
War Diary	Vieille Chapelle	06/11/1914	06/11/1914
War Diary	Chapigny	07/11/1914	14/11/1914
War Diary	Estaires	15/11/1914	15/11/1914
War Diary	Meteren	16/11/1914	16/11/1914
War Diary	Wulverghem	17/11/1914	28/11/1914
War Diary	St. Jans Cappel	29/11/1914	30/11/1914
Heading	14th Brigade. 5th Division. 1st Battalion The Devonshire Regiment December 1914		
War Diary	St. Jans Cappel	01/12/1914	04/12/1914
War Diary	Wulverghem	05/12/1914	10/12/1914
War Diary	Neuve Eglise	11/12/1914	17/12/1914
War Diary	St. Jans Cappel	18/12/1914	23/12/1914
War Diary	Wulverghem	24/12/1914	29/12/1914
War Diary	Dranoutre	30/12/1914	31/12/1914
Heading	14th Bde. 5th Div. 1st Devonshire Regt. January 1915		

War Diary	Dranoutre	01/01/1915	04/01/1915
War Diary	Bailleul	05/01/1915	10/01/1915
War Diary	Wulverghem	11/01/1915	16/01/1915
War Diary	Neuve Eglise	17/01/1915	23/01/1915
War Diary	Wulverghem	24/01/1915	26/01/1915
War Diary	Neuve Eglise	24/01/1915	31/01/1915
Heading	14th Bde. 5th Div. 1st Devonshire Regt. February 1915		
War Diary	Neuve Eglise	01/02/1915	04/02/1915
War Diary	Wulverghem	05/02/1915	07/02/1915
War Diary	Neuve Eglise	08/02/1915	11/02/1915
War Diary	Wulverghem	12/02/1915	15/02/1915
War Diary	Neuve Eglise	16/02/1915	19/02/1915
War Diary	Wulverghem	20/02/1915	23/02/1915
War Diary	Neuve Eglise	24/02/1915	27/02/1915
War Diary	Wulverghem	28/02/1915	28/02/1915
Heading	14th Bde. 5th Div. 1st Devonshire Regt. March 1915		
War Diary	Wulverghem	01/03/1915	03/03/1915
War Diary	Neuve Eglise	04/03/1915	07/03/1915
War Diary	Wulverghem	08/03/1915	11/03/1915
War Diary	Neuve Eglise	12/03/1915	15/03/1915
War Diary	Wulverghem	16/03/1915	19/03/1915
War Diary	Neuve Eglise	20/03/1915	23/03/1915
War Diary	Kemmel	24/03/1915	27/03/1915
War Diary	Locre	28/03/1915	31/03/1915
Heading	14th Bde. 5th Div. 1st Devonshire Regt. April 1915		
War Diary	Locre	01/08/1915	01/08/1915
War Diary	Kemmel	02/04/1915	03/04/1915
War Diary	Locre	04/04/1915	04/04/1915
War Diary	St. Hubertushoek	05/04/1915	07/04/1915
War Diary	Kruisstraat	08/04/1915	10/04/1915
War Diary	Oosthoek	11/04/1915	15/04/1915
War Diary	Kruisstraat	16/04/1915	20/04/1915
War Diary	Zillebeke	21/04/1915	30/04/1915
Heading	14th Bde. 5th Div. 1st Devonshire Regt. May 1915		
War Diary	Zillebeke	01/05/1915	04/05/1915
War Diary	Groenen Jaun Nr Kruisstraat	05/05/1915	06/05/1915
War Diary	Groenen Jaun	07/05/1915	10/05/1915
War Diary	Oosthoek	11/05/1915	31/05/1915
Heading	14th Bde. 5th Div. 1st Devonshire Regt. June 1915		
War Diary	Oosthoek	01/06/1915	01/06/1915
War Diary	Groenen Jaun	02/06/1915	16/06/1915
War Diary	Oosthoek	17/06/1915	30/06/1915
Heading	WO95/1565-2 5th Division 14th Infantry Bde. 1st Devon Regt. July To December 1915 (To 95 Bde 5 Div)		
Heading	14th Bde. 5th Div. 1st Devonshire Regt. July 1915		
War Diary	Oosthoek	01/07/1915	01/07/1915
War Diary	Groenen Jaun	02/07/1915	07/07/1915
War Diary	Oosthoek	08/07/1915	17/07/1915
War Diary	Groenen Jaun Nr Dickebusch	18/07/1915	23/07/1915
War Diary	Boeschepe	24/07/1915	25/07/1915
War Diary	Godewaersvelde	26/07/1915	31/07/1915
Heading	14th Bde. 5th Div. 1st Devonshire Regiment August 1915		
War Diary	Daours	01/08/1915	04/08/1915
War Diary	Dernancourt	05/08/1915	07/08/1915

War Diary	Bray Sur Somme	08/08/1915	08/08/1915
War Diary	Maricourt	09/08/1915	31/08/1915
Heading	14th Bde. 5th Div. 1st Devonshire Regiment September 1915		
War Diary	Maricourt	01/09/1915	01/09/1915
War Diary	Sailly Lorette	02/09/1915	09/09/1915
War Diary	Suzanne	10/09/1915	10/09/1915
War Diary	Maricourt	11/09/1915	23/09/1915
War Diary	Suzanne	24/09/1915	30/09/1915
Heading	14th Bde. 5th Div. 1st Devonshire Regiment October 1915		
War Diary	Suzanne	01/10/1915	08/10/1915
War Diary	Maricourt	09/10/1915	31/10/1915
Heading	14th Bde. 5th Div. 1st Devonshire Regiment November 1915		
War Diary	Maricourt	01/11/1915	04/11/1915
War Diary	Suzanne	05/11/1915	13/11/1915
War Diary	Maricourt	14/11/1915	30/11/1915
Miscellaneous	1st Devon. Regiment Intelligence Report	01/11/1915	01/11/1915
Miscellaneous	1st Devon. Regiment Intelligence Report	02/11/1915	02/11/1915
Miscellaneous	1st Devon. Regiment Intelligence Report	03/11/1915	03/11/1915
Miscellaneous	1st Devon. Regiment Intelligence Officers Report	04/11/1915	04/11/1915
Miscellaneous	Intelligence Report 1st Devon Regt.	15/11/1915	15/11/1915
Miscellaneous	1st Devon. Regiment Intelligence Report	16/11/1915	16/11/1915
Miscellaneous	Intelligence Report 1st Devon.	17/11/1915	17/11/1915
Miscellaneous	Intelligence Report 1st Devon.	18/11/1915	18/11/1915
Miscellaneous	Intelligence Report 1st Devon.	19/11/1915	19/11/1915
Miscellaneous	Intelligence Report 1/Devon.	20/11/1915	20/11/1915
Miscellaneous	Intelligence Report 1st Devon	21/11/1915	21/11/1915
Miscellaneous	Intelligence Report 1/Devon	22/11/1915	22/11/1915
Miscellaneous	Intelligence Report 1st Devon	23/11/1915	23/11/1915
Miscellaneous	Intelligence Report 1 Devon	24/11/1915	24/11/1915
Miscellaneous	Intelligence Report 1/Devon Regt	25/11/1915	25/11/1915
Miscellaneous	Intelligence Report 1st Devon.	26/11/1915	26/11/1915
Miscellaneous	Intelligence Report 1st Devon.	27/11/1915	27/11/1915
Miscellaneous	Intelligence Report 1st Devon	28/11/1915	28/11/1915
Miscellaneous	Intelligence Report 1/Devon.	29/11/1915	29/11/1915
Miscellaneous	Intelligence Report 1/Devon.	30/11/1915	30/11/1915
Heading	14th Bde. 5th Div. 1st Devonshire Regiment December 1915		
War Diary	Maricourt	01/12/1915	12/12/1915
War Diary	Suzanne	13/12/1915	14/12/1915
War Diary	Maricourt	15/12/1915	20/12/1915
War Diary	Suzanne	21/12/1915	24/12/1915
War Diary	Maricourt	25/12/1915	30/12/1915
War Diary	Suzanne	31/12/1915	31/12/1915
Heading	WO95/1565/2		
Heading	WO95/1565-3 Pt III 5th Division 14th Bde. 5th Cheshires From UK 1915 Feb-1915 Dec. To 56 Div Troops (Pioneers)		
Heading	14th Bde. 5th Division. Joined=14th Bde on 19th February 1915 from Army Troops. 5th Cheshires. February 1915		
War Diary	Cambridge	14/02/1915	14/02/1915
War Diary	Southampton	14/02/1915	14/02/1915
War Diary	Havre	15/02/1915	17/02/1915

War Diary	Bailleul	18/02/1915	19/02/1915
War Diary	Neuve Eglise	21/02/1915	05/03/1915
Heading	5th Cheshires March 1915		
War Diary	Neuve Eglise	06/03/1915	20/03/1915
War Diary	Kemmel	23/03/1915	23/03/1915
War Diary	Locre	24/03/1915	24/03/1915
War Diary	Kemmel	24/03/1915	01/04/1915
Miscellaneous	A Form. Messages And Signals.		
Miscellaneous	To The Adjutant 5th Cheshire Regt.	31/03/1915	31/03/1915
Heading	April 1 & 2		
Heading	14th Bde. 5th Division. 5th Cheshires April 1915		
War Diary	Kemmel	03/04/1915	05/04/1915
War Diary	Dickebusch	07/04/1915	07/04/1915
War Diary	Ypres	08/04/1915	22/04/1915
War Diary	Kruisstraat	23/04/1915	27/04/1915
War Diary	Kruisstraat near Ypres	28/04/1915	30/04/1915
Heading	14th Bde. 5th Division. 5th Cheshires May 1915		
War Diary	Ypres	01/05/1915	23/05/1915
War Diary	Boeschepe	24/05/1915	31/05/1915
Heading	14th Bde. 5th Division. 5th Cheshires June 1915		
War Diary	Ypres	01/06/1915	28/06/1915
Heading	14th Bde. 5th Division. 5th Cheshires July 1915		
War Diary	Ypres	01/07/1915	24/07/1915
War Diary	Reninghelst	25/07/1915	25/07/1915
War Diary	Eecke	26/07/1915	28/07/1915
Heading	14th Bde. 5th Division. 5th Cheshires August 1915		
War Diary	Daours	04/08/1915	04/08/1915
War Diary	Treux	05/08/1915	08/08/1915
War Diary	Suzanne	09/08/1915	29/08/1915
War Diary	Suzanne-Vaux	30/08/1915	30/08/1915
War Diary	Vaux	31/08/1915	31/08/1915
Heading	14th Bde. 5th Division. 5th Cheshires September 1915		
War Diary	Suzanne	02/09/1915	03/09/1915
War Diary	Trenches	09/09/1915	30/09/1915
Heading	14th Bde. 5th Div. 5th Cheshires October 1915		
War Diary	Maricourt	01/10/1915	29/10/1915
Heading	14th Bde. 5th Div. 5th Cheshires November 1915		
War Diary	Maricourt	01/11/1915	13/11/1915
War Diary	Suzanne	15/11/1915	18/11/1915
War Diary	Vaux	20/11/1915	29/11/1915
War Diary	Bray	30/11/1915	30/11/1915
Heading	5/Cheshires Intell Report Nov 1915		
War Diary	Vaux	17/11/1915	18/11/1915
War Diary	Vaux	17/11/1915	27/11/1915
Heading	5th Div. Pioneers. 5th Cheshires December 1915		
War Diary	Bray	03/12/1915	31/12/1915

14 INFANTRY BRIGADE.

1 BN DEVONSHIRE REGT.

1914 AUG TO 1915 DEC.

5 BN CESHIRE REGIMENT.

1915 FEB TO 1915 DEC.

1565

14 INFANTRY BRIGADE.

1 BN DEVONSHIRE REGT.

1914 AUG TO 1915 DEC.

5 BN CESHIRE REGIMENT.

1915 FEB TO 1915 DEC.

1565

WO 95/15651

WO 95/1565

5th Division

14th Infantry Bde.

1st Devon Regt.

1914 - AUG - 1915 JUNE

8th Brigade.

3rd Division.

Battalion disembarked HAVRE 21.8.14.

1st BATTALION

THE DEVONSHIRE REGIMENT

AUGUST 1 9 1 4

Army Form C. 2118.

WAR DIARY
or
INTELLIGENCE SUMMARY

(Erase heading not required.)

1/4 Br. Boorshire Regiment

1914

Hour, Date, Place	Summary of Events and Information	Remarks and References to Appendices
11 a.m. 21st August 6/14 Jersey.	The Battalion left Jersey immobilized and arrived at Havre at about 11 p.m. Strength 21 Officers, 446 other ranks, including 5 R.A.M.C. and 1 A.O.C. attached. The Battalion disembarked and spent the night in the Hangar aux Cotons.	...
4.30 a.m. 22nd August Havre.	The Battalion marched to no 1 Rest Camp, where 56 g Army Reservists, with 5 Officers and 10 other serving soldiers joined the Battalion from there. 2 Officers and 54 other ranks joining with mobilization equipment etc from Honfleur. at 2.30 p.m. D Company, under Major C.C.M.Maynard, D.I.O., strength 5 officers and 221 other ranks proceeded by train to BUSIGNY.	...
23rd August HAVRE	The Battalion remained in Camp.	...
24th August HAVRE	Headquarters, the Machine gun Section & B Company proceeded by train to AMIENS, strength 12 Officers and 338 other ranks; the above were billeted on arrival.	...

Army Form C. 2118.

WAR DIARY
or
INTELLIGENCE SUMMARY.
(Erase heading not required.)

1st Devonshire Regt

1914

Hour, Date, Place	Summary of Events and Information	Remarks and references to Appendices
24th Aug. HAVRE	½ of "C" Company, 3 officers 116 other ranks, proceeded by train to BOULOGNE. ½ of "C" Company, 2 officers, 111 other ranks, proceeded by train to ROUEN. A Company, 5 officers 221 other ranks, remained at HAVRE, together with 1 officer and 63 other ranks, being details left at the base.	
25th August AMIENS	In billets at AMIENS, battalion employed on various L of C duties.	
26th August AMIENS	as above	
27th August AMIENS	H.Q., M.G. section and B Company, 11 officers 337 other ranks, proceeded by train to ROUEN and billeted there, meeting there ½ Coy of "C" Coy.	
28th August AMIENS ROUEN	On arrival in billets at ROUEN, battalion employed on various L of C duties.	
29th August ROUEN	2 officers and 106 other ranks, proceeded to rear advanced base at LE MANS by steamer	LEMANS
30th August ROUEN	1 officer and 50 other ranks of B Coy proceeded to by steamship. PLOUSSA via S. NAZAIRE	

Army Form C. 2118.

WAR DIARY
or
INTELLIGENCE SUMMARY
(Erase heading not required.)

1st Devonshire Regiment

1914

Instructions regarding War Diaries and Intelligence Summaries are contained in F. S. Regs., Part II. and the Staff Manual respectively. Title pages will be prepared in manuscript.

Hour, Date, Place	Summary of Events and Information	Remarks and references to Appendices
31st August. ROUEN.	H.Q., B Coy, & M.G. Section embarked transport, horses & baggage on S.S. TEVIOT at about 8.30 p.m.	—

C.W.W. Corlein Lt Col
Cmdg. 1st Devonshire Regt.

> **SECRET.**
>
> **THIS DOCUMENT IS THE PROPERTY OF H.B.M. GOVERNMENT** and is intended only for the personal information of _____
>
> and of those Officers under him whose duties it affects. He is personally responsible for its safe custody, and that its contents are disclosed to those Officers and to them only.

APPENDIX K 10.

INSTRUCTIONS

FOR THE

INSPECTOR-GENERAL OF COMMUNICATIONS.

This gives the date July 1914.

[A 1770]   (B173) 110 7/14 H&S 817wo

SECRET.

APPENDIX K 10.

INSTRUCTIONS

FOR THE

INSPECTOR-GENERAL OF COMMUNICATIONS.

[A 1770]

(B173) 110 7/14 H&S 817wo

CONTENTS.

	PARA.
PART I.—MOBILIZATION—	
Time and place of reporting	1—5
PART II.—PRELIMINARY AND GENERAL—	
Co-operation with the French	1, 2
Object of arrangements made	3
Lines of Communication units	4
Station of the I.G.C.	5
Channels of communication with French railways	6
Headquarters of administrative services	7
PART III.—EMBARKATION AND DISEMBARKATION—	
Naval staffs	1—13
Base commandant	14
Military landing officer	15
Commission de Port	16, 17
General control of the movement	18
Ports of embarkation	19
Approximate dates of departure of troops, &c.	20
Disembarkation	21
Disembarkation Tables	21A
Approximate dates of arrival of troops, &c.	22
Capacity of the ports	23—26
Military factors affecting disembarkation	27
Rest camps	28
Stores	29
Mechanical transport	30
Portable derricks, slings and petrol	31—33
Pilots, tugs, stevedores, &c.	34—36
Frozen meat vessels	37
Telegrams	38—41
Progress reports	42
Return of transports to United Kingdom	43, 44
Codes, postal, cash arrangements	45—48
PART IV.—MOVEMENT TO THE AREA OF CONCENTRATION, DETRAINMENT AND BILLETING—	
General	1, 2
Concentration movement by rail	3—5
"Commission régulatrice de débarquement"	6
Control of billeting arrangements	7
British officers at detraining stations	8
French officers for duty	9
Detrainment at the advanced base	10
Details of detraining duties	11, 12
Concentration movement by road	13
Temporary landings for aircraft	14
Supply	15
Interpreters	16
	SUB-SECTION.
PART V.—ORGANIZATION OF THE LINES OF COMMUNICATION—	
General	1
Director of Army Signals	2
Director of Supplies	3
Director of Ordnance	4
Director of Transport	5
Director of Railway Transport	6
Director of Works	7
Director of Remounts	8
Director of Veterinary Services	9
Director of Medical Services	10
Finance, Account and Pay Services	11
Postal Services	12
Censorship	13

NOTE.—The following abbreviations have been used—

Inspector-General of Communications	I.G.C.
Base Commandant	B.C.
Military Landing Officer	M.L.O.
Principal Naval Transport Officer	P.N.T.O.
Divisional Naval Transport Officer	D.N.T.O.
Gare régulatrice	G.R.
Gare régulatrice de débarquement	G.R.D.

I. 1

INSTRUCTIONS FOR THE INSPECTOR-GENERAL OF COMMUNICATIONS.

Owing to the conditions governing the scheme of operations it has not been possible to acquaint officers during peace time with the details of their duties. These instructions have accordingly been drawn up in greater detail than would otherwise have been necessary.

PART I.—MOBILIZATION.

1. If not previously summoned to attend, the following officers concerned with Line of Communication duties will report at the War Office, not later than noon on the first day of mobilization, to receive their instructions:—

(a.) Headquarters of Inspector-General of Communications.

The Inspector-General of Communications with Aides-de-Camp and General Staff Officers, 1st, 2nd and 3rd Grade, cipher officers, and the Principal Naval Transport Officer report to Director of Military Operations
- London accommodation—Hotel Metropole, Northumberland Avenue.
- Mobilizing office—Dolphin Hotel, Southampton.

(b.) Headquarters, Line of Communication Defences.

Commander and Aide-de-Camp, General Staff Officer, 2nd Grade, report to M.O. 1
- London accommodation—Hotel Metropole.
- Mobilizing office—Flower's Hotel, Queen's Park, Southampton.

(c.) Headquarters of Bases.

Each Base Commandant, and the Divisional Naval Transport Officer for each Base, report to M.O. 1
- Mobilizing offices—
  - Headquarters, No. 1 Base—Crown Hotel, High Street, Southampton.
  - Headquarters, No. 2 Base—Crown Hotel, High Street, Southampton.
  - Headquarters, No. 3 Base—Star Hotel, High Street, Southampton.

(d.) Headquarters of Advanced Base.

Commandant reports to M.O. 1 — Mobilizing office—Flower's Hotel, Queen's Park, Southampton.

(e.) Headquarters of Administrative Services and Departments.

Place of mobilization and office in each case—Kensington Palace Hotel.

Director of Army Signals reports to	M.O. 1.
Director of Supplies reports to	D.S.Q.
Director of Ordnance Services reports to	D.E.O.S.
Director of Transport reports to	D.T.M.
Director of Works reports to	D.F.W.
Director of Remounts reports to	D.R.
Director of Veterinary Services reports to	D.G.A.V.S.
Director of Medical Services reports to	D.G.A.M.S.
Director of Postal Services reports to	?
Paymaster-in-Chief reports to	?
Financial Adviser reports to	?
Principal Naval Transport Officer reports to	D.M.O.

2. The remainder of the personnel of the above headquarters report at the place of mobilization of the unit.

A list has been prepared by the Mobilization Branch giving the detail of the personnel for the information of the Commander of each headquarter unit.

3. The instructions received are to be studied by the officers before the embarkation of their headquarters, which are arranged as under:—

Base Commandants ..
Principal Naval Transport Officer ..
Divisional Naval Transport Officers } 2nd day.
Advanced Base Commandant
Director of Army Signals ..

Inspector-General of Communications } 3rd day.
Headquarters of Administrative Services and Departments

Times of departure by train from London have been fixed for the Director of Army Signals and for the Headquarters of Administrative Services and Departments. These times are known to the mobilizing officers. Officers whose headquarters mobilize at Southampton will proceed to that port by ordinary train.

4. The naval personnel for duties at the port of disembarkation (*vide* Part III., paragraph 13) will travel with the headquarters of the Base Commandant.

5. Descriptions of the ports of disembarkation have been prepared for the Base Commandants and their staffs.

PART II.—PRELIMINARY AND GENERAL.

1. **Co-operation with the French.**—The organization of this campaign has been worked out in conjunction with the French. These instructions contain a description of the arrangements made, with a statement of some points which still require attention, and are designed to show *in general outline* the procedure designed to secure co-operation between the British and French authorities and between the different staffs, services and departments of the British Army and Navy.

The details can be read in the separate instructions given to various executive officers.

No names beyond the advanced base are mentioned, but these are contained in the confidential papers and maps issued personally to the Inspector-General of Communications.

2. It is necessary to realize clearly the degree to which the British Army is, and must be, dependent on the French Government for its concentration and subsequent supply. The entire railway service is manned and controlled by the French, who undertake the work of construction, repair, maintenance, traffic management and protection, not only in French territory, but beyond the frontier.

The local "Commandants d'armes" at each base have been responsible in peace time for preparations for our reception, providing rest camps, sites and buildings for depôts, &c.

3. **Object of the arrangements made.**—The area of concentration having been chosen the main objects of all arrangements made have been—

   (i.) To concentrate the Expeditionary Force, and
   (ii.) Simultaneously to build up the Lines of Communication service.

4. **Lines of Communication units.**—Orders have been given for an initial distribution of all Lines of Communication units. This distribution is given in detail in Appendix L 2, and has been adopted after consultation with the French authorities as being most suitable for the concentration period, when transport facilities are limited. The allocation after concentration is completed will rest with the Inspector-General of Communications, but, as will be noted later, the Advanced Base will not be filled up unnecessarily.

5. **Station of the Inspector-General of Communications.**—The Headquarters of the Inspector-General of Communications lands at Port C and should proceed to the Advanced Base. No advanced party has been arranged for.

The French General Officer attached to British General Headquarters will be at the advanced base from the 1st day of French mobilization, and the Headquarters of the Inspector-General of Communications should move there and get into touch with him forthwith.

6. **Channels of communication with French Railways.**—During the period of concentration a "Commission de Ligne," which comprises officers of the French staff and technical railway officials, will be at the advanced base and will control the railway movement. Subordinate to this body are, a "délégation à l'embarquement" at each port of landing, and a "commission régulatrice de débarquement" at a junction near the area of concentration.

At the Advanced Base the General Staff of the Inspector-General of Communications will be the sole channel of communication between the British authorities and the "Commission de Ligne."

For this purpose the General Staff Officer, 1st Grade, will act as the Inspector-General of Communication's representative, the French having particularly requested that a senior staff officer of the Inspector-General of Communications should be nominated for this work. To assist this officer the General Staff Officer, 2nd Grade, who will be an officer from the Directorate of Military Operations at the War Office, will be with the General Staff Officer, 1st Grade. He will be conversant with all details of the plans for movement.

At the ports the Base Commandants will be the sole channels of communication between the British and the "délégations à l'embarquement," which have local control of the railways.

Similarly at the "gare régulatrice de débarquement," the Assistant Quartermaster-General of the advanced party of General Headquarters will be the British representative.

After concentration, the system of communication at the advanced base and at the ports remains practically the same, the only change being that the "Commission de Ligne" is replaced by a "Commission Régulatice," whilst at the ports the "délégations à l'embarquement" disappear and Base Commandants deal with the local "commissions de gare."

7. **Headquarters of Administrative Services and Departments.** — The detailed distribution of the headquarters of each administrative service and department is given in Part V. in connection with the description of the work of his department.

PART III.—EMBARKATION AND DISEMBARKATION.

(Identical in "Instructions for Base Commandants" (K 1) and "Instructions for the Inspector-General of Communications" (K 10).)

1. **Naval Staffs.**—The responsibility of the Admiralty and of the Naval Officers concerned with the transport of the troops is defined in Article 1226, King's Regulations and Admiralty Instructions, and in Chapter II. of the Manual of Combined Naval and Military Operations. It must be understood that the instructions given in both these regulations refer primarily to disembarkations in a British or enemy country, and that, in considering the question of landing in a friendly country, with the active assistance of the local authorities, they must be taken as indicating the spirit in which the operations are to be carried out rather than the strict letter of the law.

2. The Principal Naval Transport Officer (P.N.T.O) is the representative of the Director of Transports in the country of disembarkation, and is generally responsible that orders and instructions issued by the Admiralty from time to time for the conduct of the sea transport of the expedition are duly carried out.

He should establish his headquarters at C, but this will not preclude his visiting other ports if he considers it necessary to do so.

3. The scheme of operations has been worked out and agreed to between the Admiralty and War Office, on the one hand, and the French authorities, on the other, and the arrangements there made must be adhered to as rigidly as circumstances will allow. The transport by sea is a small part only of the whole scheme of concentration, and any disarrangement of it will have far-reaching effects on collateral arrangements on both sides of the Channel, and must in consequence be avoided if possible.

4. At the same time it is recognized that *circumstances may occur which will render some modification inevitable*, and in such a case the P.N.T.O. and the Inspector-General of Communications, as representing the naval and military authorities respectively, must agree as to the best course of action. The P.N.T.O. will state the various alternatives that, in his opinion, are feasible from a naval point of view, and the I.G.C. will then decide which of them he will accept.

5. Care must be taken to carry the French authorities with us, and it will therefore be necessary to consult the "Commissions de Port," concerned, before a decision is made.

6. No large alterations of plans, such as changing the destination of transports from C to B or A, is allowed without the sanction of the Admiralty in consultation with the War Office.

7. *Provided that circumstances necessitate them*, changes from C to R, or *vice versâ*, and changes from B to A, may be made without previous reference to the Admiralty, after the concurrence of the I.G.C. and the "Commissions de Port" concerned has been obtained. The P.N.T.O. is to inform the Director of Transports, Admiralty, by telegraph if any such alterations are made.

8. In order to avoid the delay which would occur in trying to communicate with ports and officers at a distance from the place at which the P.N.T.O. may happen to be at the moment, the Divisional Naval Transport Officer (D.N.T.O.) is to be considered as the deputy of the P.N.T.O. at all ports or districts at which the latter is not actually present.

9. The P.N.T.O. will take steps to see that the I.G.C. or his local representative is informed as soon as possible of anything which may arise with regard to the efficiency or movements of the transports, the state of the sea, weather, or tides, or other circumstances which may impede the working of the pre-arranged plan of movement.

10. The P.N.T.O. will issue general instructions for the guidance of the D.N.T.O. when acting as his deputy. In order to secure decentralization, these instructions should give the D.N.T.O. as free a hand as possible.

11. The D.N.T.O. will take steps to see that the P.N.T.O. and the Base Commandant are informed as soon as possible of anything which may arise with regard to the efficiency or movements of the transports, the state of the sea, weather, or tides, or other circumstances which may impede the working of the estimated time-table.

12. The P.N.T.O. will leave London after consulting with the D.M.O., and will arrange to obtain the necessary information as to his passage from the Enquiry Officer, Southampton.

On arrival at his destination the P.N.T.O. will at once get into touch with the local French authorities.

13. The following is the Naval Transport Staff for overseas ports:—

Principal Naval Transport Officer		1
Secretary to P.N.T.O. (Accountant Officer, R.N.)		1
Writers		2
Orderlies (privates, R.M.L.I.)		6
Servants to P.N.T.O. (privates, R.M.L.I.)		2
Servant to Secretary to P.N.T.O. (private, R.M.L.I.)		1
Interpreters (arranged by War Office)		1

	A.	B.	C.	R.
Divisional Naval Transport Officers (Captains, R.N., retired)	1	1	1	1
Transport Officers (Commanders, R.N., retired)		4	6	4
Secretaries to D.N.T.Os. (Accountant Officers, R.N.)	1	1	1	1
Writers	1	2	2	2
Orderlies (privates, R.M.L.I.)		6	6	6
Servants (privates, R.M.L.I., one to each officer)	2	6	8	6
Interpreters (arranged by War Office)	1	1	1	1

NOTES—

    Officers and orderlies will be provided with bicycles.

    The French have arranged for hotel and office accommodation of the Naval Transport Staff at oversea ports.

    Interpreters will join at oversea ports.

14. **Base Commandant.**—A Base Commandant with a suitable staff is appointed for each of the Ports C, R and B. He is responsible to the I.G.C. for the reception and accommodation of all troops at the port and for discipline and interior economy generally. He is the sole channel of communication between the British troops and the French railway authorities at the port.

The B.C. of Port C is responsible, in addition, for advising the P.N.T.O. as to military requirements in the co-ordination of traffic between Ports C and R. Should it be necessary, on account of naval or other considerations, to depart from the pre-arranged scheme of disembarkation, the necessary modifications will be carried out by the P.N.T.O. in consultation with the B.C., in accordance with the principles laid down in paragraph 4 of these instructions.

15. **Military Landing Officer.**—A Military Landing Officer with such assistant M.L.O.'s as may be necessary, is appointed to the staff of each Base Commandant. He is responsible for carrying out all executive details on shore with regard to the disembarkation of troops, in consultation with the D.N.T.O., and conveys orders to the troops for their movements to rest camps or quarters.

During the disembarkation he will—

(i.) Advise the Divisional Naval Transport Officer, if necessary, as to the distribution of men and horse brows, stevedores, &c., and see that the necessary labour for moving the brows is provided.

(ii.) See that the troops clear the quays as required by the Naval Transport Officers and detail them to forming up places as necessary.

(iii.) Arrange, through the Base Commandant, for horse or other transport to clear off the quays the baggage or stores of units having no transport of their own.

(iv.) Collect the landing returns and nominal rolls of officers prepared by each unit or detachment of a unit; these are to be forwarded to the 3rd Échelon, General Headquarters, at Port C.

(v.) Receive from the Base Commandant or the "Commandant d'Armes," a statement as to the rest camps to be occupied by troops landing. Each unit will be warned. The French have undertaken to provide each with a guide, and in some cases an interpreter, to conduct their units to their camps, and the Military Landing Officers arrange for them to meet the units. The routes to be marked in a manner suitable for night or day.

(vi.) Issue orders as to the routes to be followed in the docks to the dock exits.

(vii.) Supervise the erection of latrines and urinals on the quays. Tubs, &c., are being sent across early for this purpose.

(viii.) Be the channel for ascertaining and complying with the requirements of the officers in charge of depôts, at which stores are unloaded so far as stevedores, dock labour, &c., are concerned.

III. 3

16. **"Commission de Port."**—At each French port a "Commission de Port" will be formed to regulate the approach to the port, the entry of the Expeditionary Force ships, and the landing of troops and material. It will be constituted as follows:—

(a.) The "Commandant d'Armes," or Military Governor of the Port, President.
(b.) French Members—

(i.) "L'Officier de Marine commandant le front de Mer," or Naval Officer Commanding the Coast Defences.
(ii.) Two French Military Officers.
(iii.) "L'Ingénieur chef du Service maritime de la Navigation," or Senior Civil Engineer of the Docks and Harbour Board.
(iv.) The Captain of the Port.

Subordinate officers and interpreters are also attached to the Commission under conditions laid down by the "Commandant d'Armes."

(c.) British members—

(i.) The D.N.T.O.
(ii.) The Senior Military Landing Officer, *i.e.*, the D.A.A.G. of the headquarters of the base.

The D.N.T.O. will, as a rule, be the channel of communication between the British authorities and the "Commission de Port."

17. The general instructions for the entry, berthing and discharge of the transports will be drawn up by the "Commission de Port," as far as may be necessary, after receiving information from the D.N.T.O., in consultation with the Military Landing Officer, as to any special requirements, such as the precedence to be given to particular ships.

The respective responsibilities of the French and British members of the "Commission de Port" are defined as follows:—

The French representatives are responsible for ensuring—

The evacuation of quays and basins.
The entry of vessels into the port.
The allotment of berths to each ship.
The berthing of vessels.
The sailing of vessels.

Decisions on these points are given by French representatives, the functions of the British members in these matters being advisory.

Responsibility for disembarking the troops and discharging cargo rests with the British members, who will be furnished by the French with the necessary workmen, and all available cranes and other appliances. (For Brows, *see* paragraph 35.)

The British officers will issue orders to French workmen engaged in unloading. Interpreters are placed at their disposal for the purpose if required.

18. **General control of the movement.**—*Owing to the many considerations which have had to be taken into account in deciding the order of despatch of the troops, every effort must be made to carry out the prearranged programme, unless some extremely grave event should take place, such as the blocking of the River F.*

Should minor delays at the ports occur, it will probably be better to proceed with the programme as planned than to make alterations at the last moment.

The control of the transport of the army by sea as a whole rests with the Admiralty in consultation with the War Office.

19. **Ports of embarkation.**—The Expeditionary Force will embark from Southampton, Newhaven, Avonmouth, Liverpool, Belfast, Dublin, Queenstown, Cork, and Glasgow.

20. **Approximate dates of departure of troops and military supplies.**—The order in which the movement is to be carried out is generally as follows:—

(a.) The staffs and units necessary for the first organization of the lines of communication and the advanced portions of various headquarters embark on the first, second and third days of military mobilization.

(b.) Some supplies and stores are sent on the first day.
(c.) The Infantry (less 4th Division) and some lines of communication units embark on the fourth, fifth and sixth days.
(d.) The Cavalry and the remainder of the fighting troops (less 4th Division) embark between the seventh and eleventh days, both inclusive.
(e.) The 4th Division embarks on the 12th and 13th days.
(f.) The "Base Detachments" (details left at the base) are due to embark on the 13th and 14th days.

21. **Disembarkation.**—(a.) The disembarkation will take place at Ports C, R and B. Arrangements have been made for using Port A as an alternative to Port B, if the naval situation allows, and if such a change is found imperative.

(b.) Port C is the principal base and Port R is a subsidiary base. It is intended to make use of Port B mainly during the period of concentration, but it may be necessary to make use of it for supplies and stores during the period of operations as well.

21A. **Disembarkation Tables.**—The attached disembarkation tables and key (Appendix L 1) show the units which are to land each day at the various ports. The key should be destroyed as soon as the details affecting the particular port have been entered in the tables.

All units, on disembarkation, will proceed to a rest camp before continuing the journey, except in the case of advanced portions of staffs and such units of the Lines of Communication as arrive on the earlier days and are detailed to proceed to the advanced base or beyond; such units will continue their journey at once, if possible.

The disembarkation tables show the troops which may be expected to land each day under the following headings:—

(a.) For the area of concentration.
(b.) For the Advanced Base.
(c.) To remain at the port.

Stores and supplies are not mentioned in the tables. These mostly come *via* Newhaven, and lists of the probable daily arrivals are given in the Tables A for each port.

The disembarkation tables do not show shiploads. The number of ships, anticipated to arrive each day at each port, conveying troops, stores or mechanical transport, is given in the Table B for each port.

Troops shown as arriving between noon on one day and noon on the next are those which embarked at Southampton or Newhaven on the first day named. Thus:

Troops embarking on the $\begin{Bmatrix} \text{6th day at Southampton} \\ \text{5th day at Dublin} \end{Bmatrix}$ will be shown as disembarking between noon on the 6th day and noon on the 7th.

An exception to the above rule is made in the case of ships conveying mechanical transport to Port R from Avonmouth or Liverpool, and of ships to any port from Glasgow, when an extra day is allowed for the voyage.

"Serial numbers for sea movement" are shown in the second column of each page of the disembarkation tables. These numbers are arranged according to British trainloads and are used solely as a telegraphic code between Embarkation and Base Commandants (*vide* paragraphs 38 to 40 below).

In the last column on each page are shown grouped "serial numbers for rail movement," for reference only to the rail movement papers, the tables D. The detailed numbers given in the latter will be used by the French to designate units selected for rail movement forward.

The two principles followed in allotting these (oversea rail movement) serial numbers are:—

(a.) The first digit of the number indicates the division, &c., to which the unit belongs;
(b.) One or more complete numbers form a French trainload, *i.e.*, no number has to be split up to go into two or more trains.

Copies of the disembarkation tables will be in the hands of some of the higher British officials but not in the hands of French officials, who have been provided with the information given in the Tables D, together with the port of landing and the probable date of arrival of each unit.

III. 5

22. Approximate dates of arrival of troops and military supplies.—The approximate time of arrival of transports may be estimated from the following:—

Average steaming time:—
To Port C—
From Newhaven			80 miles,	say 8 hours	$\frac{1}{3}$ day.
,, Southampton	..	..	114 ,,	10 ,,	$\frac{1}{2}$,,
,, Avonmouth*	..	..	435 ,,	40 ,,	$1\frac{1}{2}$ days.
,, Liverpool*	..	..	539 ,,	48 ,,	2 ,,
,, Belfast	..	..	560 ,,	50 ,,	2 ,,
,, Dublin*	..	..	466 ,,	42 ,,	2 ,,
,, Queenstown or Cork	..		391 ,,	36 ,,	$1\frac{1}{2}$,,
,, Glasgow*	..	..	585 ,,	53 ,,	$2\frac{1}{4}$,,

To Port R—
From Port C *add* 8 to 20 hours.

To Port B—
From Newhaven			59 miles,	say 6 hours	$\frac{1}{4}$ day.
,, Southampton	..	.	124 ,,	11 ,,	$\frac{1}{2}$,,
,, Avonmouth*	..	..	495 ,,	44 ,,	2 days.
,, Liverpool*	..	..	599 ,,	56 ,,	$2\frac{1}{2}$,,
,, Belfast	..	..	620 ,,	58 ,,	$2\frac{1}{2}$,,
,, Dublin*	..	..	526 ,,	48 ,,	2 ,,
,, Queenstown or Cork	..		451 ,,	42 ,,	2 ,,
,, Glasgow*	..	..	645 ,,	60 ,,	$2\frac{1}{2}$,,

23. Capacity of the ports.—The daily capacity of each port for the purposes of this scheme has been estimated at the following:—

Port C—30 ships.
Port R—20 ships (12 by day, 8 by night).
Port B—11 ships.

The list of ships due to arrive at each port has been kept at about these limits.

24. Port A.—The limit for Port A is eight ships, exclusive of "Class C" ships (stores from Newhaven) which can be berthed in the avantport at all conditions of tide.

No military base staff or supplies have been arranged for Port A (the naval staff for that port is shown in paragraph 13). It is proposed to use Port A as an alternative to Port B, only when owing to bad weather or congestion at the latter place it is absolutely necessary. The Base Commandant at Port B will, in such circumstances, arrange for the movement to Port A of any stores and supplies and of such portion of his headquarters as may be necessary for the reception of the troops, he will also decide whether troops will rail or march to Port B, according to circumstances.

25. Port G.—The French have been asked to arrange for ships conveying mechanical transport to be allowed, if absolutely necessary owing to congestion, to discharge at Port G. The vehicles would then proceed by road to Port R. This question is now (July, 1914), under consideration.

It is not proposed to land troops at Port G, as the necessary railway arrangements cannot be made, and, in view of the additional 150 miles of road thereby entailed, the use of this port would in any case be confined to great emergencies.

26. Ports C and R.—*If an alteration in the programme of disembarkation between Ports C and R becomes absolutely necessary* (*vide* paragraph 14), the P.N.T.O., in consultation with the Base Commandant at Port C, who acts as the representative of the I.G.C. in the matter, will redistribute the traffic between the two ports. Should such changes be necessary, the following points must be borne in mind:—

(a.) The component parts of a French trainload should land at the same port (*vide* paragraph 27).
(b.) Forty trains a day can be despatched from Port C and Port R *combined*. Though it is possible to run the whole of this number from Port C only, such a procedure would entail a heavy strain on the railway, and it is most desirable that as many trains as possible, up to a maximum of 15 per diem, should be despatched from Port R.

---

* For mechanical transport ships half a day should be added.

(c.) The cranes at Port R are not capable of lifting out tractors or weights exceeding 5 tons.

(d.) Ammunition for ammunition parks (mechanical transport) is being sent to Port R in separate ships from those carrying the vehicles. Therefore, any vehicles which may happen to be landed at Port C or Port G will have to go to Port R to be loaded up.

(e.) Stores and food should be landed as arranged, as far as possible.

(f.) The interpreters to be attached permanently to units are being sent by the French to the ports according to the disembarkation plan. Hence, in the event of any departure being made from the prearranged plan, special arrangements must be made for them to rejoin their units.

27. **Military factors affecting disembarkation.**—Troops are embarked by British trainloads. Each trainload of troops on embarking will be complete in food, &c., for the voyage. Different trainloads of the same unit will not necessarily embark in the same ship; it follows, therefore, that the component parts of a French trainload, which is bigger than, but bears no fixed relation to, a British trainload, may travel in more than one ship. The French trainloads are shown in the Tables D (Appendix L, 9), and a rough comparison between these and the British ones can be seen in the Disembarkation Tables (Appendix L, 1).

Units will be assembled at the ports of disembarkation, whenever possible.

The main supply depôt is at C, and subsidiary supply depôts are at B and R. A portion of the harbour contiguous to the railway has been told off for each.

It is desirable that store ships should be assigned berths near the hangars or areas available for the storage of their cargoes.

28. **Rest Camps.**—Troops other than those to remain at the ports will go into rest camps on disembarkation previous to proceeding by rail. Stores will be placed in depôts. The details concerning the rest camps (which will be prepared by the French, with the exception of pitching the tents) are given in the Instructions to Base Commandants.

On the second day of military mobilization tents are despatched from Southampton as follows:—

> For 8,000 men to Port R.
> For 10,000 men to Port B.
> For 29,000 men to Port C.

The lines of communication battalions sent to the ports on the second day of military mobilization will pitch the tents. On completion of this duty they will be available for such work as the Base Commandant may order, but certain detachments have to be made to the Advanced Base and "railheads," details of which are given in the Instructions for Base Commandants, Part IV., paragraph 5.

29. **Stores.**—The stores and supplies to be sent with the Force are given in detail in the Instructions to Base Commandants and Military Heads of Departments.

30. **Mechanical transport.**—The majority of the mechanical transport is destined for Port R, but as the two heavy cranes at that place have not sufficient lift or reach to take the tractors or workshop trucks out of a ship's hold, all vehicles of this type have been ordered to Port C in special ships, there being three big cranes (besides the floating ones) at the latter port capable of lifting them.

Except the two mentioned above, the cranes at Port R will not lift more than 5 tons, but there are many which will lift that weight.

It is hoped that the ships conveying the mechanical transport will be capable of lifting it out, but the above arrangements have been made in case it should prove that they cannot do so.

31. **Portable derricks.**—To enable mechanical transport to be handled at oversea ports lacking sufficient cranage power, the following portable derricks, lifting capacity 10 tons, will be carried to the ports indicated from Southampton in the earliest transports, and will be retained there for use on board ships in disembarking the vehicles, &c.:—

> A .. .. —
> B 2
> C 2
> R 6

The derricks are 50 feet long, and the heel fits into a shoe hollowed to take it, fitted with eyebolts and rings for securing to the deck.

32. Slings for mechanical transport.—The following slings for handling mechanical transport will also be despatched from United Kingdom ports in early transports, to be landed for use at the ports indicated:—

	Slings to lift 7-ton tractors.	Slings to lift 4½-ton lorries.
C	9	4
R	..	39
B	7	3

33. Petrol for mechanical transport.—All mechanical transport vehicles, including motor cars, embark with sufficient petrol in tins to enable them to clear the docks on landing.

34. Pilots, tugs and lighters.—Pilots, tugs and lighters will be allocated by the "Commission de Port" as required.

The tugs required and available are as follows:—

	Minimum required.	Available locally.	To be sent from United Kingdom.
Port C	30	12	18
Port R	20	10	10
Port B	8	3	5
Port A	2	2	..

35. Gangways and horse brows.—Gangways and horse brows are essential for quickly unloading men and horses. As the French have not any, the British are entirely dependent on those sent with the Force or manufactured locally.

The following is a list of the gangways and horse brows which are held at Southampton in peace time for despatch to the ports of landing in the first ships sailing thither:—

	Gangways.			Horse brows.		
	40 feet.	36 feet.	26 feet.	40 feet.	36 feet.	26 feet.
C	..	18	12	..	18	12
R	..	6	6	..	6	6
B	..	6	6	..	6	6
A	3	..	3	3	..	2

Gangways and brows for Port A will be shipped on board transports bound for Port B. After the troops, &c., have been disembarked at Port B the transport will land the brows at Port A before returning to England.

36. Stevedores.—The following is the estimated number of stevedores required:—

Port C	3,000
Port R	1,000
Port B	500
Port A	500

The French have undertaken that no man required for work in the docks shall be mobilized, and the number of stevedores promised are as follows:—

Port C	3,000
Port R	1,000
Port B	300
Port A	150

The best arrangements possible under the circumstances to provide any shortage of labour on board the transports must be made by the D.N.T.O. in consultation with the Base Commandant and the "Commission de Port." If labour is not likely to be forthcoming from the French, it may be demanded from the United Kingdom or temporarily from His Majesty's naval or military forces. French officials will control French labourers, crane mechanics, &c.

37. **Frozen meat vessels.**—The vessels despatched from the United Kingdom with frozen meat are to be used as storage depôts for it at Ports C, B and R respectively.

38. **Telegrams.**—On the sailing of a transport from the United Kingdom a telegram, addressed to both the D.N.T.O. and the Base Commandant of the port of disembarkation, will be sent by the Embarkation Commandant of the port of embarkation, giving the following information in the order shown :—

Name and number of transport.
Probable date of arrival (in words).
Probable time of arrival.

(NOTE.—In the case of ships ordered to R the probable date and time of arrival at C should be inserted in place of the date and time of arrival at R.)

Draught.
Serial number of military units (separated by the word "and").
Tonnage and general description of stores on board, *e.g.*, ammunition, hospital stores, food supplies, &c.

The headings will not be telegraphed, and a telegram would thus read as follows :—

Argus 157.
Fourth December.
8 A.M.
23 feet.
Units 57 and 49 and 53.
Hospital stores, 30 tons.

(Any other information, as necessary.)

NOTE.—In the case of mechanical transport, the numbers of men (including officers), tractors, tenders, heavy lorries, light lorries and motor cars respectively, will be specified in addition to the unit.

If the ship's appliances cannot deal with the heaviest lift on board, the word "insufficient" should be added at the end of the telegram. If this word is not telegraphed it will be assumed that the ship's appliances are sufficient to deal with the heaviest lift. The information contained in this telegram will be handed by the B.C. and D.N.T.O. at the port of disembarkation, to the Commandant d'Armes and the Commission de Port respectively.

39. For ships sailing at any time previous to midnight of the second/third day these telegrams will be addressed to the "Commandant d'Armes" of the port of disembarkation.

40. The telegrams from the ports of embarkation notifying the despatch of ships for Port R. will be addressed both to Port R and Port C, so that the "Commission de Port" at the latter place may arrange for the necessary pilotage up the River F.

41. All naval and military telegrams in the oversea country should be forwarded through the British Army Signal Service for transmission over special Army lines. Military telegraph forms will be supplied as necessary by the Base Commandant.

42. **Progress reports.**—(*a.*) The P.N.T.O. will send daily reports to the Director of Transports on Form T 175. Any important trouble must be reported at once by telegram.

(*b.*) The D.N.T.Os. will report daily to the Director of Transports concerning the work at their ports, as well as to the P.N.T.O., using the Form T 175. They will report any important trouble by telegram to the Director of Transports and P.N.T.O.

(*c.*) Base Commandants will each telegraph a short daily report to the Inspector-General of Communications, and to "Heeltool, London," stating the progress of the movement. In particular, any alteration in the fixed programme of disembarkation or extraordinary delay in the berthing and clearance of shipping, or in the movement of troops by rail, should be mentioned in the report.

43. **Return of transports to United Kingdom.**—Transports are to return to the ports in the United Kingdom indicated in their sailing orders. If it is found

necessary to order a transport to a different port, the Director of Transports, the D.N.T.O. at the port to which she was originally to return, and the D.N.T.O. at the new port, are to be at once informed. The master should be given such instructions in writing.

It is important that transports should not be retained at oversea ports except for urgent reasons, of which the Director of Transports should be at once informed.

With regard to vessels which have disembarked at R, and which are not scheduled for a return journey, the D.N.T.O. may retain them at R until the majority of the ships have arrived, if room can be found to moor them, so as to avoid the risk of too much congestion in the River F.

44. On the sailing of a transport for the United Kingdom the P.N.T.O. is to cause the port to which she is returning to be informed by wire as follows :—

        Name and number of transport.
        Date and time of leaving.
        Probable date of arrival.
        (Any further information necessary.)

The telegram will be addressed to the following :—

    Director of Transports, Admiralty.
    D.N.T.O. ⎫ of the port to which the
    Embarkation Commandant ⎭ transport is returning.

45. **Codes and cyphers.**—For secret messages between the Director of Transports, Naval Transport Officers and His Majesty's ships, Cypher C will be used, and for those between Naval Transport Officers and Military Officers the Playfair Cypher will be used. The Playfair Code words will be given by the Director of Transports to the P.N.T.O. and D.N.T.Os., and by the War Office to General Headquarters, each Base Commandant and the Inspector-General of Communications; also to the Embarkation Commandant for communication to the Senior Military Officer on board each transport, whose duty it will be to encypher or decypher telegrams sent or received. The Base Commandants have been instructed that the method of calling up may be communicated to the French, if necessary, but not the code words.

Instructions for communication by wireless telegraphy are given in the enclosure to Instructions to Masters.

All wireless messages are to be in cypher, other telegraphic communications are to be in cypher if secret, and *en clair* if not secret.

46. **Postal.**—The base post office will be at Port C. A stationary post office is detailed for duty at each of the Ports B and R.

47. **Censorship.**—Censorship of communications emanating from British naval and military sources is put into force at the ports under British military censors, who are on the staff of the I.G.C.

48. **Cash arrangements.**—An officer of the Army Pay Department is attached to each base staff for the purpose of opening imprest accounts in the administrative base areas. Arrangements have been made by which these officers will be able to obtain from the local "Trésorier-Payeur General, Receveur des Finances ou Percepteur" French currency in exchange for the cheque brought with them from England, under instructions of the Army Paymaster-in-Chief.

PART IV.—MOVEMENT TO THE AREA OF CONCENTRATION, DETRAINMENT AND BILLETING.

1. The Secret Map, No. 1, issued personally to the I.G.C., shows the concentration areas, by twin divisions, of the Field Army.

Appendix L 2 shows the distribution of the Line of Communication services and troops.

2. All mechanically propelled vehicles proceed to the area of concentration by road. The active aeroplanes of the Royal Flying Corps move by air.

The remainder of the Expeditionary Force moves by rail.

3. **Concentration movement by rail.**—The entire railway service is manned and controlled by the French, who undertake the work of construction, repair, maintenance, traffic management and protection, not only in French territory, but beyond the frontier. The British Railway Transport Establishment is provided to act merely as intermediaries between the French and the British troops. The system to be followed has been worked out in peace, and the necessary action on the part of the British officers is given in—

>Instructions for Base Commandants. (Appendix K 1.)
>Instructions for Advanced Base Commandant. (Appendix K 4.)
>Instructions for Advanced Parties, &c. (Appendix K 5.)

In addition to this, the General Staff officer, 2nd Grade, Headquarters, I.G.C., is familiar with all necessary details.

4. The area of concentration, the area allotted to divisions, &c., and the detraining stations are shown on Secret Map No. 1 (*vide* paragraph 1), which is to be shown only to those whose duty requires the knowledge.

5. The system of movement is described in "Railway concentration movement of the British Army" (Appendix L 17), of which the following is a summary :—

(*a*.) The movement is controlled by the "Commission de Ligne" at the advanced base.

(*b*.) The maximum number of trains available from the ports each day is—

>From Port B 20
>„ Port C ⎫ combined .. 40
>„ Port R ⎭

>N.B.—The number of trains from Port C and Port R combined must not exceed 40. The whole of this number can, in case of urgent necessity, be despatched from Port C, 15 is the maximum from Port R.

>All trains given above as starting from Port B have starting times arranged for Port A, if required for troops landed there.

(*c*.) The movement can commence at 0 *heures* on the 7th day of French mobilization. French time runs from midnight to midnight, 0 *heures* to 24 *heures*.

(*d*.) The list of troops which can be railed from a port on the (n)th day is made out by a committee of British and French officers (*see* Appendix L 17) at the port at noon on the (n—2)th day, *i.e.*, at least 36 hours before any unit's train leaves the port.

(*e*.) Lists as in (*d*) are telephoned to the "Commission de Ligne" from all ports and that body returns, the same evening, a list of troops which will be railed from each port on the (n)th day and the train times allotted to them.

>In the case of a list being made out for, say, the 11th day, it would include—
>(i.) Units which from any cause have been left out of previous lists.
>(ii.) Units which have landed since the completion of the previous list.
>(iii.) Units whose transports will, in the opinion of the Base Commandant, be in harbour either berthed or ready to come alongside *by* 24 *heures on the 9th day*.

>>In the case of units not landed this opinion must be based on the telegrams from Embarkation Commandants announcing the despatch of ships, or on telegraphic reports from the ships themselves.

>>In certain cases proviso (iii.) will enable troops to be included which are practically certain to be ready *to entrain late* on the 11th, but which do not come within its strict meaning.

(*f.*) All trains pass through one station which is the "gare régulatrice de débarquement" (G.R.D.), or "detrainment regulating station." The time tables for each unit as far as the G.R.D. are worked out and allotted by the Commission de Ligne, who for this purpose assume provisional detraining stations. But the final allotment of detraining stations is made at the G.R.D. by the "Commission régulatrice de débarquement," who arrange matters to suit the billeting areas of units as far as possible. *See* "Instructions for Advanced Parties, &c." (Appendix K 5.)

6. **The "Commission régulatrice de débarquement."**—The "Commission régulatrice de débarquement" at the "G.R.D.," working under the "Commission de Ligne," is responsible for the railway arrangements in connection with detrainment. This body has the final voice in deciding the detraining stations to be used, as railway interests must finally prevail. The billeting of the troops, however, has to be given as much weight as possible, and therefore British and French personnel, to carry out the billeting duties, work in connection with this "Commission."

7. **Control of the billeting arrangements.**—The British Assistant Quartermaster-General, General Headquarters, will, in conjunction with the "Commission," be in general charge of the undermentioned arrangements:—

(*a.*) The allotment of billets to units arriving by train and by road.
(*b.*) Fixing march routes, for units arriving by rail, between detraining stations and billets.
(*c.*) Arranging routes to enable mechanical transport vehicles and motor cars, when reporting to him, to reach their billets or units.
(*d.*) Special orders for the supply of units prior to the arrival of the supply columns (mechanical transport). (*Vide* "Supply System"—Appendix L, 16.)
(*e.*) The modification of billeting areas should such a course be necessitated by interruption or breakdown of the railway.

The Assistant Quartermaster-General, General Headquarters, will be assisted by the advanced parties of headquarter units. These parties work in the various sub-areas allotted to divisions, detaching the "billeting officers" to the "gare régulatrice de débarquement."

8. **British officers at detraining stations.**—One D.A.D.R.T. and 24 British officers, drawn from the railway transport establishment, will be sent to the "Gare régulatrice de débarquement" for duty at the 12 detraining stations as railway transport officers. They will receive their orders from the A.Q.M.G., General Headquarters.

9. **French officers, &c., for duty.**—The senior staff officer to the French General attached to British General Headquarters, together with a staff called "officiers de cantonnement," will assist the British Assistant Quartermaster-General, General Headquarters.

General Headquarters and other headquarters of the field army will be joined in the area of concentration by—

(i.) French "officiers de liaison."
(ii.) Interpreters for headquarter units.
(iii.) Gendarmerie.

Their detailed distribution is given in "Instructions for Advanced Parties."

10. **Detrainment at the Advanced Base.**—Some troops detrain at the Advanced Base. These will receive instructions from the Advanced Base Commandant, who acts for them, under the "Commission de Ligne," as the Assistant Quartermaster-General, General Headquarters, does for troops detraining in the area of concentration. (*See* "Instructions for Advanced Base Commandant.")

11. **Details of detraining duties.**—A detailed description of the method of detraining and billeting troops in the area of concentration is given in "Instructions for Officers of Advanced Parties, &c."

12. It will be seen from the above that British co-operation in the railway movement is practically limited to—

(i.) Stating what troops are available to move from the ports.
(ii.) Acting as intermediaries at the entrainment and detrainment.
(iii.) Assisting in the detrainment by arranging the billets.

The British have nothing whatever to do with the working of the railways.

13. **Concentration movement by road.**—All mechanically propelled vehicles are to receive their orders for movement from the Base Commandant at the port of landing. Printed forms showing the route have been prepared. All cars and vehicles proceed to the "G.R.D." where they receive instructions from the British Assistant Quartermaster-General of General Headquarters as to their final destination.

Vehicles, &c., from Port B go through direct in one day; those from Port R and Port C halt one night at the advanced base.

14. **Temporary landing station for aircraft.**—A locality (H) has been selected to form a temporary landing station for aircraft moving by air to the place of concentration. An advanced party of R.F.C. personnel, with the necessary equipment for repairs and a supply of petrol and lubricants, will be sent there to make arrangements for the reception of such machines as may require to replenish or refit.

15. **Supply.**—The arrangements regarding the despatch of supplies by rail from the ports both during concentration and subsequently are shown in Appendix L 16.

16. **Interpreters.**—Units are joined by their interpreters at the ports, as shown in the "Instructions for Entrainment and Embarkation, Part II." (Appendix J 9.)

PART V.—ORGANIZATION OF THE LINE OF COMMUNICATIONS.

(1.) General.

1. Appendix L, 2, shows the distribution of Line of Communication units in the theatre of operations up to the time when concentration is completed.

2. This distribution has been made in accordance with the detailed instructions prepared for each Director, Base Commandant, &c., and the stores and supplies of all kinds which are due to arrive are shown in the tables at the end of the instructions for each Base Commandant.

3. During the concentration period the Advanced Base will be kept clear of stores and supplies with the exception of—

    (a.) A first reserve of gun and rifle ammunition, which will be kept on railway vehicles in its vicinity (*vide* under Deputy Director of Ordnance Services).

    (b.) One day's reserve supplies for the whole of the Expeditionary Force, including petrol, which will be kept there on railway vehicles (*vide* Appendix L, 16, "Supply System").

4. In the following sections the work of each directorate and administrative service is described, fuller details being given in the instructions to the individual directors.

N.B.—While the head of each administrative service at the Advanced Base will correspond direct with his representatives at the bases on technical matters, any orders given by them involving demands for railway transport must invariably be notified at the same time to the General Staff, I.G.C., for purposes of co-ordination and communication to the French railway authorities.

(2.) Director of Army Signals.

1. The headquarters of the Director of Army Signals sails on the 2nd day for Port C, where a French officer of the Department of Posts and Telegraphs will be waiting with diagrams of the telegraphic circuits.

2. An Assistant Director should remain at Port C. The Deputy Director and his headquarters (less the Assistant Director) should proceed to the Advanced Base. The Director and his headquarters should join General Headquarters on its arrival, in the first instance accompanying the Inspector-General of Communications to the Advanced Base.

3. The diagram (Appendix L, 18) shows the system which it is proposed should be in working order by the 12th day of mobilization, exclusive of the communications in the area of concentration.

4. A French officer of the Post and Telegraphs Department is due to meet the Director at Port C on the 2nd day, when the advanced party of the Signal Company, Line of Communications, arrives. This party has to start and run the system until the arrival of the remainder of the company.

British operators from the General Post Office are being sent to the cable landing places.

A through line from General Headquarters to England, manned entirely by British operators, is provided for in the scheme.

It will be necessary, in the first instance, to use such local telephone systems as may be needed, especially at the ports, but special arrangements are being made to erect a British telephone system at Port C.

The French have agreed to accept British official messages, if stamped or signed, for despatch over their lines subject to their regulations for their own similar telegrams.

5. A method of communication between the Navy and Army has been agreed upon and the keywords fixed. These are given in Appendix L, 4; this appendix has been given to the three Base Commandants and to General Headquarters.

(3.) Director of Supplies.

1. The headquarters of the Director of Supplies will be distributed as under—

Detail.	Officers.	Other ranks.	Horses.	Destination.
Director of Supplies	1	1	1	Advanced Base.
Deputy-Assistant Director of Supplies	1	1	1	
Clerks	..	5	..	
Motor car and driver	..	1	..	
Assistant Director of Supplies	1	1	1	Port C.
Clerks	..	1	..	

2. The distribution of the headquarters of the Deputy Director of Supplies is—

Detail.	Officers.	Other ranks.	Horses.	Destination.
Deputy Director of Supplies	1	1	1	To join General Headquarters on its arrival.
Clerks	..	6	1	
Motor car and driver	..	1	..	
Assistant Director of Supplies	1	1	..	With Assistant Quartermaster-General, General Headquarters, at the "gare régulatrice de débarquement."
Clerks	..	3	..	
Motor car and driver	..	1	..	
Deputy-Assistant Director of Supplies	1	1	..	Port B.
Clerks	..	1	..	

3. The supply arrangements during concentration and during operations have been worked out between the British and French General Staffs. A description of the system is given in Appendix L, 16 ("Supply System").

(4.) Director of Ordnance Services.

1. The headquarters of the Director of Ordnance Services will be at the Advanced Base, and no representative will be sent to General Headquarters unless specially ordered.

2. The headquarters of the Deputy Director will remain at Port C, detaching to Port R as necessary.

3. The main Ordnance Depôt is at Port C, where space has been reserved for the stores, vehicles, &c., given in the schedules, and for ammunition and explosives, according to the requirements given in the Base Commandant's instructions.

Some local workshops have also been reserved for our use.

The detail of these is in the hands of the French Commandant d'armes and the British Base Commandant.

4. Some ammunition is being landed at Port B and will be sent on to the Advanced Base as soon as possible—

4th day .. .. 207 tons rifle ammunition ($5\frac{3}{4}$ million rounds S.A.A.).
6th day .. .. 412 tons gun ammunition (60 rounds per Q.F. gun, 40 rounds per howitzer, 30 rounds per heavy gun, a first reserve of demolition equipment).

This will be stored on railway wagons at, or near, the advanced base as the first Line of Communications reserve.

The ammunition to form the loads of the ammunition parks is being shipped to Port R, where it is to be put into the vehicles which will travel loaded to the area of concentration.

The remainder of the Line of Communications reserve is being sent to Port C, where it will remain until concentration is completed.

5. No stores, except the ammunition mentioned above, will be sent to the Advanced Base during the concentration period. Instructions regarding the forwarding of stores after that period will be issued by the Inspector-General of Communications; but essentials only will be sent to the Advanced Base, as that place is to be kept as clear as possible.

6. Certain deficiencies of stores, &c., may have to be made good at the beginning of the campaign. These include—

(i.) The provision of extra horse and men brows for disembarkation purposes if required at the ports of landing. The Base Commandants should be consulted.

(ii.) Entraining stores, such as handspikes, tackles, large scotches with handles, eyebolts and tools for improvising arm racks in railway wagons, cordage and skids.

(iii.) Arrangements for fitting up the ambulance trains, which should be ready by the time the Field Army advances; the provision of ambulance fittings for lorries and making up the deficiency of stretchers. *These matters are urgent,* and it is necessary to ascertain immediately the requirements of the Director of Medical Services (*see* Sub-section (10)) dealing with these services).

(iv.) After consultation with the French department of "Ponts et Chaussées" and with General Headquarters, the preparation of materials likely to be required during the advance for the repair of bridges, culverts, &c. The Director of Works should be consulted.

(5.) Director of Transport.

1. The duties of the Director of Transport, during the concentration period, fall into two broad divisions:—

(i.) Supervising the despatch of mechanical transport and motor cars of units to the area of concentration; and

(ii.) Organizing transport for immediate requirements at the bases, &c., or for eventual needs (*e.g.*, movement of hospitals) in the neighbourhood of the Field Army.

2. The initial distribution arranged for the mechanical transport depôts and the headquarters personnel is as under:—

(i.) The Advanced Mechanical Transport Depôt sends an advanced portion of one officer and 30 other ranks to land at Port B on the 2nd day and proceed to the Advanced Base.

(ii.) The Base Mechanical Transport Depôt is due to arrive at Port R on the 5th day. Some of this may eventually be required at Port C.

(iii.) The first mechanical transport units begin to arrive about the 7th day.

(iv.) The headquarters of the Director of Transport arrives at Port C on the 3rd day and should be distributed as follows:—

(*a*.) The Director and his Assistant Director to proceed to the "gare régulatrice de débarquement."

(*b*.) The Deputy Director to proceed to the Advanced Base.

(*c*.) The Assistant Director (2nd Echelon) to proceed to Port R.

(*d*.) The Deputy-Assistant Director of Transport (2nd Echelon) to remain at Port C.

(*e*.) The Deputy-Assistant Director of Transport (1st Echelon) to proceed to Port B.

3. The vehicles of supply columns and ammunition parks, as well as the motor cars of units, are to move up to the "G.R.D." by road as soon as possible after landing. The "Order for movement by road," in the hands of the Base Commandants, shows the routes to be followed. From Port B to the "G.R.D." is one day's run; vehicles proceeding from Ports C and R stop one night at the Advanced Base and then proceed.

4. The distribution in paragraph 2 is based on the following description of the duties to be carried out:—

(i.) The whole of the billeting of the army in the area of concentration is to be carried out under the Assistant Quartermaster-General, General Headquarters, at the "G.R.D." There he will be in close touch with General Headquarters.

(ii.) On landing all mechanical transport and motor cars will be sent by road to the "G.R.D.", as mentioned in paragraph 3 above, where they will receive instructions as to their destination or billets through the Assistant Quartermaster-General, General Headquarters.

(iii.) The Base Commandants at each port have in their possession forms showing the roads to be followed, distances, halts, &c., completed except for the insertion of the detail of the unit or party proceeding. The Assistant Director of Transport, or Deputy-Assistant Director of Transport, at each of the ports will, whenever he has a party to send off, complete one of the forms, get it signed by the Base Commandant and the French "Commandant d'armes" (whose signature is necessary to authorize local authorities *en route* to render help if needed), and give it to the officer in charge of the party. The Assistant Director of Transport or Deputy-Assistant Director of Transport at a port is therefore under the Base Commandant to organize the reception and despatch of all mechanical transport vehicles and motor cars landing at that port.

(iv.) Vehicles proceeding from Port B travel through to the "G.R.D." in one day. Vehicles proceeding from Port C and Port R will halt for the night at the advanced base, moving to the "G.R.D." the next day. Consequently the Deputy Director of Transport at the Advanced Base is responsible, under the Advanced Base Commandant, for organizing a suitable control at or near the Advanced Base for the reception of vehicles or units stopping a night and for the replenishment of petrol, &c., as required.

(v.) The Assistant Quartermaster-General, subject to the advice of the Director of Transport and instructions from General Headquarters, is responsible for allotting the billets for the supply columns, ammunition parks, and reserve parks (which travel by rail), and for directing motor cars to their units.

The Director of Transport must therefore get into touch with General Headquarters as to the distribution of the mechanical transport units to meet the demands of any immediate or eventual movements.

His Assistant Director of Transport should assist the Assistant Quartermaster-General, General Headquarters, by establishing the control necessary to receive and replenish the vehicles and to issue promptly their instructions regarding billets or their distribution. The position of this control need not necessarily be at the "G.R.D.", but might be on the road by which vehicles arrive, according to the instructions of the Assistant Quartermaster-General, General Headquarters. *No personnel for this control has been detailed*, but if it cannot be furnished by the Assistant Quartermaster-General it might be found by ordering up, for temporary duty, some of the advanced mechanical transport depôt from Port R.

5. The majority of the mechanical transport is being sent to Port R, but all tractors and trucks are being sent to Port C. Motor cars are landed at all the ports, and the mechanical transport of the Royal Flying Corps is being landed at Port B. The ammunition for the ammunition parks is being shipped to Port R, where it will be loaded on to the vehicles of the parks.

6. The petrol, lubricants, &c., are being landed according to arrangements with which the Director of Supplies is acquainted, and one of the first duties of the Director of Transport will be to ensure a suitable distribution of them to enable the vehicles to be supplied. In the matter of petrol supply we have to be independent of the French, except in circumstances regarding which the Director of Supplies has been informed.

7. Before the supply columns leave the ports it must be ascertained whether any petrol or other supplies have to be taken up to the Advanced Base or beyond.

Petrol is not to be pumped into the tanks of mechanical transport vehicles from railway wagons; the French railway authorities lay great stress on this point.

8. As regards transport for supply purposes in the area of concentration, units must supply themselves from railheads ("gares de ravitaillement"), so long as they are stationary, by means of their supply and baggage wagons prior to the arrival of the supply columns. This, however, entails heavy work; for this transport and supply columns are to be sent up as soon as possible.

9. The Advanced Horse Transport Depôt is being sent to Port R, arriving about the 3rd day.

The Base Horse Transport Depôt will be divided between Ports C, R and B with the object of replacing casualties amongst the horses of units landing. The various portions should land on the 2nd or 3rd days.

10. The French have promised to supply transport to meet the first needs of the

Base Commandants of the ports and at the Advanced Base. A considerable portion of this may belong to the French troops. No understanding as to the organization of this transport has been come to and this matter requires attention.

11. The organization of the transport required by hospitals, &c., is a question which must receive attention during the concentration period. During this time it may not be possible to bring up any vehicles or horses by rail, but such can immediately follow the last troops.

12. Until otherwise ordered by the Inspector-General of Communications, the Director of Transport will act as Director of Inland Water Transport.

(6.) Director of Railway Transport.

1. No Director of Railway Transport will be appointed, as the French are entirely responsible for all railway arrangements.

2. The distribution of the Railway Transport Establishment will be as under:—

One Deputy-Assistant Director of Railway Transport will be sent for duty to each of the Ports C, R and B, to the Advanced Base and to the G.R.D.

One Deputy-Assistant Director of Railway Transport will remain at Southampton.

The remainder of the officers of the Railway Transport Establishment will be despatched to the G.R.D. and will be distributed by the Deputy-Assistant Director of Railway Transport at that place for duty at the detraining stations.

(7.) Director of Works.

1. The Director of Works and his headquarters are to proceed to the Advanced Base; the Deputy Director and his headquarters to remain at Port C.

2. The 15 officers of the Royal Engineers, to accompany the Director of Works from England, will be distributed as under:—

9 officers and 9 bâtmen	..	..	Port C } Attached to headquarters of bases.
3 ,, 3 ,,	..	..	,, R
3 ,, 3 ,,	..	..	,, B

Twenty officers will be despatched on the 10th day and 20 more on the 14th day, all for Port C, to be allotted as required by the Director of Works.

3. It has not been possible to make any detailed estimate of the work of the Director of Works' personnel. Certain stores, shown in Item 11 of the Quartermaster-General's War Reserve Schedule, are being despatched on the 3rd day *et seq*. They are sent as equipment for demolitions, water supply, entrenching and siege requirements to be held by the Ordnance as special Engineer reserve.

4. The Director of Ordnance Services has been instructed to make good certain deficiencies, in which the help of the Director of Works may be required. They include—

(i.) The provision of extra gangways and horse brows at the ports if required, and not available from home.

(ii.) Entraining stores, such as handspikes, tackles, large scotches with handles, eye bolts and tools for improvising arm racks in railway carriages, cordage and skids.

(iii.) Ambulance fittings for lorries; also stretchers as required by Director of Medical Services.

(iv.) Materials likely to be required for the repair of bridges and culverts.

5. No arrangements have been made for the early supply of stores for purely Works Services, and these would have to be obtained by purchase on mobilization.

(8.) Director of Remounts.

1. The Director of Remounts and his headquarters are to be at the Advanced Base, the Deputy Director and his headquarters at Port C.

2. For location of units, *see* Appendix L, 2.

(9.) Director of Veterinary Services.

1. The Director of Veterinary Services and his headquarters are to be at the Advanced Base, the Deputy Director and his headquarters at Port C.

2. For location of units, *see* Appendix L, 2.

(10.) Director of Medical Services.

1. The Director of Medical Services and his headquarters are to be at the Advanced Base; the Deputy Director and his headquarters at Port C.

2. The above arrangement would be the best during the commencement of concentration. During this period the eventual medical situation must be considered and decided, as the arrangements at present made may not be considered suitable to meet with battle casualties.

The existing distribution has been based on three factors—

(i.) The necessity of economizing rail transport during concentration.

(ii.) The need for keeping the area between the Advanced Base and the army as clear as possible, coupled with the reluctance of the French to agree to the scattering of our hospitals about the country, which, it must be recollected, is filled with their troops.

(iii.) The difficulty of mobilizing the medical units and consequently their late embarkation.

3. To explain the influence of these factors it is necessary to recapitulate the present arrangements from Appendix L, 2. They are—

Ordered to remain at Port C.

		Day.
Nos. 9 and 10 Stationary Hospitals	arriving about	6th—7th*
Nos. 1 and 3 Stationary Hospitals	,, ,,	11th—12th*
Nos. 4, 6, 8, 11, 12 Stationary Hospitals	,, ,,	19th—20th*
No. 2 General Hospital	,, ,,	6th—7th†
No. 6 General Hospital	,, ,,	9th—10th*
No. 1 General Hospital	,, ,,	11th—12th*
No. 9 General Hospital	,, ,,	12th—13th*
Nos. 8 and 10 General Hospital	,, ,,	14th—15th*
No. 1 Sanitary Section	,, ,,	5th—6th†
Nos. 1 to 11 Sanitary Squads	,, ,,	5th—6th†
Nos. 1 to 3 Base Depôts Medical Stores	,, ,,	12th—13th†
Convalescent Depôt	,, ,,	6th—7th*
Nos. 1 to 3 Hospital Ships	,, ,,	12th—13th*

Ordered to remain at Port R.

No. 3 General Hospital	arriving about	6th—7th†
No. 5 General Hospital	,, ,,	9th—10th*
Nos. 4, 11, 12 General Hospital	,, ,,	15th—16th*

Ordered to remain at Port B.

No. 2 Stationary Hospital	arriving about	5th—6th†
No. 2 Sanitary Section	,, ,,	5th—6th†

Ordered to proceed to, and remain at, the Advanced Base.

No. 7 General Hospital	arriving about	9th—10th†
Nos. 5 and 7 Stationary Hospitals	,, ,,	8th—9th*
Nos. 1 to 6 Ambulance Trains	,, ,,	8th—9th
Nos. 1 to 6 Clearing Hospitals	,, ,,	12th—13th*
Nos. 1 to 3 Advanced Depôts Medical Stores	,, ,,	12th—13th*

NOTE.—Units marked * are not to be established until ordered by the Director of Medical Services. Units marked † are to be established at once.

4. Previous to the arrival of the earliest of the above units at the ports, the medical charge of troops first sent devolves on the medical officers of the Line of Communication battalions.

One field ambulance for each Division is despatched from home amongst the first mounted troops, *i.e.*, on the 7th or 8th day.

5. It is not expected that *heavy* battle casualties will be incurred before the completion of the concentration, but the Cavalry Division and the 1st and 2nd Divisions are available for employment a day or two earlier. It is impossible accurately to foresee the course of events, but the above dates may be taken as a guide.

6. The problems before the Inspector-General of Communications and the Director of Medical Services are—

> (i.) To decide the best eventual location for the hospitals in view of the battle casualties expected.
>
> (ii.) To organize the means of evacuating the wounded.

7. The location cannot be settled without consulting the French as to the places which may be occupied by us and without reference to General Headquarters so far as the plan of operations and available railway facilities are concerned. It is necessary first to find out the area outside of which we cannot go. It is certain that places must be chosen on the railway system serving our army and that, without express permission from General Headquarters, no General Hospitals are to be established beyond the Advanced Base.

8. The system of evacuation of the sick *during the period of concentration* is—

> (i.) The sick of units will be taken back to railheads—
>> (a.) Before the arrival of the field ambulances and supply columns, on the "train" wagons with units.
>>
>> (b.) Subsequently, by means of the ambulances of the first field ambulance to arrive (*vide* paragraph 4 above), or by vehicles of supply columns.
>
> (ii.) From railheads they are taken back to the Advanced Base in the railway trains which brought up supplies.
>
> (iii.) For this purpose one or more wagons will be attached at the Advanced Base to each supply train, fitted with apparatus and stretchers provided by the British. Until such fitted wagons are ready, special arrangements must be made by the A.Q.M.G., General Headquarters, for the transport of the sick by rail to the advanced base.
>
> (iv.) Sick likely to be able to rejoin shortly may be kept at the Advanced Base; but those who may be sick longer and who can be moved will be sent back to Ports C and R.

9. The system of evacuation *during operations* is as follows:—

> (i.) The daily sick will be dealt with by the supply columns and supply railway trains, as in paragraph 8 above.
>
> (ii.) Battle casualties will be evacuated in special trains, "trains sanitaires improvisés," organized at the "Gare Régulatrice," by the Inspector-General of Communications. These trains will be sent to the "gares d'évacuation" on the demand of the Inspector-General of Communications, addressed to the "Commission Régulatrice."
>
> All the wounded will be sent to the "Gare Régulatrice," where those who may rejoin shortly will be kept, whilst those not likely to be well soon will be sent to the base.
>
> (iii.) Clearing and Stationary Hospitals will be sent up near the army as required by arrangement between the Inspector-General of Communications and the "Commission Régulatrice," to clear the field ambulances and take charge of such wounded as cannot be moved.

10. The "trains sanitaires improvisés," mentioned above, are made up of ordinary covered trucks, fitted with an apparatus of the type of the French Bréchot-Desprez-Ameline fitting.

Stores sufficient for six "trains sanitaires improvisés," each carrying 396 lying-down cases, will be sent from England. The trains must be ready by the 16th day at latest.

These fittings are also required for the daily railway supply trains, *see* paragraph 8 (iii.).

(11.) Finance, Account and Pay Services.

1. If a financial adviser is appointed, he should accompany the Inspector-General of Communications to the Advanced Base.

2. The Paymaster-in-Chief will be at Port C.

No date has been fixed for the despatch of the Army Pay Department units, owing to mobilization difficulties in England, but it is necessary to open imprest accounts on the Line of Communications, and with formations, immediately. To meet this need an advanced portion of the Army Pay Department unit is being sent to each port of disembarkation, respectively, on the 2nd day (*see* paragraph 7 below).

Further, the field cashiers attached to Divisions, &c., must be provided with currency, as explained below, at the earliest possible date, in order to provide for local purchases, requisitions, &c.

No field cashier is detailed for the Advanced Base.

3. As it will be necessary for the British Army to be in possession of currency for immediate payments in France, the following arrangements have been made between the Treasuries of the two countries.

4. A representative of the French Treasury will be attached to the British Paymaster-in-Chief from the date of the latter's arrival in France.

5. The French Treasury will arrange for French currency to be placed at the disposal of the British Paymaster-in-Chief, or any other officer designated by the latter, in exchange for cheques made payable in pounds sterling. The pounds sterling will be calculated at par (25 francs 22 centimes), subject to any subsequent adjustment, in accordance with the conditions for the negotiation of cheques, *i.e.*, the profit or loss resulting from the operation will accrue to the British Treasury.

6. The British must inform the French Minister for War, immediately mobilization is ordered, as to its first requirements in currency at each of the ports or elsewhere. This will enable the French Minister for War to warn the French Treasury as to the requirements, so that they can be met.

It is also necessary that the name of the British Paymaster-in-Chief shall be communicated immediately to the French Minister for War for the information of the French Minister of Finance.

7. The portions of the base Army Pay Department unit (1 officer and 2 other ranks each) sailing on the 2nd day for each of the three ports are despatched for the purpose of providing a paymaster for each base Commandant, and are to provide money to the naval transport officers if required.

These paymasters are to present themselves to the accountant of the French Treasury at each port (Trésorier Payeur Général, Receveur des finances ou percepteur) who will hand them the French currency in exchange for the cheque brought with them.

It is consequently necessary for the Paymaster-in-Chief to provide these paymasters with the cheques before they sail, in accordance with the terms of the notice he has sent the French War Office (*see* paragraph 6 above).

8. During the campaign the British Paymaster-in-Chief can demand from the French Finance Minister (telegraphic address—Ministre des Finances, Direction du mouvement des Fonds, Paris), at least 48 hours in advance, the sums which are required, indicating the locality where the currency should be handed over, choosing whenever possible a town of some importance.

The French Finance Minister will then take steps so that the British Paymaster-in-Chief, or his representative, can obtain the currency at the place named.

This procedure will allow the paymasters with divisions, &c., to draw the money required for local purchases, requisitions, &c.

9. The above outline gives the arrangements made. The Paymaster-in-Chief is responsible for issuing the necessary instructions for the service.

(12.) Postal Services.

1. No special arrangements have been made regarding the postal services. It is considered that the general principle contained in our regulations will suffice, but the Director of Postal Services will be responsible for initiating any necessary arrangements with the French.

2. Censorship will be carried out to some degree in the military post offices, and attention is directed to the instructions given on that subject.

(13.) Censorship.

1. Censorship in the theatre of operations is under the direction of the Commander-in-Chief.

The censorship of all postal and telegraphic communications of the forces in the field, press correspondents and foreign attachés is controlled by the Chief Censor, who is in charge of Sub-section I. (*d*) of the General Staff at General Headquarters. All licenses to press correspondents must be countersigned by the Chief Censor. This officer is assisted by—

(*a*.) A postal censorship establishment.
(*b*.) A " press officer," in charge of press correspondents.
(*c*.) An officer in charge of foreign attachés.

2. As regards the troops, every communication that emanates from any individual is read by the officer in immediate command of him, *e.g.*, his squadron or company commander. This officer is responsible that the communication contains no information that might conceivably be of use to the enemy should it fall into his hands. He franks the communication at the end of the text to show that he has censored it, and also on the cover, if any. In the latter case a special rubber stamp is used, the postal authorities having orders not to forward any communication that has not been so stamped.

3. In order to deal with independent communications and also to act as a check on the censorship carried out by units, the following censorship will be provided on the Line of Communications:—

At the Advanced Base	1 General Staff Officer, 3rd Grade.
At the principal base	1 attached officer.
At each stationary post office	1 attached officer.
Assistants to the above	Retired or Officers Training Corps officers.

4. Provision has been made for—

(A.) A special "Urgent" envelope (Army Form A 2043).
(B.) A Field Service post card (Army Form A 2042). (*See* Field Service Regulations, Part II., Appendix VIII.)

The former, (A), which is for use in case of urgent business, is not delayed when once it has been properly censored by the Officer Commanding the unit to which the sender belongs.

The latter, (B), is designed to replace the ordinary letter that individuals generally wish to send to their friends and relations. Providing that the sender deletes that printed portion which he does not wish to send and writes nothing on the post card except his name and the address to which it is to be sent, the postal authorities will forward the card without delay for censorship.

5. The arrangements for censorship of the communications of the civilian inhabitants will be made by the Commander-in-Chief, in conjunction with the local authorities, and will be communicated to all concerned.

8th Brigade.

3rd Division.

The battalion transferred to 14th Brigade,
5th Division - 1.10.14.

1st BATTALION

THE DEVONSHIRE REGIMENT

SEPTEMBER 1 9 1 4

1/Bn Devon Regt
1st to 30th Septr 1914.

Diary   8/3

1st Sept.   Hd. Qrs. & D. Coy awaiting embarkation on S.S. "Teviot"
             Lieut. Hozell & 3 other ranks of D Coy embarked on board
             S.S. "Mellifont"

2nd Sept.   Left Rouen on S.S "Teviot" at 2.20 a.m. & passed Havre
             at 2.30 p.m.

3rd Sept.   At Sea.

4th Sept.   Arrived at St Nazaire about 4.30 p.m. & anchored.

5th Sept.   At anchor & awaiting orders.

6th Sept.   Hd. Qrs & D. Coy. on board S.S "Teviot" entered docks at St
             Nazaire. 11 other ranks of Batt. joined Hd. Qrs, from Havre
             (employed as Telephone Operators at No's 6, 7 & 8 Rest Camps)
             Disembarked about 5.30 p.m, unloaded ship, marched
             about 2 miles out of the town & bivouaced for the night.

7th Sept.   Bivouaced for the day, 3 men of B Coy admitted to hospital.
             About 4 p.m, ½ of C. Coy strength 3 Officers. 115 other ranks,
             Draft 1 Officer 91 other ranks, Details 19 other ranks
             & 1 man of D. Coy from hospital joined the Batt. Total
             Strength 4 Officers, 226 other ranks.

8th Sept.   Hd. Qrs A, B & ½ C Coy strength 14 Officers 619 other ranks
             56 horses & 14 Vehicles, left St. Nazaire by train about
             2. p.m. for Melun.
             Major M. Doyle P.O.W.C left Batt. to join No 11 Stationary
             Hospital at St. Nazaire
             Lieut H. Crofton R.A.M.C joined Batt.

9th Sept.   Travelling by train

10th Sept   Arrived by train at Coulommiers, detained & bivouaced
             Lieut. A.7 Northcote joined Hd. Qrs as Asst Provost Marshal
             & Littlewood & Capt Odam joined Brigadier Provost Staff
             D Company Strength 5 Officers & 210 other ranks joined the
             Batt. Capt G.F Grey & 11 other ranks of C Coy joined the Batt.
             No 7650 Pte J G Harding of D. Coy reported missing on journey
             from Pemain

11th Sept.	The Batt. marched from Coulomiers to Sacie distance about 16 miles on its way to join the 8th Brigade 3rd Division, 2nd Army Corps. Arriving there about 3 p.m. & occupied empty houses for the night. 4 other ranks admitted to Hospital here. 3 R.G.A. men joined the Batt, A German soldier was taken prisoner here by Batt. & handed over to Civil Authorities on Batt. leaving next morning.
12th Sept.	Batt. marched from Sacie to Monthiers distance about — miles & billeted in a large house for the night. 1 man admitted to Hospital. The following joined the Batt. during the march from other Corps:- 11th Hussars 2 other ranks & 2 Horses, D.C.L.I. 1 man. 2/B Royal Scots 1 man. 2/Bn Royal Irish Regt. 1 man.
13th Sept.	Batt. marched from MONTHIERS to OULCHY'LA'VALLE distance about 12 miles & occupied empty houses for the night. 5 other ranks admitted to Hospital. A German Soldier name KARL FRIEDRICH WILHELM TIMM 14th Prussian Infantry, Dramberg, was captured & made prisoner of war.
14th Sept.	Batt. marched from OULCHY'LA'VALLE to BRAINE distance about 15 miles arriving about 7 p.m. & bivouaced, moving off again about 11 p.m. to take up a position about 5 miles away towards the firing line of the 3rd Division. The Batt here joined the 8th Brigade.
15th Sept.	The Batt. joined the firing line, Capt. R. Luscombe & 16 other ranks wounded.
16th Sept.	Wounded 24 other ranks.
17th Sept.	Killed No 7880 Sgt. A. Kingdom B Coy. Wounded other ranks 2.
18th Sept.	Wounded other ranks 1.

19th Sept. Killed:- Lieut. H.L. Hopkins R.A.M.C. (M.O.) Attd.
No 4878 C.O.M. Sgt. A. Cornish B Coy
" 8971 Private S. Adams A "

Wounded:- Other ranks 4.
Two Officers & 184 other ranks (2nd & 3rd Reinforcements) joined the Battalion.

20th Sept. Killed:- Capt H.G. Elliot
No 8198 Sgt A. Jeck A Coy.
" 7028 Pvt. J. Kilgannon A Coy) Died from
" 7156 " H. Joy D " } wounds
" 9109 Pte. S.C. Targett B "

Wounded:- Lieut. W.A. Fleming & Other ranks 4.

Accidentally injured Other ranks 1.

21st Sept. Killed:- No 7695 Pte. G. Kiff D Coy
" 7614 " A. Moga D Coy (Died from wounds)

Wounded:- Lieut G.S. Dixon (slightly wounded & doing duty)
- " S.H. Yeo — " —
- " C.F.W. Lang — " —

Other ranks 14.

22nd Sept. No 7631 Pte. W. Donovan D Coy.} Died from wounds
" 8144 " A. Trowle D " }

Wounded:- Other ranks 5.

23rd Sept. Nil

24th Sept. Nil

25th Sept. Wounded Capt. S.B. Davis
Lieut & Adjt. R.E.L. Tratton (& doing duty)
Other ranks 2.

26th Sept. Severely Wounded. Lieut. V.A. Beaufort.
- " - Other ranks 4.

The Batt. relieved in the trenches by R.S. Fusiliers & marched to Courcelles for a rest.
5 other ranks admitted to Hospital.

27th Sept.	In Billets at Courcelles, 2 other ranks admitted to Hospital. 62 other ranks (1st Reinforcements) joined the Battalion.
28th Sept.	In Billets at Courcelles, 9 other ranks admitted to Hospital.
29th Sept.	In Billets at Courcelles, 9 other ranks admitted to Hospital.
30th Sept.	The Battalion marched from Courcelles to JURY, distance about 10 miles, 17 other ranks admitted to Hospital before the Battalion marched off. On arrival at JURY the Batt. was Billeted, 2 other ranks admitted to hospital. Information was received of the death of No 8733 Pte E Jarvis J Coy who died at No 10 General Hospital St. Nazaire 29/9/14.

14th Brigade.

5th Division.

Battalion came from 8th Brigade 1.10.14.

1st BATTALION

THE DEVONSHIRE REGIMENT

OCTOBER 1914.

Army Form C. 2118.

WAR DIARY
or
INTELLIGENCE SUMMARY.
(Erase heading not required.)

Hour, Date, Place	Summary of Events and Information	Remarks and references to Appendices
1914. 1st October	The Battalion marched from COURCELLES to JURY, about 10 miles and joined the 14th Infantry Brigade, 5th Division, in relief of Suffolk Regt. and relieved Major C.C.M. Maynard D.S.O. left to take up the appointment of A.A. & Q.M.G. 3rd Division.] 5 men returned from hospital, and 8 men admitted.	Mob. 30/SS INS Sheet 33.
2nd October	The 14th Infy Brigade marched in the evening from JURY to NAMPTEUIL about 11 miles where the Battalion bivouacked for the night in a field. [Lieut G.E.R. Grior left on Special duty under Buford Smith] Capt BR Jeffreys and 4 other rank's were admitted to hospital.	
3rd October	The Brigade marched to LONGPORT by night about 16 miles and billeted there. 5 men were admitted to hospital.	
4th October	The Brigade marched to FRESNOY-LA-RIVIERE, by night, about 8¾ miles, and billeted. Lieut G.E.R. Grior rejoined from Special duty.] 9 men admitted to hospital. [No 9790 Pte H. Dore W'doy, reported missing on line of march.]	
5th October	The Brigade rested at FRESNOY-LA-RIVIERE. No 9790 Pte H. Dore rejoined, notification received of death of No 9686 Pte W. Rogers at BRAINE from Gun Shot-Wound in action at VAILLEY on 22nd September 1914.] 12 men admitted to hospital, 4 men returned from hospital	
6th October	The Brigade marched to VERBERIE at 3 p.m and billeted [in a match factory.] 1 man was admitted to hospital.	

Army Form C. 2118.

WAR DIARY
or
INTELLIGENCE SUMMARY.
(Erase heading not required.)

Instructions regarding War Diaries and Intelligence Summaries are contained in F. S. Regs., Part II. and the Staff Manual respectively. Title pages will be prepared in manuscript.

Hour, Date, Place	Summary of Events and Information	Remarks and references to Appendices
4th October	The Battalion marched to LONGUEVIL ST MARIE, [via PORT SALUT,] pontoon Bridge] and entrained by 9 a.m, obtained at ABBEVILLE at about 4 p.m. and marched to billets in VAUCHELLES-LES-QUESNOY, in which neighbourhood the rest of the 14th Infantry Brigade assembled. Notification received of the appointment of Majors R.A. Wright and Nogber Lepl. E. Spilsbury to Lieutenants in the Regiment.	map BEAUVAIS sheet 32. map. ABBEVILLE sheet 11. map. AMIENS sheet 12.
8th October	The Brigade marched to VITZ-VILLEROY, VAULX area, and the Battalion billeted in the latter place. 4 other Ranks to hospital.	map ARRAS sheet 4. Later.
9th October 10th October	The Brigade left VAULX in the evening and proceeded by motor lorries to DIEVAL, distance about 30 miles, and billeted. The Battalion and part of the Brigade was carried beyond DIEVAL to DIVION, and had to march back. The Battalion (D Coy) furnished outposts to the N,E, and S of DIÉVAL. 8 men were admitted to hospital.	later.
10th October	The Brigade remained in Billets at DIÉVAL [a continual stream of Belgian refugees chiefly from LILLE, passed through the village in a S.W direction] Captain H. A. Chichester Lieutenants W.V. Stennell and D.R.L. Quentin, all from 3rd (Reserve) Bn. ⊕ around Service Regiment joined the Battalion. 8 men admitted to Hospital.	later
11th October	The Battalion acted as Advanced Guard to the Brigade and marched via CAMBLAIN-CHATELAIN and CHOQUES, and HINGES to LOCON, arrived & later it was billeted, placing outposts covering the canal. 9 men were admitted to hospital.	later

WAR DIARY or INTELLIGENCE SUMMARY.

(Erase heading not required.)

Army Form C. 2118.

Hour, Date, Place	Summary of Events and Information	Remarks and references to Appendices
12th October.	The Battalion was detached from the 14th Infy. Bde. and placed in Divisional Reserve at GORRE close to the CHATEAU. 2 Companies under Major L.G. William were subsequently placed under the orders of the O.C. 13th Infy. Bde. E.Bn. Coned Gds Brigade, at LETOURET, where Lieut C.C. Haynes & No 9099 Sergt W. Lemon were wounded.	Map ARRAS Sheet Y.
13th October.	The Battalion, less 2 Coys remained in Divisional reserve, and dug trenches to the East of the CHATEAU. 1 man wounded, 3 men admitted to hospital.	
14th October.	The Battalion less 2 Coys remained in Divisional reserve as above.	
15th October.	The Battalion less 2 Coys was moved forward about 1½ miles along the LA BASSEE CANAL.	
16th October.	The Battalion, less 2 Coys, remained as before. At 6pm the Battalion was assembled for a night advance in the direction of the LA BASSEE Canal bridge South of CANTELEUX, and entrenched on the rising ground East of GIVENCHY.	

WAR DIARY or INTELLIGENCE SUMMARY.

(Erase heading not required.)

Army Form C. 2118.

Hour, Date, Place	Summary of Events and Information	Remarks and references to Appendices
14th October.	At 5.30 a.m. the Battalion started to advance, in conjunction with the French on the South side of the Canal and the Bedford Regt. on the left. "B" & "D" Coys formed the firing line and supports. The enemy fire was heavy. At 2 p.m. the advance was continued but had to be abandoned on account of Lack of Support. 3 men were killed and Lieuts. P.R. Worrall and R.O. Anstey with 16 others ranks wounded.	Map ARRAS Sheet 4.
18th October.	At 10 a.m. the French battalion crossed to the North side of the Canal, and when the latter had deployed for attack, the Battalion supported their advance which, was brought to a standstill by the German fire. The Norfolk Regt. was on the left of the Battalion. The advance was resumed at dusk and a line running approximately N and S though CANTELEUX was entrenched, with the right flank bent back in a S.E. direction. 2 men were Killed and 4 wounded.	
19th October.	The battalion improved its position, and after nightfall the line was straightened by advancing the right Company, in conjunction with the French on the right of the Battalion. 1 Man was killed and 1 man wounded. Lieut. P.R. Worrall returned from hospital.	

WAR DIARY or INTELLIGENCE SUMMARY.

(Erase heading not required.)

Army Form C. 2118.

Instructions regarding War Diaries and Intelligence Summaries are contained in F.S. Regs., Part II. and the Staff Manual respectively. Title pages will be prepared in manuscript.

Hour, Date, Place	Summary of Events and Information	Remarks and references to Appendices
20th October.	Our guns opened soon after dawn, but their fire was returned at about 9 a.m. by a heavy cannonade on the left Bn. the Battalion and the Norfolk Regt; meanwhile an attack on the Cheshire Regt. from their to the left was developed. While assisting at placing the houses at the Western end of CANTELEUX village in a state of defence and in taking other defensive measures there, Capt. H.A. Chichester was killed, and Lt.Col. C.M. Brooke and Lieut A. Tillett were wounded; Major P.G. William therefore assumed Command, 3 other ranks also were killed, and 10 wounded. During the afternoon our own guns dropped some shell in our line. The night was quiet.	Maps ARRAS Sheet 4.
21st October.	The trenches were heavily shelled during the day, but the night was quiet. Killed other ranks 2; wounded other ranks 9; died from wounds other ranks 1.	
22nd October.	Very heavy shelling all day by the Germans who attacked the Cheshire Regt. and the trench on the S. side of the canal. The Germans gained some ground to the N.E. near VIOLAINES, and on the S. bank of the canal. Orders were received to withdraw to the GIVENCHY line at midnight in conjunction with the French on the N. bank of the canal, and	

Army Form C. 2118.

WAR DIARY
or
INTELLIGENCE SUMMARY.
(Erase heading not required.)

Instructions regarding War Diaries and Intelligence Summaries are contained in F.S. Regs., Part II. and the Staff Manual respectively. Title pages will be prepared in manuscript.

Hour, Date, Place	Summary of Events and Information	Remarks and references to Appendices
22nd October.	and the Norfolk Regt. to our left. The withdrawal was carried out without incident, and a line running approximately North from the Q of GIVENCHY was entrenched. During the day 6 men were killed and 10 wounded. Captain G.H. Green was wounded.	Map ARRAS. Sheet 4.
23rd October.	Two Coys (A&B) entrenched in the position covering GIVENCHY, with Head "A" Coy in support in the village. The Germans were seen advancing during the day but did not press home their attack; their shell fire was at times heavy. D. & A. Coys were subsequently moved up into close support in consequence of orders received from G.O.C. 15th Bde. During the day Lieut R.E. Hancock performed an act of gallantry in leaving his trench, picking up a wounded man and carrying him 100 yards to a place of safety. Killed other ranks 4, wounded other ranks 19. Missing other ranks 4.	
24th October.	Considerable shell and rifle fire during the day. In the evening in accordance with the plan of making the trench supported from the defence of GIVENCHY, "C" Coy and part of "A" Coy was relieved by French troops during the evening. Killed Lieut D.A.R. Abadee, other Ranks 15, Wounded other ranks 29. from hospital other ranks 3.	

WAR DIARY
or
INTELLIGENCE SUMMARY.
(Erase heading not required.)

Army Form C. 2118.

Hour, Date, Place	Summary of Events and Information	Remarks and references to Appendices
23rd October.	The Battalion maintained its position in front of GIVENCHY, with "A" (?Sehow) and "B" Coy in the firing line. The enemy's fire was generally heavy but the German did not press home their attack. No Hill Sergt H.W. Bet killed in Commanding "B" Coy after his Officers had been killed. [Lieut. O.T.W. Hay made a good reconnaissance to report on the situation of ourselves and the enemy in the evening.] Killed Captain B.H. Beatty, Lieut. E.O. Gerald, other ranks 6; Wounded other ranks 14; Missing other ranks 1. Died from Wounds other Ranks 3. To Hospital other ranks 4.	
26th October.	A quiet day on the whole. In the evening the Battalion was relieved, as the defence of GIVENCHY was to be given over to the French entirely, and reached billets at FESTUBERT (ca# N. 9 LE PLANTIN) about midnight. The following message from Sir Horace Smith-Dorrien Commanding 2nd Army Corps. was received. "Congratulations to Col. Ballard and Norfolks, Devons, and D.L.I. Wellingtons for the splendid way they have maintained their position round GIVENCHY in spite of heavy losses." Killed other ranks 1, Wounded other ranks 5, To Hospital other Ranks 5.	10#
27th October.	The Battalion remained in billets in reserve with 2 Coys ready to turn out at short notice. [Pte Horgan rejoined Batt. having been reported missing 25/10/14]	10#

WAR DIARY or INTELLIGENCE SUMMARY.

Army Form C. 2118.

Hour, Date, Place	Summary of Events and Information	Remarks and references to Appendices
28th October.	The Batt. remained in billets in reserve, with 2 Coys ready to turn out at short notice, until 12.15 p.m. when a message was received relieving the urgency. During the evening the Battalion relieved the 1/Manchesters. Capt. (Robert Brunner) in the trenches which run South for about 400x from the road leading E and N.E. from FESTUBERT CHURCH, and about 1 mile from that point; the road was exclusive. Capt. H.C. Whitfield to hospital	
29th October.	The firing line consisted of "D" Coy, "B" Coy, 1 platoon of "A" Coy and "C" Coy, with 3 platoon of "A" Coy, in support, the trenches were bad and badly sited with a poor field of fire. During the day the Germans attacked and got within very close quarters, particularly on the left, where they could practically only be fired on by "C" Coy from the right enfilade. The enemy were kept off at the cost of considerable losses. Orders were received to hand over the left fire trench to a company of Ghurkas in the evening. This never happened to be the worst sited of any, was very wide and difficult of access. "D" Coy was moved back into the support trench. Killed Lieut. G.S. Armstrong & Lieut R.S. Hancock, Other Ranks 4. Wounded Lieut. L. Spilsbury, Other Ranks 6.	

WAR DIARY
or
INTELLIGENCE SUMMARY.
(Erase heading not required.)

Army Form C. 2118.

Hour, Date, Place	Summary of Events and Information	Remarks and references to Appendices
30th October	The Germans renewed their attack, particularly on the Tunnel now held by the Junction; a platoon of "C" Coy, under Lieut. B.E. Mulcett was therefore sent up to reinforce at considerable risk, but arrived to find the Germans practically in occupation of the tunnel; took the further Officers had been killed or wounded. Lieut. T.O.B. Silvin then brought up the remainder of "B" Coy, and with these Mulcett's platoon was able to press the left which was somewhat threatened as a result of the German attack on the further trench - Rats in the afternoon reinforcements of the West Riding and Bedford Regt. were brought up. Killed other ranks 39, Wounded other ranks 45.	
31st October	A quiet day, during the evening the Battalion was relieved by the 104th Pioneers and marched to POPRE. Killed other ranks 4, Wounded other ranks 6, Missing other ranks 3.	

E.G. Williams Lt. Colonel
Commdg. 1/D Devon Regt.

14th Brigade.

5th Division.

1st BATTALION

DEVONSHIRE REGIMENT

NOVEMBER 1914.

Army Form C. 2118.

WAR DIARY
or
INTELLIGENCE SUMMARY.
(Erase heading not required.)

Instructions regarding War Diaries and Intelligence Summaries are contained in F.S. Regs., Part II. and the Staff Manual respectively. Title pages will be prepared in manuscript.

Hour, Date, Place	Summary of Events and Information	Remarks and references to Appendices
1st November 1914 FESTUBERT.	Battalion was relieved in trenches at FESTUBERT by 104th Inniskilling, marched to GORRE and billeted near the Chateau by 6 a.m. At 6.30 p.m. Battalion marched via LE TOURET, LA COUTURE, and VIEILLE CHAPELLE to LESTREM where it rejoined 14th Infantry Brigade and billeted.	Map "ARRAS" Sheet 4. Map. ST. OMER, Sheet H.
2nd November 1914 LESTREM.	At 12.30 p.m. Battalion marched for CLAPBANCK, ½ mile S.E. of 0 in BAILLEUL sq via ESTAIRES, DOULIEU, PONT WEMEAU, NOOTE BOOM, BELLE CROIX FE, But was halted at D'où PETIT BOIS and subsequently ordered to return to LESTREM and occupy the same billets as before. 6 other Ranks to Hospital. Capt. E. Granville & Capt. H.a.S. Longe and 14 O. other ranks (4th & 5th Reinforcements) joined the Batt.	
3rd November 1914 LESTREM.	The Battalion marched at 6.20 a.m. and billeted at VIEILLE CHAPELLE. 5 other ranks to Hospital.	
4th November 1914 VIEILLE CHAPELLE	The Battalion rested in billets at VIEILLE CHAPELLE; at 2.30 p.m. Battalion marched to CROIX BARBEE where it halted and then proceeded to billets at East end of LA COUTURE as Divisional Reserve to Meerut Division. 2 other Ranks to Hospital.	

Army Form C. 2118.

WAR DIARY
or
INTELLIGENCE SUMMARY.
(Erase heading not required.)

Instructions regarding War Diaries and Intelligence Summaries are contained in F.S. Regs., Part II. and the Staff Manual respectively. Title pages will be prepared in manuscript.

Hour, Date, Place	Summary of Events and Information	Remarks and references to Appendices
5th November 1914 LA COUTURE	The Battalion returned to billets at VIEILLE CHAPELLE at 8 a.m. 2 other Ranks to hospital.	—
6th November 1914. VIEILLE CHAPELLE	The 14th Infantry Bde. relieved the 8th Infantry Bde. in the trenches S.E. of LAVENTIE in neighbourhood of CHAPIGNY and FAUQUISSART. Battalion relieved Suffolk Regt. in trenches running N.E. and S.W. about 300 yards E. of CHAPIGNY, as extended letter places Bn. H.Q. were placed. "A" & "C" Coys. went into firing line, and "B" & "D" into Support and reserve respectively. Killed 1 other Rank, 1 wounded 1 other Rank.	—
7th November 1914 CHAPIGNY.	Battalion held trenches and improved them. A quiet day.	—
8th November 1914. CHAPIGNY.	A quiet day; Battalion continued to improve trenches. "B" & "D" Coys relieved "A" & "C" Coys. in firing line. 3 other ranks to hospital.	—
9th November 1914. CHAPIGNY	A quiet day; Battalion continued to improve trenches etc. Wounded 6 other Ranks 3. To Hospital 7 other ranks. 1. Information received of the death of No 8672 Sgt. R. Copley at 1st General Hospital BOULOGNE. Reqd. at M. Humfrey & 52 other ranks (15th Reinforcements) joined the Batt.	—
10th November 1914. CHAPIGNY.	A quiet day; Battalion continued to improve trenches. etc. "A" and "C" Coys. from Support and reserve relieved "B" and "D" Coys. in firing line. Slightly wounded and doing duty 1 other Rank. 1, Information received of the death of No 7134 Pte J. Somers at BETHUNE.	—

Army Form C. 2118.

WAR DIARY
or
INTELLIGENCE SUMMARY.
(Erase heading not required.)

Instructions regarding War Diaries and Intelligence Summaries are contained in F.S. Regs., Part II. and the Staff Manual respectively. Title pages will be prepared in manuscript.

Hour, Date, Place	Summary of Events and Information	Remarks and references to Appendices
11th November 1914. @ CHAPIGNY.	In accordance with orders received overnight a continuous stream of rifle fire on the enemy's trenches was kept up by alternate platoons &c. between 1 a.m. and 2 a.m. as part of a demonstration in support of operation carried out by Meerut division South of NEUVE CHAPELLE. Some good scouting work towards enemy's trenches was done by No 8506 Pte. H. Tuffley and No 8632 Pte. A. Tellyn. The day passed quietly. To Hospital other ranks 5.	.....
12th November 1914. @ CHAPIGNY.	A quiet day except for some shelling. Battalion continued improvement of trenches etc. "B" & "D" Coys relieved "A" & "C" Coys in fire trenches. Wounded other ranks 4. To Hospital other ranks 4.	.....
13th November 1914. @ CHAPIGNY.	A quiet day; nothing of note to record. Killed other ranks 1, wounded other ranks 1. Information received of the death of No 4654 Pte L. Fuller at WESTMINSTER-LATOUQUES 11-11-14.	.....
14th November 1914. @ CHAPIGNY.	A quiet day on the whole. In the morning it was found that the enemy had sapped towards the left of the position (D Coy) and had dug a parallel at about 50x at some points from our fire trench. For about 10 yards during the night, which was dark and stormy, attempts at counter-sapping were stopped by shell fire. No 8499 Sergt W. Simmon D Coy, did good work in reconnoitring and reported the German parallel as unoccupied and of negligible dimensions. During evening Bde was relieved by 2nd Rawath Regt, assembled at	.....

79
3298

Army Form C. 2118.

WAR DIARY
or
INTELLIGENCE SUMMARY
(Erase heading not required.)

Instructions regarding War Diaries and Intelligence Summaries are contained in F. S. Regs., Part II. and the Staff Manual respectively. Title pages will be prepared in manuscript.

Hour, Date, Place	Summary of Events and Information	Remarks and References to Appendices
14th November 1914. CHAPIGNY.	at LAVENTIE and marched to ESTAIRES, which was reached at about 3 a.m. 15th. Wounded other ranks 3.	
15th November 1914 ESTAIRES	The Battalion arrived at about 3 a.m. billeted, and marched off at 4.30 a.m. to march with Brigade [via TROU BAYARD DOULIEU, NOOTE BOOM, BAILLEUL so] to METEREN where it was billeted after having halted and waited some considerable time pending the arrival of II Bde Staff Officer. A cold and very wet march.]	MAP. FRANCE. OSTEND.
16th November 1914. METEREN.	Brigade marched at 3.30 p.m. to relieve French 136th Regt. and French 39th Division in trenches West of MESSINES. "B" Coy was placed at disposal of Manchester Regt. on right of Battalion, "A" "C" Coy were placed in firing line and "D" in reserve. D.C.L.I were on left of Battalion. To Hospital other ranks 6.	
17th November 1914. WULVERGHEM.	Quiet day. During evening "B" Coy relieved left Coy of Manchester Regt. and came under Devon Command again during evening. Wounded other ranks 14. To Hospital other ranks 21.	
18th November 1914. WULVERGHEM.	Nothing of note to record. Battalion continued improvement of trenches. 2/Lt. Lt. Col. H.C. Whipple joined Batt. from Hospital. Killed other ranks 6. Wounded other ranks 4. To Hospital other ranks 4.	

Army Form C. 2118.

WAR DIARY
or
INTELLIGENCE SUMMARY
(Erase heading not required.)

Instructions regarding War Diaries and Intelligence Summaries are contained in F. S. Regs., Part II. and the Staff Manual respectively. Title pages will be prepared in manuscript.

Hour, Date, Place	Summary of Events and Information	Remarks and References to Appendices
19th November 1914. WULVERGHEM.	A quiet day. Nothing of note to record. Wounded other Ranks 2. To Hospital other ranks 2.	
20th November 1914. WULVERGHEM.	A quiet day. In accordance with orders received, during the evening "D" Coy. (from reserve) took over the left hand of Mandeville Regt. on right of "B" Coy, and a Coy. of D.C.L.I. took over left devon lines, thus relieving "C" Coy. which was placed in reserve vice D. Batt. H.Q. which had previously been in Lone Farm an D.C.L.I. who moved to more central spot, further to right, to suit new arrangement. Dangerously wounded Capt. H.C. Whipple. Killed other Rank 1, Wounded other Ranks 8. (Self inflicted 1.) To Hospital other ranks 2.	
21st November 1914. WULVERGHEM.	Nothing of note to record, quiet day. Wounded 3 (self inflicted) To Hospital other ranks 8.	
22nd November 1914 WULVERGHEM.	A quiet day. A hostile aeroplane descended about 400 yards in rear of firing line between Devon and D.C.L.I. position at about 9.30 a.m. D.C.L.I. took charge of the two aviators, document's etc. and a party of R.F.C. came subsequently to remove the machine and equipment. Wounded 1. To Hospital other Rank 1. (Information received of the death of No 7349 Pte. A. Coombes at No 3 Ambulance Train 14-11-14.)	

Army Form C. 2118.

WAR DIARY
or
INTELLIGENCE SUMMARY
(Erase heading not required.)

Instructions regarding War Diaries and Intelligence Summaries are contained in F. S. Regs., Part II. and the Staff Manual respectively. Title pages will be prepared in manuscript.

Hour, Date, Place	Summary of Events and Information	Remarks and References to Appendices
23rd November 1914. WULVERGHEM.	Nothing of note to record; quiet day. Killed other ranks 1, Wounded other ranks 4.	
24th November 1914. WULVERGHEM.	Nothing of note to record, quiet day. Killed other ranks 1, Wounded other ranks 1, to Hospital other ranks 16.	
25th November 1914. WULVERGHEM.	Nothing of note to record quiet day. Wounded other ranks 1, Information received of the death of No 9341 Cpl. R. Abraham at No 14 General Hospital BOULOGNE 24/11/14.	
26th November 1914. WULVERGHEM.	Nothing of note to record. Injured other ranks 1, to Hospital other ranks 6. Information received of the death of Capt H.C. Whipple at No 2. Clearing Hospital BAILLEUL 25/11/14. Capt R.J. Nuttall and 123 other ranks (1st Reinforcements) joined the Batt.	
27th November 1914. WULVERGHEM.	Fairly quiet day; a shell exploded in one of "B" Co.'s fire trenches. Killed other ranks 3, Wounded other ranks 6, To Hospital other ranks 1.	
28th November 1914. WULVERGHEM.	Quiet day. During evening the Battalion was relieved in the trenches by the East Surrey Regt. assembled by companies at NEUVE EGLISE and marched to billets at ST. JANS CAPPEL. To Hospital other ranks 16.	

Army Form C. 2118.

WAR DIARY
or
INTELLIGENCE SUMMARY
(Erase heading not required.)

Instructions regarding War Diaries and Intelligence Summaries are contained in F. S. Regs., Part II. and the Staff Manual respectively. Title pages will be prepared in manuscript.

Hour, Date, Place	Summary of Events and Information	Remarks and References to Appendices
28 November 1914 WULVERGHEM	Information received of the death of No 5119 C.S.M. A. Shore at No 8 Clearing Hospital BAILLEUL 8/11/14. No 5382 C.S.M. W. Chandler and No 4050 Sergt. H. Salt were granted furlough from 29-11-14. To 5-12-14 with permission to proceed to England.	
29 November 1914 ST. JANS CAPPEL	Battalion rested in Billets. To Hospital Other ranks 3.	
30 November 1914 ST. JANS CAPPEL	Battalion rested in Billets. Information received of the death of No 9194 Pte. W.O.S. Gardiner at BAILLEUL 26/11/14.	

Strength hoppiel Nov. 98

E.A. Williams Lt.Colonel.
Commdg. 1st Devon Regt.

14th Brigade.

5th Division.

1st BATTALION

THE DEVONSHIRE REGIMENT

DECEMBER 1914.

Army Form C. 2118.

WAR DIARY
or
INTELLIGENCE SUMMARY
(Erase heading not required.)

Instructions regarding War Diaries and Intelligence Summaries are contained in F. S. Regs., Part II. and the Staff Manual respectively. Title pages will be prepared in manuscript.

Hour, Date, Place	Summary of Events and Information	Remarks and References to Appendices
1st December 1914. ST. JANS CAPPEL.	The Batt. rested in billets. To Hospital Capt. S. G. Mullock. Other ranks 6.	Nil.
2nd December 1914. ST. JANS CAPPEL.	The Batt. rested in Billets. During the afternoon the Commander-in-Chief, Sir John French addressed the Battalion, thanking them personally and on behalf of the country for the part they had taken in the campaign and stating his conviction that they would respond with equal readiness in the future whatever the task demanded of them. Captain C. G. C. Eley & Seven Rifl. joined the Batt. and was posted to B. Coy. To Hospital other ranks 3.	Nil.

WAR DIARY
or
INTELLIGENCE SUMMARY

(Erase heading not required.)

Army Form C. 2118.

Hour, Date, Place	Summary of Events and Information	Remarks and References to Appendices
3rd December 1914. ST. JANS CAPPEL.	The Battalion rested in billets. [In the afternoon H.M. King George V. presented honours and awards etc. in a field 700 yards N.E. of ST JANS CAPPEL. The Battalion furnished one Company at full war strength composed of a platoon from each company with the following Officers. Capt. J.R.J. Milne, Capt. H.M. Hempstead (3rd Hants Regt), Lieut. O.P.W. Kaye, Lieut. S.H. Jeg, Lieut. W.J. Alexander, Lieut. G.E. Mulock (S.R.) Lieut. G.P.R. Drury D. 45th R.F.) Lieuts. G.P.R. Drury, W.B. Stennell (Special Res.) and Lieut. O.H. Foster were in charge of a draft of 100 men keeping the ground cleared.] [The remainder of the Batt. was formed up in single rank on the North side of the road leading WEST from ST.JANS. CAPPEL Church, with its left at that point, and cheered H.M. as he left the ground in his motor car.] To Hospital Capt. C. Granville, Other ranks 1.	1/"

WAR DIARY
or
INTELLIGENCE SUMMARY

(Erase heading not required.)

Army Form C. 2118.

Hour, Date, Place	Summary of Events and Information	Remarks and References to Appendices

4th December 1914
ST JANS CAPPEL
	The Batt. marched at 1 p.m. via BAILLEUL and LE LEUTHE for NEUVE EGLISE, where it went forward and relieved the R. West Kent Regt. in the trenches about 1 mile East of WULVERGHEM, between the WULVERGHEM-MESSINES road and the river DOUVE.
	
	Distribution
	
	FROM WULVERGHEM. TO MESSINES.
	
	                   C. Coy.
	B. Coy.
		D. Coy.
		                       A. Coy.
		
		          DOUVE RIVER
		
		"A" and "C" Coys in the firing line with "B" and "D" Coys in support.
		To Hospital Other Ranks 6.
			men

Army Form C. 2118.

WAR DIARY
or
INTELLIGENCE SUMMARY

(*Erase heading not required.*)

Instructions regarding War Diaries and Intelligence Summaries are contained in F. S. Regs., Part II. and the Staff Manual respectively. Title pages will be prepared in manuscript.

Hour, Date, Place	Summary of Events and Information	Remarks and References to Appendices
5th December 1914. WULVERGHEM.	Situation as yesterday. A quiet day, much rain. To Hospital Other Ranks 6.	
6th December 1914. WULVERGHEM.	Quiet night, except for some sniping. Enemy quiet during day. During the evening "D" Coy relieved "A" and "B" Coy "C" in the firing line. Lieut N. Botibol, Transferred from 1/R.W. Kent Regt. to 1st Devon Regt. Killed other ranks 1, Wounded other ranks 2.	
7th December 1914. WULVERGHEM.	Quiet night except for some sniping. Enemy quiet during the day. To Hospital other ranks 9, from Hospital other ranks 1.	

Army Form C. 2118.

WAR DIARY
or
INTELLIGENCE SUMMARY

(Erase heading not required.)

Instructions regarding War Diaries and Intelligence Summaries are contained in F. S. Regs., Part II. and the Staff Manual respectively. Title pages will be prepared in manuscript.

Hour, Date, Place	Summary of Events and Information	Remarks and References to Appendices
8 December 1914. WULVERGHEM.	All quiet during the night. Enemy quiet during day except for some shelling of WULVERGHEM. During evening A. Coy relieved D. Coy, and E. Coy. "B" Coy. in the fire trenches. Wounded: other Ranks 1.	
9 December 1914. WULVERGHEM.	All quiet during the night and day. At 6.30.p.m. 2 platoons of "B" Coy under Lieut. G.B.P. Green and Lieut. T.W.B. Delman, with one machine gun under Lieut W.V. Stewell, were moved into a position facing EAST and at right angles to the left of the trenches of "C" Coy, which face NORTH along the WULVERGHEM — MESSINES Road, with the object of supporting a reconnaissance which was made by a platoon of the Manchester Regt. on the NORTH flank of the Devon position. No fire action was however necessary and the normal positions were resumed. By order of the A.O.C. at 9.30.p.m. A message was received directing the O.O. 15" convey the	

WAR DIARY
or
INTELLIGENCE SUMMARY
(Erase heading not required.)

Army Form C. 2118.

Hour, Date, Place	Summary of Events and Information	Remarks and References to Appendices
9th December 1914	Brigadier General's appreciation of good work and information obtained by him during reconnaissance the night before last. (1st R Infy. Bde. No. D.M.G. 49 dated 9/12/1914) Wounded other Ranks 2. To Hospital other Ranks 6.	
10th December 1914. WULVERGHEM.	A quiet day. In the evening the Batt. was relieved by the 1st East Surrey Regt, and then proceeded by companies etc. independently to billets at NEUVE EGLISE. "A" and "B" companies remained on the position while digging support trenches 150 yards in rear of the fire trenches. One platoon of "B" Coy was detained to dig a dug-out for the O.C. and another look out from the East Surrey Regt, a post on the NEUVE EGLISE - WULVERGHEM road. Wounded other Ranks 3. To Hospital other Ranks 3.	

WAR DIARY or INTELLIGENCE SUMMARY

Army Form C. 2118.

(Erase heading not required.)

Hour, Date, Place	Summary of Events and Information	Remarks and References to Appendices
11th December 1914. NEUVE EGLISE	The Batt. rested in billets. To hospital Other Ranks 1. Capt. R.J. Mehui? Lieut W.A. Fleming and 40 other Ranks (4th Reinforcements) joined the Battalion.	
12th December 1914. NEUVE EGLISE	The Batt. rested in billets. During the evening "B" and "D" Coys. were employed in digging reserve trenches on the position recently occupied by the Batt. Wounded Accidentally Other Ranks 2. To Hospital Other Ranks 2.	
13th December 1914. NEUVE EGLISE	The Batt. rested in billets. During the evening "A" and "C" Coys. were engaged in digging reserve trenches on the position recently occupied by the Batt. To Hospital Other Ranks 2.	

Army Form C. 2118.

WAR DIARY
or
INTELLIGENCE SUMMARY
(Erase heading not required.)

Instructions regarding War Diaries and Intelligence Summaries are contained in F. S. Regs., Part II. and the Staff Manual respectively. Title pages will be prepared in manuscript.

Hour, Date, Place	Summary of Events and Information	Remarks and References to Appendices
14th December 1914. NEUVE EGLISE	The Batt. stood by in billets from 4 a.m. while the 3rd Division and 16th French Corps attacked the MESSINES position from the Northwards. During the afternoon the Batt. moved from its billets in the Southern portion of the town to billets in the Northern portion, to make room for the Norfolk Regt. and other units of the 15th Infantry Brigade. During the evening "B" and "D" Coys. were employed in digging a reserve trench on the position originally prepared by the Batt. To Hospital other ranks 4. No 7416 Pte. W.R.Pond, transferred to No 5 Signal Coy R.E. authy G.O.C 14th Infy. Bde. dy 14–12–14.	when
15th December 1914. NEUVE EGLISE	The Batt. stood by in billets from 4 a.m. "A" and "B" Coys. were employed digging reserve trenches EAST of WULVERGHEM during the evening. To Hospital other ranks 1.	when

Army Form C. 2118.

WAR DIARY
or
INTELLIGENCE SUMMARY
(Erase heading not required.)

Instructions regarding War Diaries and Intelligence Summaries are contained in F. S. Regs., Part II. and the Staff Manual respectively. Title pages will be prepared in manuscript.

Hour, Date, Place	Summary of Events and Information	Remarks and References to Appendices
16th December 1914. NEUVE EGLISE	"B" and "D" Coys relieved Coys of the 6th Bn. Yorkshire Regt. (T.F.) in trenches, coming under command of O.C. S.C.L.I. and Manchesters respectively at 5 a.m. "A" and "C" Coys employed at digging communication trenches East of WULVERGHEM during evening. Accidentally wounded Other ranks 1, To hospital Other ranks 5.	
17th December 1914. NEUVE EGLISE	The Coyt. less "B" and "D" Coys under O.C. Cornwalls & Manchesters respectively left by in billets at NEUVE EGLISE. At 12.30 p.m. the Regtl. Transport, billeting representatives and a few rest marched to fresh billets at ST JANS CAPPEL and at 2 p.m. the Battalion less the above, followed. During the evening "B" and "D" Coys were relieved and marched to ST JANS CAPPEL, where the Batt. with the rest of the 14th Infantry Bde. was held in divisional reserve. No.9933 Pte. S. Geary A.Coy transferred to 1/Devon Regt. Authy. D.C. 1/Devon Regt. dated 17-12-14. Killed Other ranks 3.	

WAR DIARY
or
INTELLIGENCE SUMMARY
(Erase heading not required.)

Army Form C. 2118.

Hour, Date, Place	Summary of Events and Information	Remarks and References to Appendices
18th December 1914 ST JANS CAPPEL.	The Batt. rested in billets ready to turn out at half an hour's notice. Inoculation against enteric fever was started. The following joined the Batt. Lieut. F.A. Hellaby (3/Auckland Regt.) N.Z. Loose Forces, Attd., 3 Coppers (13 Reg.) Lieut M.F.C. Perry Second Lieut. and 130 other ranks (9th Reinforcements). Other ranks 1. To Hospital other ranks 2.	1/"
19th December 1914. ST JANS CAPPEL.	The Batt. rested in billets in reserve, nothing of note occurred. To Hospital other ranks 4.	
20th December 1914. ST JANS CAPPEL.	The Batt. rested in billets, in reserve. [Voluntary Church Parades were held.] To Hospital other ranks 4.	

Army Form C. 2118.

WAR DIARY
or
INTELLIGENCE SUMMARY
(Erase heading not required.)

Instructions regarding War Diaries and Intelligence Summaries are contained in F. S. Regs., Part II. and the Staff Manual respectively. Title pages will be prepared in manuscript.

Hour, Date, Place	Summary of Events and Information	Remarks and References to Appendices
21st December 1914. ST. JANS CAPPEL	The Batt. rested in billets in reserve. 1 other rank to hospital.	
22nd December 1914. ST. JANS CAPPEL	The Batt. rested in billets. Played 14th Field Ambulance at Association Football and beat them by 4 goals to 1. To Hospital Lieut. V.R.W. Johnston, other ranks 3.	
23rd December 1914.	Batt. left billets at ST JANS CAPPEL at 1-45 p.m. Marched via DRANOUTRE, and lost one part of 2 wheeled transport by order of Wellington's West Riding Regt. and part of these received by 9th Queen Victoria Rifles (T.F.). Two Coys of Manchester Regt., "B" & "C" were placed under orders of O.C. 1 Devons as a reserve. "D" & "C" Coys with part of "A" were in firing line, and remainder of "A" Coy & "S" Coys in support and reserve. The Transport was billeted at DRANOUTRE.	

Army Form C 2118.

WAR DIARY
or
INTELLIGENCE SUMMARY
(Erase heading not required.)

Instructions regarding War Diaries and Intelligence Summaries are contained in F. S. Regs., Part II. and the Staff Manual respectively. Title pages will be prepared in manuscript.

Hour, Date, Place	Summary of Events and Information	Remarks and References to Appendices
23rd December 1914. WULVERGHEM.	A quiet day except for some sniping. During the evening the trenches on the left rear were occupied by "B" Coy, part of "D" Coy and the M.G. Section were handed over to the 2/South Lancashire Regt. and the two Manchester Coys received under the command of their own C.O. Two platoons of "C" Coy then took on part of the line and support trenches to the right of "A" Coy from the 2/Manchester Regt. and the M.G. Section was moved to a flank position in the firing line. The remaining 2 platoon of "C" Coy were placed in the farm about 400 yards North of W. in WULVERGHEM. Bn. H.Q. were moved to a house about 400 yards N.W. of that point and D Coy. was moved to a farm about 900 yards N.W. of the last named point. Work was on the improvement of trenches was continued. Dug from which the water might be collected for the purpose of boiling out were dug, and the parapets improved. Killed: Other Ranks 9, Wounded & Hernialii. 2, To Hospital Other Ranks 2.	MW

Army Form C. 2118.

WAR DIARY
or
INTELLIGENCE SUMMARY
(Erase heading not required.)

Instructions regarding War Diaries and Intelligence Summaries are contained in F. S. Regs., Part II. and the Staff Manual respectively. Title pages will be prepared in manuscript.

Hour, Date, Place	Summary of Events and Information	Remarks and References to Appendices
25th December 1914. WULVERGHEM.	A particularly quiet day. Beyond a few shells fired at WULVERGHEM during the early morning there was practically no firing in our section. Considerable progress was made in improving trenches etc. The day was frosty and misty. Wounded: other Ranks 2. To Hospital other Ranks 8.	Wm
26th December 1914. WULVERGHEM.	A quiet day which enabled some improvement in drainage of fire trenches to be carried out during daylight. During evening all men not on fire or support trenches were employed under R.E. supervision in digging a new fire trench in advance of existing one, mostly to right of Town and in front of Manchester's improving Communication trench, also in bringing up 25 wooden whale light troughs to the fire trenches abutting on the WULVERGHEM - WYTSCHAETE Road. The above Battn. comprised the Battalion less (2 N.C.O. and 23 men under Lieut. W.V. Stennett) 2 platoon of C Coy. and D Coy. left the Battalion support. The Coy. D.C.L.I. was employed on conversion of existing ditch into Communication trench at night of Devon trenches.	Wm

Army Form C. 2118.

WAR DIARY
or
INTELLIGENCE SUMMARY
(Erase heading not required.)

Instructions regarding War Diaries and Intelligence Summaries are contained in F. S. Regs., Part II. and the Staff Manual respectively. Title pages will be prepared in manuscript.

Hour, Date, Place	Summary of Events and Information	Remarks and References to Appendices
26th December 1914. WULVERGHEM.	After noon "D" Coy relieved "C" Coy; any relief as between "A" and "B" Coy, was considered impracticable on the whole as affording insufficient promise of rest to the men relieved. To Hospital Other Ranks 3.	
27th December 1914. WULVERGHEM.	The day passed quietly and some improvement was made in the trenches, but owing to wet much work was again undone. During the evening work was carried out on lines similar to those in force yesterday. During evening the Brig. General visited the trenches and later the V Divl Signal Officer came to lay a new telephone line consisting of a single strand of galvanized and enamelled wire similar to that used by the Germans, and made by Siemens Ltd. The line was to be so laid as to place all stations on a circle, so that line would always be available in event of a break being made. The use of the wire was unsatisfactory owing to the frequency with which fracture occurred then during the duration of the test. Slightly wounded and doing duty Other Ranks 1. To Hospital Other Ranks 6.	

Army Form C. 2118.

WAR DIARY
or
INTELLIGENCE SUMMARY

(Erase heading not required.)

Instructions regarding War Diaries and Intelligence Summaries are contained in F. S. Regs., Part II. and the Staff Manual respectively. Title pages will be prepared in manuscript.

Hour, Date, Place	Summary of Events and Information	Remarks and References to Appendices
28th December 1914. WULVERGHEM.	A quiet day on the whole. The Batt. Sappers and remainder of Batt. not in fire or support trenches was employed digging new fire trench etc. Under supervision of R.E. during evening but work was interrupted by enemy opening fire. Wounded Other Ranks 6. To Hospital Lieut M. McJerry, other Ranks 10.	
29th December 1914. WULVERGHEM.	During early hours of morning Captain H. du R. Sponge made a reconnaissance of part of enemy position and obtained information as to types of wire entanglements etc. During evening the Battalion was relieved by 2/ East Surrey Regt. and went into Brigade Reserve in billets at DRANOUTRE. To Hospital Lieut S.H. Yeo, Other Ranks 1. Died of Wounds. Other Ranks 1. Ranks 9.H.	

WAR DIARY
or
INTELLIGENCE SUMMARY
(Erase heading not required.)

Army Form C. 2118.

Hour, Date, Place	Summary of Events and Information	Remarks and References to Appendices
30th December 1914. DRANOUTRE	Nothing of note occurred. Captain R.J. Milne with 2 N.C.O's and 23 Privates who were considered unfit for duty in the trenches were sent to join H.Q. 2nd Army Corps for duty with a Company in process of formation there. To Hospital Other Ranks 29.	
31st December 1914. DRANOUTRE	Nothing of incident occurred. 4 men from each platoon received a full lesson at H.Q. of 39th Company, R.E. in the use of Grenades. To Hospital Other Ranks 6. (Total for month 157 O.R.)	

E.W. Serocold
Lt. Colonel
Commdg. 1st Devon Regt.

14th Bde.
5th Div.

1st DEVONSHIRE REGT.

January

1915

Army Form C. 2118.

WAR DIARY
or
INTELLIGENCE SUMMARY
(Erase heading not required.)

Instructions regarding War Diaries and Intelligence Summaries are contained in F. S. Regs., Part II. and the Staff Manual respectively. Title pages will be prepared in manuscript.

Hour, Date, Place	Summary of Events and Information	Remarks and References to Appendices
1st January 1915. DRANOUTRE.	The Batt. remained in billets. Nothing of importance occurred. Lieut A.H. Cope (late) 2/Devon Regiment joined Batt. for duty. To Hospital Other Ranks Y.	W
2nd January 1915. DRANOUTRE.	The Batt. remained in billets. To Hospital Other Ranks 14.	W
3rd January 1915. DRANOUTRE.	The Batt. remained in billets. Nothing of note occurred. To Hospital Other Ranks 4.	W
4th January 1915. DRANOUTRE.	The Batt. marched from DRANOUTRE to BAILLEUL with 14th Infy. Brigade and billeted. Attached to 5th Division R.E. at BAILLEUL as Carpenters. Other Ranks H. To Hospital Other Ranks 2. Lieut & Adjt. L.E.L. Nator, Lieut E.E.R. Prior, Lieut. C.F.W. Lang, No 6740 C.S.M. B. Todd, No 5803 C.S.M. B. Thod., No 6993 C.Q.M.S. J. Riley, & No 9320 Sgt. O.J. Sanders, granted leave to England from 4-1-15 to 10-1-15.	W

Army Form C. 2118.

WAR DIARY
or
INTELLIGENCE SUMMARY
(*Erase heading not required.*)

Instructions regarding War Diaries and Intelligence Summaries are contained in F. S. Regs., Part II. and the Staff Manual respectively. Title pages will be prepared in manuscript.

Hour, Date, Place	Summary of Events and Information	Remarks and References to Appendices
5th January 1915. BAILLEUL.	The Batt. in billets. Attached to 5th Division Head Quarters for course of instruction in use of telephones, other Ranks 2. To Hospital other Ranks 2.	/1/
6th January 1915. BAILLEUL.	The Batt. in billets. To Hospital other Ranks 1.	/1/
7th January 1915. BAILLEUL.	The Batt. in billets. To Hospital other Ranks 2, from Hospital other Ranks 1.	/1/
8th January 1915. BAILLEUL.	The Batt. in billets. To Hospital other Ranks 14.	/1/
9th January 1915. BAILLEUL.	The Batt. in billets. To Hospital other Ranks 14.	/1/

Army Form C. 2118.

WAR DIARY
or
INTELLIGENCE SUMMARY

(Erase heading not required.)

Instructions regarding War Diaries and Intelligence Summaries are contained in F. S. Regs., Part II. and the Staff Manual respectively. Title pages will be prepared in manuscript.

Hour, Date, Place	Summary of Events and Information	Remarks and References to Appendices
10th January 1915. BAILLEUL.	The Brigade marched from BAILLEUL to WULVERGHEM about 1-30 p.m. and Batt. took over trenches on right of WULVERGHEM — MESSINE roads from R. West Kent Regt. Transport billeted at NEUVE EGLISE. Lieut. C. Bertram Bore 5C.R.S., Lieut. C.F. Dingwall 1/8. Surrey Regt. and Lieut. G.A. Davies of Manchester Regt. attached temporary to Battalion. To Hospital Other Ranks 6.	
11th January 1915. WULVERGHEM.	The Batt. in trenches by WULVERGHEM. Shelled during day. Killed other Ranks 1. Wounded other Ranks 6. Lieut. C.F.W. Rang, No 6740 C.Sm. E. Tabb, No 5803 C.Sm. R.T. Rodes, No 6993 C.Q.M.S. J. Ridley, & No 9520 Sgt. O.J. Sanders rejoined from leave. To Hospital other Ranks 2.	
12th January 1915. WULVERGHEM.	The Batt. in trenches at WULVERGHEM. To Hospital Lieut. C.F.W. Rang, other Ranks 2.	

Army Form C. 2118.

WAR DIARY
or
INTELLIGENCE SUMMARY
(Erase heading not required.)

Instructions regarding War Diaries and Intelligence Summaries are contained in F. S. Regs., Part II. and the Staff Manual respectively. Title pages will be prepared in manuscript.

Hour, Date, Place	Summary of Events and Information	Remarks and References to Appendices
13th January 1915. WULVERGHEM.	The Batt. in trenches. Killed other Ranks 1, Wounded other Ranks 2. To Hospital other Ranks 3. Lieut. & W.J. Gallon and 45 other Ranks (10th Reinforcements) joined Battalion.	
14th January 1915. WULVERGHEM.	The Batt. in trenches. Heavy shelling. Killed Lieut. T.O.S. Ditmas, other Ranks 9. Wounded other Ranks 6. (The following did good work to day in keeping dig out the men from the supporting point after it had been blown in. There was heavy rifle fire at the time. Lieut. M. D. Hannon, Lieut L. West, Sgt. J. B. Sullivan all of the 28th County of London Artists Rifles who were attached temporary for 24 hours to Battalion.) To Hospital Capt. H. de L. Sholye, other Ranks 18.	
15th January 1915. WULVERGHEM.	The Batt. in trenches. To Hospital other Ranks 3, from hospital other Ranks 2.	

Army Form C. 2118.

WAR DIARY
or
INTELLIGENCE SUMMARY
(Erase heading not required.)

Instructions regarding War Diaries and Intelligence Summaries are contained in F. S. Regs., Part II. and the Staff Manual respectively. Title pages will be prepared in manuscript.

Hour, Date, Place	Summary of Events and Information	Remarks and References to Appendices
16th January 1915. WULVERGHEM.	The Batt. in trenches, relieved from trenches by 1/E. Surrey Regt., and retired to billets at NEUVE EGLISE. Lieut. J. T. Cole, Lieut. A. W. Fisher, attached to Batt. on probation from 16-1-15, to 6-2-15. Killed other Ranks 1, To Hospital other Ranks 3.	W
17th January 1915. NEUVE EGLISE.	The Batt. in billets. To Hospital other Ranks 11. from Hospital other Ranks 1.	W
18th January 1915. NEUVE EGLISE.	The Batt. in billets. Lieut. A. Tullett joined Batt. To Hospital other Ranks 1. From Hospital other Ranks 1.	W
19th January 1915. NEUVE EGLISE.	The Batt. in billets. From Hospital other Ranks 1. Pro H466 Sgt. Major & Lead and No. 4424 Sgt. A. Barry granted leave to proceed to England 19-1-15. to 26-1-15.	W

WAR DIARY or **INTELLIGENCE SUMMARY**

Army Form C. 2118.

(Erase heading not required.)

Hour, Date, Place	Summary of Events and Information	Remarks and References to Appendices
20th January 1915. NEUVE EGLISE.	The Batt. in billets. To Hospital Other Ranks 3, from Hospital Other Ranks 5. [Information received of the death of No 8628 Pte. J. William at 13 General Hospital BOULOGNE.] Lieut. C.C. Haynes and 60 other ranks (11th Reinforcements) joined the Batt.	W
21st January 1915. NEUVE EGLISE.	The Batt. in billets. To Hospital Lieut. G. McLarin, Other Ranks 3. From Hospital Other Ranks 3.	W
22nd January 1915. NEUVE EGLISE.	The Batt. in billets. To Hospital Lieut. J.T. Cole (on probation.) Other Ranks 3.	W
23rd January 1915. NEUVE EGLISE	The Batt. in billets. About 4.30 p.m. they marched towards WULVERGHEM and relieved the 1/E. Surrey Regt. in trenches. Lieut. C.F. Dingwall rejoined 1/E. Surrey Regt. from temporary duty with Batt. To Hospital Lieut. A. Tibbits, Other Ranks 6, from Hospital Other Ranks 1.	W

WAR DIARY
or
INTELLIGENCE SUMMARY
(Erase heading not required.)

Army Form C. 2118.

Hour, Date, Place	Summary of Events and Information	Remarks and References to Appendices
24th January 1915. WULVERGHEM.	The Batt. in lines near WULVERGHEM. Wounded other ranks 1. To Hospital other ranks 8. From Hospital other ranks 9.	/N
25th January 1915. WULVERGHEM.	The Batt. in lines near WULVERGHEM. To Hospital Lieut. C. Benham Done (attached temporary for duty) from Hospital other ranks 2.	/N
26th January 1915. WULVERGHEM.	The Batt. was relieved in the lines by 2/ Manchester Regt. about 4 p.m. and retired to billets at NEUVE EGLISE. Wounded 1. (who afterwards died of wound). To Hospital other ranks 2. Lieut. W.S. Sherwell, Lieut. O.A. Bopp, No 8657 C.S.M. Booth, No 3907 C.Q.M. Sgt L. Aralio, No 6737 Sgt L. Gould, No 4426 Q.M.S. R. Bowie, granted leave and furlough to England 26-1-15 to 3-2-15.	/N

WAR DIARY
or
INTELLIGENCE SUMMARY
(Erase heading not required.)

Army Form C. 2118.

Hour, Date, Place	Summary of Events and Information	Remarks and References to Appendices
24th January 1915. NEUVE EGLISE.	The Batt. in billets. To Hospital other ranks 4. [The following N.C.O and men of the Batt. have been awarded the DISTINGUISHED CONDUCT MEDAL. No 8099 Lspl. W. Simmonds, No 3942 Bandsman W. Dunster, & No 9311 Pte. W. B. Worsfold. Awly. List No.10 dated 23-1-15.]	
28th January 1915. NEUVE EGLISE.	The Batt. in billets. Lieut. D.M. Gray and 10+ other ranks (12 Reinforcements) joined the Batt. To Hospital other ranks 6. No 653 Sp. W.S. Whitley transferred to No 5 Signal Coy. R.E. dated 22-1-15.	
29th January 1915. NEUVE EGLISE.	The Batt. in billets. To Hospital other ranks 2, from Hospital other ranks 2.	

Army Form C. 2118.

WAR DIARY
or
INTELLIGENCE SUMMARY
(Erase heading not required.)

Instructions regarding War Diaries and Intelligence Summaries are contained in F. S. Regs., Part II. and the Staff Manual respectively. Title pages will be prepared in manuscript.

Hour, Date, Place	Summary of Events and Information	Remarks and References to Appendices
30th January 1915. NEUVE EGLISE.	The Batt. in billets. A few shells were fired into NEUVE EGLISE. To Hospital other ranks 3, from Hospital other ranks 1.	M
31st January 1915. NEUVE EGLISE.	The Batt. in billets. 16 other ranks proceeded to Base for employment on lines of Communication, being unfit for duty in the Trenches. (Authy. A. G. G.H.Q. No A/1135 dated 24-1-15.) To Hospital other ranks 2.	M

1/1.

6 + 207 friend
6 + 182 6 mt
25 km

K 1 + 23
W 17
Dth 26
───────
tot + 1 off, 55 o.r.

tot + 1 off, 55 o.r.

[signature]
Lieut. Colonel.
Commdg. 1st Devon Regt.

14th Bde.
5th Div.

1st DEVONSHIRE REGT.

FEBRUARY

1915

Army Form C. 2118.

WAR DIARY
or
INTELLIGENCE SUMMARY
(Erase heading not required.)

Instructions regarding War Diaries and Intelligence Summaries are contained in F. S. Regs., Part II. and the Staff Manual respectively. Title pages will be prepared in manuscript.

Hour, Date, Place	Summary of Events and Information	Remarks and References to Appendices
1st February 1915. NEUVE EGLISE	The Batt. in Quitters. 2 Coys. B & C. went into Reserve Trenches in support of 11th Surrey Regt. to Hospital the Rankers 2.	W
2nd February 1915. NEUVE EGLISE	Head Quarters of Batt. A & D. Coys. in billets B & C Coys. in Reserve Trenches to Hospital the Rankers 12.	W
3rd February 1915. NEUVE EGLISE	Hd. Qrs. A. & D. Coys. in billets. B & C Coys in Reserve Trenches. Capt. V.R. Savage, Armstrong H. Leinster Regt. and Lieut. B.J. Bond 3/ Devon Regt. joined the Batt. to Hospital the Rankers 1.	W
4th February 1915. NEUVE EGLISE	Hd. Qrs. A & D. Coys. in billets. B & C. Coys. in Reserve Trenches. Lieut. J.P.R. Orton rejoined the Batt. from leave. Lieut. W.V. Shewill. Lieut. E.A. Bolton. No. 8657. L/S.M. W. Bolton. No.3956. C.Q.M.S. A. Hastli. No.6757. Sgt. F. Gould, No.4426 Q.M.S.R. Dowle rejoined the Batt. from leave. A.O. "A"&D Coys went into billets near WULVERGHEM, they were then joined by	W

Army Form C. 2118.

WAR DIARY
or
INTELLIGENCE SUMMARY
(Erase heading not required.)

Instructions regarding War Diaries and Intelligence Summaries are contained in F. S. Regs., Part II. and the Staff Manual respectively. Title pages will be prepared in manuscript.

Hour, Date, Place	Summary of Events and Information	Remarks and References to Appendices
4th February 1915.	by "B." "C." Coys about 4 p.m. relieving 1/6 E Surrey Regt. Ad. Pm. of Batt. were at L.A. PLUS, DOUVE FARM. To Hospital other Ranks 4. From Hospital other Ranks 2.	W
5th February 1915. WULVERGHEM.	The Batt. in Trenches. A good deal of shelling during day. Lieut. W. V. Stewell wounded. Killed other ranks 1. Wounded other ranks 3. (1 died of wounds). No 4119 Sgt. W. Littlewood joined Batt. from Military Prison. Duties at G. H. Qrs. To Hospital Lieut. B. L. Bond, other Ranks 2.	1/1" W
6th February 1915. WULVERGHEM.	The Batt. in Trenches. Ravailles red Hospital Kd.	W
7th February 1915. WULVERGHEM.	The Batt. in Trenches. The Batt. was relieved in trenches by the 2/Hampshire Regt. and 1/D.C.L.I. Killed other ranks 1. To Hospital other ranks 1 from Hospital other ranks 1. Lieut. & QMr. S. Downing, Lieut. S. Bolitho Leave to England 8-2-15 to 15-2-15. No 7810 Q.Q.M.S. J. Hand & No 8446 Sgt. L. Britton furlough to England 8-2-15 to 12-2-15.	W

Army Form C. 2118.

WAR DIARY
or
INTELLIGENCE SUMMARY

(Erase heading not required.)

Instructions regarding War Diaries and Intelligence Summaries are contained in F. S. Regs., Part II. and the Staff Manual respectively. Title pages will be prepared in manuscript.

Hour, Date, Place	Summary of Events and Information	Remarks and References to Appendices
8th February 1915. NEUVE EGLISE.	The Batt. in Billets. Capt. H. Rushmore, Lieut. G.O. Anstey, Lieut. O.O.S. Davey, Lieut. G.D. Coleman and 50 other ranks (1st A. Reinforcement) joined the Batt. 4o Hospital other ranks 7.	W
9th February 1915. NEUVE EGLISE.	The Batt. in Billets. To Hospital other ranks 14.	W
10th February 1915. NEUVE EGLISE.	The Batt. in Billets. Wounded and doing duty other ranks 1. To Hospital other ranks 5.	W 1/11 1"
11th February 1915. NEUVE EGLISE.	The Batt. in Billets, relieved the 1/D.C.L.Infy. in Trenches near WULVERGHEM. about 8 p.m. To Hospital other ranks 9. From Hospital other ranks 1. No 1376. Pte. P.R.W. Grange, No 1401 Pte R.W. Davis, Pte. G.V. Carlton + Pte. G.R. Arnot, 2nd County of London Artists Rifles, [service Batt. attached to Batt. from 11-2-15 to 12-2-15.]	W

WAR DIARY or INTELLIGENCE SUMMARY

Army Form C. 2118.

(Erase heading not required.)

Instructions regarding War Diaries and Intelligence Summaries are contained in F. S. Regs., Part II. and the Staff Manual respectively. Title pages will be prepared in manuscript.

Hour, Date, Place	Summary of Events and Information	Remarks and References to Appendices
12th February 1915 WULVERGHEM.	The Batt. in trenches. To Hospital other ranks 3, [No.1019 L/C. A. Brown, No.893 Pte. R.A. Hallewort, No.1319 Pte. H.H. Friend No.502 Pte. H.H. Bone. 28 County of London A/Cyc Rifles Service Batt. attached to Batt. from 12-2-15 to 13-2-15.] No.8996 Sgt. L.H. Britton rejoined Batt. from leave.	W
13th February 1915 WULVERGHEM.	The Batt. in trenches. Wounded other ranks 1. To Hospital Lieut. J.A. Kellaby N.Z. Ex.t Forces (3 Auckland Regt.) other ranks 1. [No.1463 Pte. R. Butts, No.1519 Pte. H.C. Saulby, No.146 A/C. B.C. Molyneux, 28 County of London A/Cyc Rifles Service Batt. attached to Batt. 13-2-15 to 14-2-15.]	W
14th February 1915 WULVERGHEM.	The Batt. in trenches. Killed other ranks 1, Wounded other ranks H. To Hospital other ranks 4.	W

Army Form C. 2118.

WAR DIARY
or
INTELLIGENCE SUMMARY
(Erase heading not required.)

Instructions regarding War Diaries and Intelligence Summaries are contained in F.S. Regs., Part II. and the Staff Manual respectively. Title pages will be prepared in manuscript.

Hour, Date, Place	Summary of Events and Information	Remarks and References to Appendices
15th February 1915. WULVERGHEM.	The Batt. in trenches, relieved by 2/Manchester Regt. about 11 p.m. and marched back to billets at NEUVE EGLISE. To Hospital other ranks 3. Information received that No 9810 C.Q.M.S. Lane whilst on leave to England was admitted to Military Hospital ST. PETERS, JERSEY. 17/2/15. Lieut. J.B. Browning & Lieut. J.B. Baldie rejoined Batt. from leave.	W
16th February 1915. NEUVE EGLISE.	The Batt. in billets. To Hospital other ranks 8, from trenches other ranks 1. Lieut. J.L.P. Taylor and 33 other ranks (1st Reinforcement) joined the Batt.	W
17th February 1915. NEUVE EGLISE.	The Batt. in billets. Lieut. J. West, Lieut. R.A. Cutting & Lieut. Peters, joined the Batt. To Hospital other ranks 6.	W

Army Form C. 2118.

WAR DIARY
or
INTELLIGENCE SUMMARY
(Erase heading not required.)

Instructions regarding War Diaries and Intelligence Summaries are contained in F. S. Regs., Part II. and the Staff Manual respectively. Title pages will be prepared in manuscript.

Hour, Date, Place	Summary of Events and Information	Remarks and References to Appendices
18th February 1915. NEUVE EGLISE.	The Batt. in Billets. Capt R. J. Nibbs and 6 other ranks rejoined Batt. from Head Qrs 2nd Army. 40 Hospital other ranks 8. [From Hospital other ranks 1. [No 5763 Pte Q.F. Roberts died at No 8 Casualty Clearing Station BAILLEUL.]	W
19th February 1915. NEUVE EGLISE.	The Batt. in billets. relieved the 1/O.C.R. & left in trenches near WULVERGHEM about 4p.m. to Hospital other ranks 4.	W
20th February 1915. WULVERGHEM.	The Batt. in trenches. Head Qrs 1 Batt. heavily shelled. Wounded other ranks 4. To Hospital other ranks 4. From Hospital other ranks 3. [No 5366 C.Q.M. S. Rainford and No 8161 Sgt. G. Burch rejoined Batt. from furlough to England.]	W 1/"
21st February 1915. WULVERGHEM.	The Batt. in trenches. Wounded other ranks 2. To Hospital other ranks 4.	W

WAR DIARY
or
INTELLIGENCE SUMMARY
(Erase heading not required.)

Army Form C. 2118.

Instructions regarding War Diaries and Intelligence Summaries are contained in F. S. Regs., Part II. and the Staff Manual respectively. Title pages will be prepared in manuscript.

Hour, Date, Place	Summary of Events and Information	Remarks and References to Appendices
22nd February 1915. WULVERGHEM	The Batt. in trenches. Killed other ranks 3, Wounded other ranks 2, to hospital other ranks 9. No 5756 Sgt Dmr W. Beeds & No 9089 Sgt R. Willey Brig evacuated or furlough to England from 22-2-15 to 24-2-15.]	M
23rd February 1915. WULVERGHEM.	The Batt. in trenches relieved by 2/Manchester Regt. and returned to billets at NEUVE EGLISE about 10 p.m. To hospital other ranks 1.	M 1/11 "?"
24th February 1915. NEUVE EGLISE	The Batt. in billets. 40 other ranks 1/5th Reinforcements joined the Batt. To hospital other ranks 1, from hospital other ranks 2. Lieut. C.D. Coleman 3/Norfolk Regt. posted to 1/3rn Norfolk Regt. on appointment.	M
25th February 1915. NEUVE EGLISE.	The Batt. in billets. 4 other ranks joined the Batt. for duty from Base. To hospital other ranks 1.	M

Army Form C. 2118.

WAR DIARY
or
INTELLIGENCE SUMMARY

(Erase heading not required.)

Hour, Date, Place	Summary of Events and Information	Remarks and References to Appendices
26th February 1915. NEUVE EGLISE.	The Batt. in billets. Lieut. P.L. Kidd & Lieut. Horton L.W. Bamfylde 3/Devon Regt. and 59 other ranks (16 Reinforcement) joined the Batt. to Hospital other ranks 1.	
27th February 1915. NEUVE EGLISE	The Batt. in billets, relieved the 1/D.C.L. Infy. in trenches near WULVERGHEM about 8 p.m. to Hospital other ranks 4. [No 5708 Sgt. Dnr. W Reed & No 9089 Sgt. R. Willey rejoined from leave to England.]	
28th February 1915. WULVERGHEM.	The Batt. in trenches. to Hospital other ranks 3. from Hospital other ranks 2.	

A. Williams. Lt Colonel.
Commdg. 1st Devon Regt.

14th Bde.
5th Div.

1st DEVONSHIRE REGT.

MARCH

1 9 1 5

WAR DIARY or INTELLIGENCE SUMMARY

Army Form C. 2118.

(Erase heading not required.)

Instructions regarding War Diaries and Intelligence Summaries are contained in F.S. Regs., Part II. and the Staff Manual respectively. Title pages will be prepared in manuscript.

Hour, Date, Place	Summary of Events and Information	Remarks and references to Appendices
1st March 1915. WULVERGHEM	The Battalion in trenches. [Killed O.R. 1, Wounded O.R. 3 Wounded (during duty) O.R. 1, To Hospl O.R. 6 from Hospl O.R. 3]	
2nd March 1915. WULVERGHEM 4 Hrs	The Battalion in trenches. [Killed O.R. 1, Wounded O.R. 2, Wounded (during duty) O.R. 1, To Hospl O.R. 3, Major & Lt.Col. Radcliffe D.S.O. (?) 1369 Pte Henry Hughes 1st Battn.] Joined the Battalion [(?) 1369 Pte Wm Williamson 20th C. of London] No. 2411 Pte S.B. Wass, No. 1369 Against Rifles attached to Battalion 2-3-15 to 3-3-15.	
3rd March 1915. WULVERGHEM	The Battalion in trenches. Relieved by D.C.L.I. about 10 pm & returned to billets at NEUVE EGLISE. [O.R. 2, Local forces rejoined Battn from Hospl. To Hospl O.R. 2, from Hospl O.R. 1, Lieut L.A. Hillary N.J. Local forces rejoined Battn from Hospl]	
4th March 1915. NEUVE EGLISE	The Batt. in Billets. NEUVE EGLISE heavily shelled by the enemy. [Slightly wounded during duty Lieut A.W. Lishen O.R. 2, Wounded O.R. 1,] Lieut J.B. Botcho & Lieut O.A. Fletcher (on probation) Lieut J. Crocker & Lieut O.A. Fletcher joined Batt., To Hospl O.R. 4, From Hospl O.R. 2.]	Co 1st 4th K.L.W. & 6 Offrs from Hospls
5th March 1915. NEUVE EGLISE	The Batt. in Billets. heavily shelled. Several casualties of garrison. Wounded O.R. 1, To Hospl O.R. 9, From Hospl O.R. 1, To Base L.of C. O.R. 5.	

Army Form C. 2118.

WAR DIARY
or
INTELLIGENCE SUMMARY.
(Erase heading not required.)

Instructions regarding War Diaries and Intelligence Summaries are contained in F.S. Regs., Part II. and the Staff Manual respectively. Title pages will be prepared in manuscript.

Hour, Date, Place	Summary of Events and Information	Remarks and references to Appendices
6th March 1915. NEUVE EGLISE.	Yr. Bath in Billets. Shells out of village three hours during the day. [To Hospl. O.R. 13.] [To Convalescent Camp Other Ranks 1.]	
7th March 1915. NEUVE EGLISE	Yr. Bath in Billets owing to heavy shelling. Bath left village early and bivouaced about 1 mile S. of village. Relieved the Dt. in Trenches near WULVERGHEM about 9pm. [To Hospl. Other Ranks 8, To Convalescent Camp Other Ranks 2.]	1/1
8th March 1915 WULVERGHEM.	Yr. Bath in Trenches. [Head Quarter farm shelled. To Hospl. Other Ranks 1, To Convalescent Camp Other Ranks 1, From Hospital Other Ranks 2.]	5'8" W.1. & hop 35 to L/C 5 from Hosp 3
9th March 1915. WULVERGHEM.	Yr. Bath in Trenches. German prisoner captured by Kurd [Fd.] Fallen. [Slightly wounded rideng duty Other Ranks 1, To Hospital Other Ranks 3, To Convalescent Camp Other Ranks 4. From Hospital Other Ranks 1.]	
10th March 1915 WULVERGHEM	Yr. Bath in Trenches. Considerable shelling during the day. [Killed Other Ranks 3. Wounded Other Ranks 5, Wounded rideng duty Other Ranks 2, To Hospital Other Ranks 2, To Convalescent Camp Other Ranks 1, From Convt. Camp Other Ranks 3.]	

WAR DIARY
or
INTELLIGENCE SUMMARY.
(Erase heading not required.)

Army Form C. 2118.

Instructions regarding War Diaries and Intelligence Summaries are contained in F.S. Regs., Part II and the Staff Manual respectively. Title pages will be prepared in manuscript.

Hour, Date, Place	Summary of Events and Information	Remarks and references to Appendices
11th March 1915 WULVERGHEM.	The Battn. in trenches. Relieved by 2/Manchester Regt. and billeted in huts about 1 mile S. of NEUVE EGLISE. [To Hospital Other Ranks 4. From Grenadiers Camp Other Ranks 4.]	Ditto
12th March 1915 NEUVE EGLISE.	The Battn. in Huts. S. of NEUVE EGLISE. To Hospital Other Ranks 8. From 1 Hospital Other Ranks 1.	9th-11th Co K & W 5. to Hosp'g from Hosp 8 Ditto
13th March 1915 NEUVE EGLISE.	The Battn. in Huts. To Hospital Other Ranks 1. Draft of 60 Other Ranks joined Battalion. (1st Reinforcement)	Ditto
14th March 1915 NEUVE EGLISE.	The Battn. in Huts. To Hospital Other Ranks 1. From Hospital Other Ranks 2.	Ditto
15th March 1915 NEUVE EGLISE	The Battn. in Huts. The Battn. received the D.C.L.I. in trenches near WULVERGHEM about 9pm. [Fields] Other Ranks 1. To Hospital Other Ranks 9. From Hospital Other Ranks 2. A 2. of London Arbot. Rifles, 1 Army Service Corps, 1 London Rifle Brigade and 1 Bombay Light Horse attached to Battn. for 48 hours trench duty.	Ditto 12th-15th to Hosp'g 19 from 5

Army Form C. 2118.

WAR DIARY
or
INTELLIGENCE SUMMARY.
(Erase heading not required.)

Instructions regarding War Diaries and Intelligence Summaries are contained in F.S. Regs., Part II and the Staff Manual respectively. Title pages will be prepared in manuscript.

Hour, Date, Place	Summary of Events and Information	Remarks and references to Appendices
16th March 1915. WULVERGHEM.	The Battn in trenches. [From Hospital Other Ranks 2. 3 County of London Cadet Rifle. 1 London Rifle Brigade & Hon Artillery Company attached to Battn for 24 hours first duty.] Draft of 54 Other Ranks (1st Reinforcements) joined Battn [and billets in NEUVE EGLISE.]	
17th March 1915. WULVERGHEM.	The Battn in trenches. [Wounded Other Ranks 2. To Hospital Other Ranks 10. From Hospital Other Ranks 1. The draft of 54 Other Ranks proceeded to join the Battn in trenches.]	
18th March 1915. WULVERGHEM.	The Battn in trenches. [Wounded Other Ranks 1. To Hospital Other Ranks 3. From Hospital Other Ranks 6.]	
19th March 1915. WULVERGHEM.	The Battn in trenches. Relieved by 1/Manchester Regt. about 9.30pm [and billeted in huts S. of NEUVE EGLISE. Killed Other Ranks 1. Wounded Other Ranks 3. From Hospital Other Ranks 3. Died at H⁰ 8 Casualty Clearing Station Other Ranks 1.]	W.15.19 K 2. w 6 Ltns⁵.13 from " 12

WAR DIARY or INTELLIGENCE SUMMARY.

(Erase heading not required.)

Army Form C. 2118.

Hour, Date, Place	Summary of Events and Information	Remarks and references to Appendices
20th March 1915. NEUVE EGLISE	The Batln. in Huts. To Hospital Other Ranks 3. From Hospital Other Ranks 2. 4 Other Ranks proceeded to ST. OMER for Machine Gun Course.	WW
21st March 1915. NEUVE EGLISE.	The Batln. in Huts. To Hospital Other Ranks 1. From Hospital Other Ranks 1.	WW
22nd March 1915. NEUVE EGLISE.	The Batln. in Huts.	WW
23rd March 1915. NEUVE EGLISE.	At 6.30 pm the Batln. marched from billets at NEUVE EGLISE and relieved the 2nd the South Lancashire Regiment and part of the 1st Bn. Royal Irish Rifles of the 1st Infantry Brigade in the LOCRE-KEMMEL line, about 2,500 yards East of the latter place. Distribution :- Trenches G1. and G2. B Coy [Capt R. Sweeny] Trenches G3, G6, G7, and H1. B Coy [Lieut A.H. Cope] Trenches H2, H3, H5, and Lock House A Coy [Lieut G.S.R. Cain] Supporting Point S.H. on Eastern of KEMMEL D Coy [Captain A.R. Saloyl-Domony] Reserve in KEMMEL 8 Platoons R.D Coy [Capt R. Philney] Machine Guns one each in H.5.1 and S.H. [Lieut W.A.F. Kemmy] H.3.1	20th 11: 16 Hosp 4, from Hosp 3. WW

Army Form C. 2118.

WAR DIARY
or
INTELLIGENCE SUMMARY.
(Erase heading not required.)

Instructions regarding War Diaries and Intelligence Summaries are contained in F.S. Regs., Part II. and the Staff Manual respectively. Title pages will be prepared in manuscript.

Hour, Date, Place	Summary of Events and Information	Remarks and references to Appendices
23rd March 1915. NEUVE EGLISE (continued).	Lieut & Adjutant L.S.L. Mahon rejoined Battn at NEUVE EGLISE from leave. (without Captain) Capt. J. Short proceeded to H.Q. 2nd Army for duty. [To Hospital Other Ranks 13, From Hospital Other Ranks 1.]	
24th March 1915. KEMMEL.	A quiet day. Battalion in trenches. During night improvements on trenches was continued by thickening parapets, building [faradin?] re: tractine was brought up by 1 D.C.L.I. and of Cheshires, and 12 Coys of B.W.I. furnished a working party. The 3 platoons of 'D' Coy on reserve were employed in carrying up rations etc. [Wounded Other Ranks 4. To Hospital Other Ranks 4, From Hospital Other Ranks 1.]	
25th March 1915. KEMMEL.	Battalion in trenches a quiet day except for slight shelling by [Lazingh?] during the afternoon. During the evening D Coy. from [Brier?] relieved 'A' Company in the trenches then R.W.K. [illegible] 3/ Scoop Regt joined Battalion. [Wounded Other Ranks 3. From Hospital Other Ranks 3.]	

WAR DIARY
or
INTELLIGENCE SUMMARY.
(Erase heading not required.)

Army Form C. 2118.

Instructions regarding War Diaries and Intelligence Summaries are contained in F.S. Regs., Part II. and the Staff Manual respectively. Title pages will be prepared in manuscript.

Hour, Date, Place	Summary of Events and Information	Remarks and references to Appendices
26th March 1915 KEMMEL.	The Battalion in Trenches. A quiet day followed by a quiet evening. During the night the repair and remodelling of trenches etc. was carried on assisted by working party of D.C.L.I. and carrying parties of other Regiments. [Wounded Other Ranks 2.] To Hospital Other Ranks 13.	1/14
27th March 1915 KEMMEL	Quiet day in Trenches. The Battalion was relieved by D.C.L.I. during the evening and marched to Billets in LOCRE where it was put in Divisional Reserve. [Killed Other Ranks 2, Lieut S.F. Taylor Wounded. Other Ranks Wounded 4, To Hospital Other Ranks 21.] From Hospital Other Ranks 3.	Cas 23 — of K 2 W 14 + 13 to Hosp 32 from. 7
28th March 1915 LOCRE.	The Battalion remained in Billets at LOCRE. Lieut R.F. Hallows R.A.M.C. proceeded to 5th Divisional Train at BAILLEUL for duty. Lieut E. Seely R.A.M.C. joined Battn. To Hospital Other Ranks 6. [1 Other Rank Died of Wounds at N° 14 Field Ambulance, LOCRE.]	

Army Form C. 2118.

WAR DIARY
or
INTELLIGENCE SUMMARY.
(Erase heading not required.)

Instructions regarding War Diaries and Intelligence Summaries are contained in F.S. Regs., Part II. and the Staff Manual respectively. Title pages will be prepared in manuscript.

Hour, Date, Place	Summary of Events and Information	Remarks and references to Appendices
29th March 1915. LOCRE	The Battalion remained in Billets at LOCRE. from Hospital Other Ranks 3.	
30th March 1915. LOCRE	The Battalion remained in Billets at LOCRE. Wounded at KEMMEL during night work Other Ranks 3. To Hospital Other Ranks 3.	1/11
31st March 1915. LOCRE	The Battalion relieved the 1st D.C.L.I. in the Trenches at KEMMEL, Leaving Q.I. to H.S. without incident Other Ranks 3. Hospital Other Ranks 8. from Hospital Other Ranks 3.	W 3 27-31st to Hosp 17 from " 9 Month K. & W 1 + 36. To Hospital 157 from " 52.

E.R. Williams
Lt Colonel.
Comdg. 1st Bn. Devon Regt.

14th Bde.
5th Div.

1st DEVONSHIRE REGT.

APRIL

1915

WAR DIARY
or
INTELLIGENCE SUMMARY.
(Erase heading not required.)

Army Form C. 2118.

Instructions regarding War Diaries and Intelligence Summaries are contained in F.S. Regs., Part II. and the Staff Manual respectively. Title pages will be prepared in manuscript.

Hour, Date, Place	Summary of Events and Information	Remarks and references to Appendices
Thursday 1st April 1915 LOCRE	A fairly quiet day except for some shelling by the enemy during the course of which some 25 large shells were dropped in and round the district from buildings known as 54 damaging it very considerably but without entirely demolishing it. The garrison escaped unhurt and was relieved during the evening. Killed Other Ranks 1, Wounded Other Ranks 1, from Hospital Other Ranks 2.	
Friday 2nd April 1915 KEMMEL	An exceptionally quiet day. Wounded Other Ranks 6, to Hospital Other Ranks 5, from Hospital Other Ranks 2.	
Saturday 3rd April 1915 KEMMEL	A very quiet day. During the evening the Battalion was relieved in the trenches by the 8th Bn Sherwood Foresters. Killed Other Ranks 3, Wounded Other Ranks 1, to Hospital Other Ranks 13, from Hospital Other Ranks 4.	
Sunday 4th April 1915 LOCRE	The Battalion rested in Billets at LOCRE. To Hospital Other Ranks 4, to Convalescent Camp Other Ranks 9.	
Monday 5th April 1915 ST. HUBERTUSHOEK	The Battalion marched at 9.15 a.m. and occupied wooden huts at ST. HUBERTUSHOEK at 9.32 a.m. The weather was very wet. Lieut F.W.J. Dalton to Hospital.	

WAR DIARY or INTELLIGENCE SUMMARY.

(Erase heading not required.)

Army Form C. 2118.

Hour, Date, Place	Summary of Events and Information	Remarks and references to Appendices
Tuesday 6th April 1915. ST. HUBERTUSHOEK	The Battalion visits in the Hutments. The Comdg. Officer, the Senior Major and Adjutant attended a conference of Commanding Officers at the 14th Infantry Brigade Head Quarters in LOCRE at 5.30pm. Other Ranks 5. to Hospital	
Wednesday 7th April 1915. ST. HUBERTUSHOEK	The 14th Infantry Brigade relieved the 15th Infantry Brigade in the trenches about OOSTHOEK, 2 miles South of YPRES. The Battalion [marched at 4.50pm via HALLEBAST] to KRUISSTRAAT [and billeted there] to be in reserve to the Brigade [from Hospital Other Ranks 2]. Other Ranks 5. to Hospital	
Thursday 8th April 1915. KRUISSTRAAT.	The Battalion remained in Billets at KRUISSTRAAT. nothing of note occurred. To Hospital Other Ranks 5, from Hospital Other Ranks 1, Lieut W.A. Fleming proceeded to Head Qrs 14th Infantry Brigade to take over duties of Brigade Machine Gun Officer.	
Friday 9th April 1915. KRUISSTRAAT.	The Battalion remained in Billets at KRUISSTRAAT. Beyond a few shells falling in the vicinity of the Billets nothing of note occurred. A Company was employed as a working party on the trenches during the evening. Lieut J West accompanied by his servant and 6 Other ranks proceeded to ST. OMER for Machine Gun Course. to Hospital Other ranks 4.	

Army Form C. 2118.

WAR DIARY
or
INTELLIGENCE SUMMARY.
(Erase heading not required.)

Instructions regarding War Diaries and Intelligence Summaries are contained in F.S. Regs., Part II. and the Staff Manual respectively. Title pages will be prepared in manuscript.

Hour, Date, Place	Summary of Events and Information	Remarks and references to Appendices
Saturday 10th April 1915. KRUISSTRAAT.	The Battalion rests in Billets. Nothing of note occurred. To Hospital Other Ranks 2, From Hospital Other Ranks 5.	
Sunday 11th April 1915. OOSTHOEK	The Battalion relieved the 1st Bn. D.C.L.I. in the trenches about OOSTHOEK, Hooge go SOUTH of YPRES during the evening; the transport remained at KRUISSTRAAT. The Battalion was distributed as follows pending the extension of accommodation in the fire and support trenches and the adoption of a more forward position for the Reserve Company and Battalion H.Q. A Coy trenches 23J, 23C, 24, with one platoon in KINGSWAY. B Coy trenches 25, 26, with one platoon in KINGSWAY. C Coy KINGSWAY. D Coy BEDFORD HOUSE (Chateau) Bn H.Q. BEDFORD HOUSE (Buildings just South of Chateau) Machine Gun Team Lieut Gun Team A.2 belong in various trenches. 2nd Lieut B.M. Gray To Hospital, To Hospital Other Ranks 1, From Hospital Other Ranks 2. Killed Other Ranks 1, Wounded Other Ranks 1.	
Monday 12th April 1915. OOSTHOEK	A fairly quiet day in the trenches. Killed Other Ranks 3, Wounded Other Ranks 5. To Hospital Other Ranks 1, From Hospital Other Ranks 1.	

WAR DIARY or INTELLIGENCE SUMMARY.

(Erase heading not required.)

Army Form C. 2118.

Hour, Date, Place	Summary of Events and Information	Remarks and references to Appendices
Tuesday 13th April 1915 OOSTHOEK	A fairly quiet day in the trenches except for some slight shelling by the enemy. During the evening there was rather more rifle firing than usual on both sides, and the enemy's trench mortars were fairly active in front of trench 26. During the early hours of the morning Lt. Colonel B.G. William C.M.G. took over command of the 1st Infantry Brigade vice Br. Genl. F.S. Inglefield C.B. who received a bullet wound whilst returning from the trenches. A Coy relieved D Coy and D Coy relieved B Coy after dark in the course of which operation Captain R.J. Mills was wounded and Captain A.R. Savage Armsby (14th Kensington Regt) took over command of D Coy on his return. Killed Other Ranks 1; Wounded Other Ranks 1, to Hospital Other Ranks 2. From Hospital 4.	
Wednesday 14th April 1915 OOSTHOEK	A quiet day except that at about 11.30pm there was a considerable amount of noise emanating apparently from some part of the line to the right of the Down Farm and lasting about a quarter of an hour. By 11.45pm all was again quiet. The impression conveyed was that the explosion of a mine by one side or the other had been the occasion of a considerable fire activity on both sides. Wounded Other Ranks 6; 2 Lieut B.W.H. Wright wounded. To Hospital Other Ranks 8.	

Army Form C. 2118.

WAR DIARY
or
INTELLIGENCE SUMMARY.
(Erase heading not required.)

Instructions regarding War Diaries and Intelligence Summaries are contained in F.S. Regs., Part II. and the Staff Manual respectively. Title pages will be prepared in manuscript.

Hour, Date, Place	Summary of Events and Information	Remarks and references to Appendices
Thursday 15th April 1915 OOSTHOEK	A fairly quiet day. During the evening the Battalion was relieved in the trenches about OOSTHOEK and withdrew to the Billets at formerly occupied at KRUISSTRAAT. 2nd Lieut Sir B.R. William Bart. joined Battalion. Died of wounds other ranks 1, Killed other Ranks 1, Wounded other Ranks 5, to Hospital other Ranks 4.	
Friday 16th April 1915 KRUISSTRAAT	A fairly quiet day in Billets at KRUISSTRAAT. Wounded other Ranks 3, to Hospital other Ranks 4, from Hospital other Ranks 1.	
Saturday 17th April 1915 KRUISSTRAAT	A quiet day in Billets at KRUISSTRAAT except for heavy fire from neighbouring batteries from inwards when at about 6000 East of ZILLEBEKE the enemy's trenches about 60 yards was fired. The Battalion stood by ready to move at short notice. 2nd Lieut R.H. Cutting, Artist Rifles, to Hospital. Lt. Colonel E.G. Williamson returned and resumed command of Battalion.	
Sunday 18th April 1915 KRUISSTRAAT	The Battalion stood by in billets ready to move at short notice. Wounded other Ranks 1, from Hospital other Ranks 1.	

WAR DIARY or INTELLIGENCE SUMMARY.

Army Form C. 2118.

Hour, Date, Place	Summary of Events and Information	Remarks and references to Appendices
Monday 19th April 1915. KRUISSTRAAT.	The Battalion remained in billets in reserve to the 5th Division. During the course of the day a few heavy shells fell in close proximity to some of the billets. To Hospital other Ranks 8, from Hospital other Ranks 3.	
Tuesday 20th April 1915. KRUISSTRAAT.	The Battalion remained in billets at KRUISSTRAAT, during the day a certain number of shells of various dimensions fell in the vicinity of the billets. At 6.45 pm the Battalion moved out of billets and took shelter under the entrenchment land on the aug.(?) part on the entrenchment along the west edge of the ETANG D ZILLEBEKE, Laying now some under the orders of the 8th Bde Toridy 15th Inf Bde with a view to moving into the trenches at Hill 60, about 3000 yards South South East of ZILLEBEKE From Hospital other Ranks 1. Wounded other Ranks 3.	
Wednesday 21st April 1915 ZILLEBEKE	During the early hours of the morning the Battalion moved forward and relieved the Bedford Regt. on Hill 60 about 2000 yards South South East of ZILLEBEKE. Half of "D" and half of "B" Company went into the forward Trench and half of "B", "A" and half of "D" Coy into the rear Trench. A small party which was a few support trench, then F. Radolff & Co. took charge of the Hill, and the garrison was continuously awaited by German trench mortars and bipods, heavy shrapnel and impulsive(?) open fired all. Somewhat unimportant lived made on the position maintained. Captain G. E. P. Prior	

WAR DIARY or INTELLIGENCE SUMMARY

Army Form C. 2118.

Hour, Date, Place	Summary of Events and Information	Remarks and references to Appendices
Wednesday 21st April 1915 ZILLEBEKE (continued)	Capt. J. R. Sangr. Armstrong and Lieut. A. H. Cope wounded. Killed/Other Ranks 8, Wounded Other Ranks 54.	
Thursday 22nd April 1915 ZILLEBEKE	The Battalion continues to hold Hill 60 in spite of considerable difficulties and a fair number of casualties. The defences were very much improved, and their condition made more tolerable by the removal of dead and wounded etc. The parapet of Hill 60 so as it became to be called was frequently blown in by German field guns which were brought up to close range. A party of expert bomb throwers was sent to assist in the defence of Hill 60 by the Northumberland Fusiliers. Lieut. L/Cpt. Tanner proved himself valuable. Lieut. R. Reed and Lieut. E. A. Hall joined Battalion. Lieut. C. A. Fletcher wounded, 2/Lieut A. W. Fisher to hospital. Killed Other Ranks 10. Wounded Other Ranks 41.	
Friday 23rd April 1915 ZILLEBEKE	A day of some activity in the trenches. A certain tension made itself felt during the day as a result of German attacks on the northern face of the YPRES salient and in consequence accrued orders was received intimating the action required in case the situation about crown created a readjustment in the configuration of the line of trenches: arrangements were therefore made to conduct the movement of the Highlanders Battalion and those of the 2nd Bn Canadian Highlanders in the event of Lieut. A. Fraser joined Battalion executing. Lieut H. Fraser joined Battalion. Wounded Other Ranks 3.	

WAR DIARY or INTELLIGENCE SUMMARY.

(Erase heading not required.)

Army Form C. 2118.

Hour, Date, Place	Summary of Events and Information	Remarks and references to Appendices
Saturday 24th April 1915. ZILLEBEKE	A comparatively uneventful day so far as the Battalion was concerned. The relief of the 2nd Br. Cameron Highlanders by the Battalion which would normally have taken place during the evening did not proceed owing apparently to some mistake on the transmission of a telephone message. Draft of the Other Ranks 1/22nd Regiment joined Battalion. 1 Lieut. J West and 6 Other Ranks from Machine Gun Corps ST OMER. Wounded Other Ranks 4.	
Sunday 25th April 1915. ZILLEBEKE	The relief of the 2nd Br. Cameron Highlanders by the Battalion was carried out during the early hours of the morning and partly in day light. This was due to two casualties of a slight nature during the operation. Nothing of note occurred during the day, but there was a certain amount of shelling of support and the trenches suffered the usual amount of destruction at the hands of the German, but were repaired as usual later in the day. Draft of 50 Other Ranks 23rd Regiment joined Battalion. From Hospital Other Ranks 2. Wounded Other Ranks 9.	

WAR DIARY or INTELLIGENCE SUMMARY

Army Form C. 2118.

Hour, Date, Place	Summary of Events and Information	Remarks and references to Appendices
Monday 26th April 1915 ZILLEBEKE	A fairly quiet day in the trenches except for some annoyance caused by the enemy's trench mortars and particularly by the "Sausage" type. Numerous were thrown by them. During the evening an alarmed signal of bombing & little aggressive on Hill 60, grenades were thrown back on some members; grenade was not all that could be desired on account of uncertainty of detonation of the older pattern in use. At one time the Germans made as though they would rush forward but this movement was quickly stopped and the party scattered by the opening of rapid fire, the effect of which was all that could be desired by the General was seen to return some dozens and apparently with some casualties. Draft of 70 Other Ranks 2nd Reinforcement joined Battalion. Lieut P.W. Cuthrip Admd R.M.C. from Hospital. Shells Other Ranks 4; Wounded Other Ranks 13; To Hospital Other Ranks 3; from Hospital Other Ranks 4.	
Sunday 27th April 1915 ZILLEBEKE	During the early hours of the morning the Battalion was relieved in the trenches by the 2nd Br Cameron Highlanders and took over the support and reserve dug-outs in the vicinity of Hill 60. The day passed quietly on the whole except for occasional shelling. On the evening the working parties were employed improving the communication trenches, entangling the enemy cutting and digging an emplacement for a new type of trench howitzer. Some progress was made with the Line of trench towards the enemy from the left end of the Line. In trench held by the Battalion. Wounded Other Ranks 8; To Hospital Other Ranks 1; from Hospital Other Ranks 6.	

WAR DIARY
or
INTELLIGENCE SUMMARY.
(Erase heading not required.)

Army Form C. 2118.

Instructions regarding War Diaries and Intelligence Summaries are contained in F.S. Regs., Part II. and the Staff Manual respectively. Title pages will be prepared in manuscript.

Hour, Date, Place	Summary of Events and Information	Remarks and references to Appendices
Wednesday 28th April 1915 ZILLEBEKE	A moderately quiet day for the Battalion except for a little shell fire during the morning. In the evening various working parties were found for the purpose of improving communication trenches, carrying up S.A.A. stores, rations etc. for the Battalion and for the Camerons from 15th Infantry Brigade H.Q. The Battalion subsequently relieved the 2nd Batt. Cameron Highlanders in the trenches when the Companies resumed their original distribution except that C Coy. continued to form a platoon on the DUMP. Killed Other Ranks 1, Wounded other Ranks 3, Ranks 4. To Hospital Other Ranks 2, from Hospital Other Ranks 4.	
Thursday 29th April 1915 ZILLEBEKE	A quiet day in the trenches about Hill 60. The only circumstance worthy of note was the explosion of a mine by the enemy at about 1 am just as the relief of Hill 60 was about to take place. Beyond the fact that the ground was somewhat shaken the explosion had but little effect. No harm was caused by the explosion which formed towards the northern cell. Two heaps called Hill 60 and one nearer Zwarteleen probably to be to find to prevent any outflanking by sapping out from the ends. Ranks 15, from Hospital Other Ranks 1. Killed Other Ranks 3. Wounded Other Ranks 1. 2nd Lieut. + Lt. & Qr. Mr. S. Downing wounded.	

WAR DIARY
or
INTELLIGENCE SUMMARY.
(Erase heading not required.)

Army Form C. 2118.

Hour, Date, Place	Summary of Events and Information	Remarks and references to Appendices
Friday 30th April 1915 ZILLEBEKE	The enemy's artillery was somewhat active through the night and day, doing some damage to the parapet on Hill 60 and causing a certain number of casualties. Otherwise the day was comparatively quiet totally Killed Other Ranks 2, Wounded Other Ranks 14, from Hospital Other Ranks 3. 40 Other Ranks joined (26th Reinforcement)	1st troop 3 + 79 /wr n 1+51

C. Seward
Lt Colonel
Comdg 1 Devon Regt.

14th Bde.
5th Div.

1st DEVONSHIRE REGT.

May

1915

WAR DIARY or INTELLIGENCE SUMMARY

Army Form C. 2118.

Hour, Date, Place	Summary of Events and Information	Remarks and references to Appendices

Saturday 1st May 1915.
ZILLEBEKE

During the early hours of the morning the battalion was relieved in the fire and support trenches by the 3rd Bn Dorset Regt and then remained in local reserve in LARCHWOOD dugouts etc. During the day there was considerable artillery activity on the part of the enemy and during the evening No.2 Coy's 3 platoons of No.3 Coy and 3 platoons of No.1 Coy were sent up to reinforce the fire trenches which were then being held by the Dorset Regt as the garrison of the trenches had been considerably thinned out as a result of the use of an asphyxiating gas by the Germans.

The following is taken from the report appertaining to the 80th Div. by the 13th Bde. Genl. Comdg. 15 Infy Bde.

Report on attack on Hill 60 on 1st May 1915.

At about 7pm on 1-5-15 the enemy began a very severe bombardment of Hill 60 and the trenches right and left, and railway cutting behind our trenches, the enemy at from 900 yards with and yellow that subsequent our [illegible] off over 30, 40, 43, 45 and 46 trenches; then gas was shot in thick volumes any exceeding on to our trenches, taking many men too quickly to admit of them getting their mouth protectors on. The asphyxiating effect being practically instantaneous. The men of [illegible] 36 were taught first went on to Hill 60, [illegible] nearly the whole of three platoons were soon affected.

In all about 300 of all ranks of the Dorset Regt were completely knocked out, many of whom were dead or unlikely to recover.

Many men who had the pot mouth cover recently issued all ready to put on either had not time to adjust it

WAR DIARY or INTELLIGENCE SUMMARY.

Army Form C. 2118.

(Erase heading not required.)

Hour, Date, Place	Summary of Events and Information	Remarks and references to Appendices
Saturday 1st May 1915 ZILLEBEKE (continued)	or had them not set enough, or was affected through the pad struck down and unpenetrability lay about at the opening of trenches where the gas was completely asphyxiated them. Every man has had a protector issued, and I am satisfied that Major Lowis Commanding "D" Coy had taken the greatest trouble to explain the use of them and ensure their use of and when necessary, but the men were caught too suddenly. Most orders in Coy always wearing the pads, what is impossible. Most orders in Coy always wearing the pads, was actually standing to arms in the trenches at 7pm, to prevent the use of their arrangements, and was waiting for the arrival by train when the gas was sent out to when they were caught by the gas. Whilst the gas was taking effect, the Germans opened a rapid rifle fire all along their line for a few minutes but after 7.30 p.m. all their aid fire was concentrated on the approaches behind our trenches especially the railway cutting, the obvious object to prevent reinforcements coming up. The critical situation which was caused by the sudden asphyxiation of most of the men along a front of about 400 yards, was quickly put right by the cool and prompt action of a few officers, and the fact that supports were close at hand and a ready system organised to make a counter attack on Hill 60, to be quickly made at any moment of the enemy attacked.	

WAR DIARY or INTELLIGENCE SUMMARY

Army Form C. 2118.

(Erase heading not required.)

Instructions regarding War Diaries and Intelligence Summaries are contained in F.S. Regs., Part II. and the Staff Manual respectively. Title pages will be prepared in manuscript.

Hour, Date, Place	Summary of Events and Information	Remarks and references to Appendices
Saturday 1st May 1915 ZILLEBEKE (continued)	Captain Slosson of the 1st Bedfords, anticipating this, had I sent to the C.O. pushed support from his trenches onto the Devon trenches 45 and 46 and reinforced Hill 60 at once. Captain Batten 'Devons' and Colonel William 'Devons' turned up 6 platoons of his into trenches 39, 46 and 43. Meanwhile the situation had been temporarily saved by the fact that some of the Devons with officers had promptly jumped up on the fire platforms and opened a rapid fire on the German trenches. The men did this whilst hardly affected by the gas except to attributable to the fact that they had their teeth high, and perhaps that the firing of their rifles dissipated the gas. This is an important point to tell others. Apparently for a few minutes however critical or till to the conduct of Lieut Kinnell saved the day to the effect of gas. Lieut Kinnell saved the day to the effect of gas. Lieut Kinnell saved the day and continued fining till the reinforcements arrived. Consequently the Germans did not discover the weak situation, and in a few minutes Captain Batten brought up two platoons while Major Cowie D.S.O. commanding 'Devons' arrived and took the situation in hand. The enemy started creeping round the two ends of the trench and trying, but they were met by bombers by Devons and Dorsets and driven back. Casualties 31. (6) Killed Other Ranks 4. Wounded Other Ranks 31. (6) Hospital Other Ranks 2. from Hospital Other Ranks 1.	

WAR DIARY or INTELLIGENCE SUMMARY

Army Form C. 2118.

Hour, Date, Place	Summary of Events and Information	Remarks and references to Appendices

Sunday 2nd May 1915.
ZILLEBEKE

A fairly quiet day. At 5:30 am one Company of Liverpools arrived and was held in reserve in LARCHWOOD dugout. During the afternoon most of the Dorset Regt. who were occupied in fowl and supply trenches were relieved by Devons and the distribution of the latter regiment was as follows: A Coy 2 platoons on Hill 60 and 2 platoons in trench 39. B Coy in trench 38 and part of 39. C Coy in trench 40 Fire and support with one platoon on the dump. D Coy 3 platoons in trench 45 and one platoon in 42 support trench. 2 Lieut OO's Davy 3/Dorsett Attd. Dorset Regt. Wounded Other Ranks 18. (To Hospital Other Ranks 4 from Hospital Other Ranks 4).

Monday 3rd May 1915.
ZILLEBEKE

During the night the enemy's artillery was active and again at about 3:30 am. Considerable difficulty was caused by the interruption of telephone communication. The day was otherwise comparatively quiet. Killed Other Ranks 2, Wounded Other Ranks 6. (To Hospital Other Ranks 8, from Hospital Other Ranks 1).

Tuesday 4th May 1915.
ZILLEBEKE

A fairly quiet day except for some shelling of the trenches by the enemy with light guns. During the evening the relief of the Battalion by the Duke of Wellington's West Riding Regiment began.
(Wounded Other Ranks 4.

Army Form C. 2118.

WAR DIARY
or
INTELLIGENCE SUMMARY.
(Erase heading not required.)

Instructions regarding War Diaries and Intelligence Summaries are contained in F.S. Regs., Part II. and the Staff Manual respectively. Title pages will be prepared in manuscript.

Hour, Date, Place	Summary of Events and Information	Remarks and references to Appendices
Wednesday 5th May 1915 GROENEN JAUN Nr KRUISSTRAAT	The relief of the Battalion by the Duke of Wellington Regiment was completed by 3.40 am when the Liverpool Company was allowed to bivouac and the command of the 2oth was handed over to Major Cowie, D.S.O. Regiment. The Battalion withdrew by platoons up to 15th MY 13th etc Head Quarters and by Companies to bivouac also to GROENEN JAUN FARM arr again H.22.b. YPRES Sheet 28 4000 0.19.15am the Battalion received order to be ready to move with ½ Batn East Surrey, tremendous aeroplanes fired; and at about 10 am took over in the neighbourhood of ECLUSE No 9 on the YPRES canal when they would in reserve order and moved to the heapps and ditch afforded Wounded cover as the Ranks H. [from Hospital Other Ranks 3.	
Thursday 6th May 1915. GROENEN JAUN Nr KRUISSTRAAT	The Battalion returned from trenches No 9 YPRES canal to its bivouac at GROENEN JAUN where the remainder of the day was spent in resting and washing etc. from Hospital Other Ranks 3.	
Friday 7th May 1915. GROENEN JAUN.	The Battalion raced in Bivouac. In the evening C Coy was employed with 50 men of B Coy in digging a second line of defence in the neighbourhood of BELLEGOED Farm. In accordance with 14th Infantry Brigade Operation Order No 205 of yesterday's date and Battalion Order No 143 of the same date. A grenadier went	

WAR DIARY or INTELLIGENCE SUMMARY

Army Form C. 2118.

Hour, Date, Place	Summary of Events and Information	Remarks and references to Appendices
Friday 7th May 1915. GROENEN JAN.	Of two officers and fifty other Ranks was formed in the Battalion, in order to obviate certain phonetic difficulties experienced as a result of companies being known by the letters A, B, C, D. A numerical system was chosen this day and the four companies originally known as A, B, C, and D were numbered 1, 2, 3 and 4 respectively. Further, with a view to the elimination of complication and confusion, instructions were issued for the sections to be numbered from 1 to 4 in each platoon and not from 1 to 16 in each Company, each section to be called by two numbers, the first the platoon number and the second the section number in the platoon, thus :– one, eight four, sixteen three. The above measures were adopted as a result of experience gained throughout the war and Companies often turning out fewer Companies or a Coy. eight men short few to Hospital other Ranks 3,	
Saturday 8th May 1915. GROENEN JAN.	The Battalion rested in Bivouac. (from Hospital other Ranks 2.	

WAR DIARY
or
INTELLIGENCE SUMMARY.
(Erase heading not required.)

Army Form C. 2118.

Instructions regarding War Diaries and Intelligence Summaries are contained in F.S.Regs., Part II. and the Staff Manual respectively. Title pages will be prepared in manuscript.

Hour, Date, Place	Summary of Events and Information	Remarks and references to Appendices
Sunday 9th May 1915 GROENEN JAUN	The Battalion were in Bivouac. During the afternoon No 2 Company made up to 200 strong from No 1 Company was employed as a working party in the neighbourhood of KRUISSTRAATHOEK and during the evening No 3 and 4 Companies were similarly employed. No 4 Company in relief of No 3. Killed Other Ranks 3, Wounded Other Ranks 2, [to Field Hospital Other Ranks 1, from Hospital Other Ranks 1.]	
Monday 10th May 1915 GROENEN JAUN	The Battalion were in Bivouac. The following officers joined. Captain D.R. Jefferys, Captain H.C. Newisson and Lieut. J.L. Pim. Coffroll [3] Dunn Regt [?] Hospital Other Ranks 3. [to Field Hospital Other Ranks 3.]	
Tuesday 11th May 1915 OOSTHOEK	A quiet day spent in Bivouac. During the evening the Battalion proceeded to relieve the 5th Bn Cheshire Regiment in the trenches about OOSTHOEK abutting on the YSER CANAL. No 1 Coy took over No 24 trench and in support: No 2 Coy took over part of 28 trench. No 3 Coy took over the SPOILBANK and No 4 Coy furnished a platoon for No 28 trench, another for No 28 support, a third for 24 and 28 Reserve trench, and a fourth at the Canal Post. Wounded Other Ranks 2, [to Field Hospital Other Ranks 6, from Hospital Other Ranks 1.]	

WAR DIARY
or
INTELLIGENCE SUMMARY.
(Erase heading not required.)

Army Form C. 2118.

Instructions regarding War Diaries and Intelligence Summaries are contained in F.S. Regs., Part II and the Staff Manual respectively. Title pages will be prepared in manuscript.

Hour, Date, Place	Summary of Events and Information	Remarks and references to Appendices
Wednesday 12th May 1915. OOSTHOEK.	A fairly quiet day except for some shelling of 24. trench by the enemy at the foot of retired causeway. During the evening our own artillery unfortunately placed some shell on our own trench 28, severely wounding one man. Killed Other Ranks 3, Wounded Other Ranks 11. [To Hospital Other Ranks 5, from Hospital Other Ranks 2.	
Thursday 13th May 1915 OOSTHOEK	A quiet day. The chief intrust centred round the enemy's mining and our own report. Killed Other Ranks 1, Wounded Other Ranks 1. [To Hospital Other Ranks 5, from Hospital Other Ranks 4.	
Friday 14th May 1915 OOSTHOEK	A very quiet day. During the evening the following redistribution of Companies was started; No. 1 Coy to SPOILBANK (3 platoons) and Canal foot (1 platoon) No. 2 Coy to No. 28 two trench, right and (3 platoon) and 28 S (1 platoon) No. 3 Coy to No. 27 two trench (3 platoon) and No. 27 S (1 platoon) No. 4 Coy to No. 28 two trench Left (2 platoon) No. 27/28 R. (1 platoon) and SPOILBANK (1 platoon). Wounded Other Ranks 2. [To Hospital Other Ranks 4.	
Saturday 15th May 1915 OOSTHOEK	A quiet day in the trenches. Wounded Other Ranks 1. To Hospital Other Ranks 4. From Hospital Other Ranks 4.	

Army Form C. 2118.

WAR DIARY
or
INTELLIGENCE SUMMARY.
(Erase heading not required.)

Instructions regarding War Diaries and Intelligence Summaries are contained in F.S. Regs., Part II. and the Staff Manual respectively. Title pages will be prepared in manuscript.

Hour, Date, Place	Summary of Events and Information	Remarks and references to Appendices
Sunday 16th May 1915 OOSTHOEK.	A very quiet day in the trenches. Lieut E. Seeley R.A.M. Corps to Hospital. To Hospital Other Ranks 2, from Hospital Other Ranks 5.	
Monday 17th May 1915 OOSTHOEK	A quiet day in the trenches. The expected relief of the Battalion by the Cheshire Regiment was postponed on account of the latter Unit having contracted some malady. The relief by No 2 Coy on trenches 28 for and 28 support by No 1 Company from SPOILBANK and Canal Post was cancelled owing to the operations of the 2/Manchester Regt and 1/D.C.L.I. on the north side of the YPRES CANAL arranged for the early hours of May 18th, namely, the filling in of a breach joining two German cops in close proximity to the line held at the junction of the above two. Battalion Wounded Other Ranks 1, To Hospital Other Ranks 3, from Hospital Other Ranks 3.	
Tuesday 18th May 1915 OOSTHOEK	A quiet day in the sector occupied by the Battalion. Killed Other Ranks 1, Wounded Other Ranks 3.	

Army Form C. 2118.

WAR DIARY
or
INTELLIGENCE SUMMARY.
(Erase heading not required.)

Instructions regarding War Diaries and Intelligence Summaries are contained in F.S. Regs., Part II and the Staff Manual respectively. Title pages will be prepared in manuscript.

Hour, Date, Place	Summary of Events and Information	Remarks and references to Appendices
Wednesday 19th May 1915 OOSTHOEK	A comparatively quiet day. Nothing of note occurred in the trenches. During the evening the relief of one platoon of No 2 Company by the platoon of No 1 Company from the CANAL POST was carried out as there had not been time for it to be carried out before daylight. Wounded other Ranks 2. To Hospital other Ranks 2. To Hospital other Ranks 1.	
Thursday 20th May 1915 OOSTHOEK	A quiet day on the whole. There was a little shelling during the morning and evening on the part of the enemy. Wounded other Ranks 2. To Hospital other Ranks 4. From Hospital other Ranks 1.	
Friday 21st May 1915 OOSTHOEK	A quiet day, but a certain amount of musketry during the evening. To Hospital other Ranks 3.	
Saturday 22nd May 1915 OOSTHOEK	A quiet day except for some shelling by H.E. for hours and its support in the morning and evening. During the course of the night No 2 Company proceeded to relieve No 3 Company in trenches 24 & 25 and 27 support and No 3 Company took the place of No 2 Company at Canal Post and Shortdeck. Joined Battalion Captain M. Llewellyn from R. Roy Hellen other Ranks 1. Wounded other Ranks 6. To Hospital other Ranks 5.	

Army Form C. 2118.

WAR DIARY
or
INTELLIGENCE SUMMARY.
(Erase heading not required.)

Instructions regarding War Diaries and Intelligence Summaries are contained in F.S. Regs., Part II. and the Staff Manual respectively. Title pages will be prepared in manuscript.

Hour, Date, Place	Summary of Events and Information	Remarks and references to Appendices
Sunday 23rd May 1915 OOSTHOEK	No change to record. Killed other Ranks 3, Wounded other Ranks 1, to Hospital other Ranks 2.	
Monday 24th May 1915 OOSTHOEK	A quiet day so far as the Battalion was concerned. Major J. Radcliff D.S.O. proceeded to assume temporary command of 2nd Bn. D. of W. West Riding Regt. 13 Infantry Bde. A/Lt. the Hon. F.W. Bramfylde from Hospital to Hospital other Ranks 4.	
Tuesday 25th May 1915 OOSTHOEK	A quiet day in the trenches. 2 Other Ranks wounded by the Battalion. Lieut R.B. Lupa & D own Regt and Lt. R.E.L. Pearman H.Penn.Regt joined Battalion. Killed other Ranks 1, Wounded other Ranks 2, to Hospital other Ranks 1.	
Wednesday 26th May 1915 OOSTHOEK	A quiet day. During the night No 3 Company from SPOILBANK relieved No 1 Company in No 28 Sap and Support Trenches. Wounded other Ranks 4, to Hospital other Ranks 19, from Hospital other Ranks 2.	
Thursday 27th May 1915 OOSTHOEK	No change to record. Lieut F.A. Hillary R.V. Kent Horse proceeded to BAILLEUL for Masson Gun Course. Wounded other Ranks 1, to Hospital other Ranks 8, from Hospital other Ranks 3.	
Friday 28th May 1915 OOSTHOEK	No change to record. Killed other Ranks 1, Wounded other Ranks 1, to Hospital other Ranks 3.	

WAR DIARY
or
INTELLIGENCE SUMMARY.
(Erase heading not required.)

Army Form C. 2118.

Hour, Date, Place	Summary of Events and Information	Remarks and references to Appendices
Saturday 29th May 1915 OOSTHOEK	No change to record. The Head Quarters of one Company and 2 platoons of 4th Bn. K.R.R.C. were attached to the Battalion and divided between No. 2 and 4 Companies for 48 hours instruction in trench duties. Lieut. B. W. St. G. Malone joined Battalion for duty. Other Ranks 12. Wounded other Ranks 6. Other Ranks to Hospital 3.	
Sunday 30th May 1915 OOSTHOEK	No change to record. Killed other Ranks 1. Wounded other Ranks 2. To Hospital other Ranks 2.	
Monday 31st May 1915 OOSTHOEK	No change to record. During the evening two more platoons of the 4th Battn. K.R.R.C. were attached in relief of the Company Hd Qrs and two platoons which had been under instruction for the past 48 hours. Wounded other Ranks 1. To Hospital other Ranks 4. From other Ranks 2.	To Hosp (wont) 17-17 from 15

C. J. Williams
Lt Colonel
Comdg 1st Bn. Devon Regt.

14th Bde.
5th Div.

1st DEVONSHIRE REGT.

JUNE

1 9 1 5

Army Form C. 2118.

WAR DIARY
or
INTELLIGENCE SUMMARY.
(Erase heading not required.)

Instructions regarding War Diaries and Intelligence Summaries are contained in F.S. Regs., Part II. and the Staff Manual respectively. Title pages will be prepared in manuscript.

Hour, Date, Place	Summary of Events and Information	Remarks and references to Appendices
Tuesday June 1st 1915. OOSTHOEK	The relief of the Battalion in the trenches by the 1/5 Battalion Cheshire Regiment was begun at 10pm and complete by 11.30pm. The battalion withdrew by Companies as they were relieved to bivouac near GROENEN JAUN in Square H.28.a. YPRES Sheet 28, 1/40,000. Wounded Other Ranks 3 Hospital Other Ranks 2, from Hospital Other Ranks 6.	Sheet 28 YPRES 1:40,000.
Wednesday June 2nd 1915. GROENEN JAUN	The Battalion remained in Bivouac. to Hospital Other Ranks 3, from Hospital Other Ranks 3.	
Thursday June 3rd 1915. GROENEN JAUN	The Battalion remained in Bivouac. to Hospital Other Ranks 4, from Hospital Other Ranks 5.	
Friday June 4th 1915. GROENEN JAUN	The Battalion remained in Bivouac. Major L.F. Radcliff DSO rejoined Battalion. to Hospital Other Ranks 4, from Hospital Other Ranks 3.	
Saturday June 5th 1915. GROENEN JAUN	The Battalion remained in Bivouac. to Hospital Other Ranks 10, from Hospital Other Ranks 14.	
Sunday June 6th 1915. GROENEN JAUN	The Battalion rested in Bivouac. 2 Other Ranks proceeded to base for duty on lines of Communication. to Hospital Other Ranks 3, from Hospital Other Ranks 4.	

Army Form C. 2118.

WAR DIARY
or
INTELLIGENCE SUMMARY.
(Erase heading not required.)

Instructions regarding War Diaries and Intelligence Summaries are contained in F.S. Regs., Part II. and the Staff Manual respectively. Title pages will be prepared in manuscript.

Hour, Date, Place	Summary of Events and Information	Remarks and references to Appendices
Monday 7th June 1915 GROENEN JAUN	The Battalion rested in bivouac. To Hospital Other Ranks 6, from Hospital Other Ranks 7.	Sheet 28 YPRES 1:40,000
Tuesday 8th June 1915 GROENEN JAUN	The Battalion rested in bivouac. To Hospital Other Ranks 8, from Hospital Other Ranks 8.	
Wednesday 9th June 1915 GROENEN JAUN	The Battalion rested in bivouac. To Hospital Other Ranks 4, from Hospital Other Ranks 4.	
Thursday 10th June 1915. GROENEN JAUN	The Battalion rested in bivouac. To Hospital Other Ranks 2, from Hospital Other Ranks 2.	
Friday 11th June 1915 GROENEN JAUN	The Battalion rested in bivouac. Lieut. G.A. Anstey proceeded to Head Quarters 7th Division for duty with a Battalion on 8th inst. July 8/C Major SWH. Wilford joined Battalion and Lieut 50 Major Ranks (31st Reinforcement). To Hospital Other Ranks 6, from Hospital Other Ranks 5.	
Saturday 12th June 1915 GROENEN JAUN	The Battalion rested in bivouac. Major L.F. Radcliff DSO. and Major H. Luxmore rejoined Battalion from leave. Lieut Col B.R. Williams Bart proceeded to BAILLEUL for Court Martial enquiry on M. Gun Section (10 days). Lieut E.C. Hope-Hall to Hospital 11th Field Ambulance. Killed Other Ranks 1, wounded Other Ranks 1. To Hospital Other Ranks 4, from Hospital Other Ranks 3.	

WAR DIARY or INTELLIGENCE SUMMARY.

Army Form C. 2118.

(Erase heading not required.)

Hour, Date, Place	Summary of Events and Information	Remarks and references to Appendices
Sunday 13th June 1915 GROENEN JAUN	The Battalion went on Bivouac. Major Wm Goodwyn proceeded to Adv. Qrs 8th Infy Bde on appointment as temporary command of 2nd Bn Cheshire Regiment. Captain D.P. Jefferys to Hospital 14th Field Ambulance. 3 Other Ranks proceeded to Base for duty on lines of Communication. To Hospital Other Ranks 14. From Hospital Other Ranks 4.	Sheet 28 YPRES 1 : 40,000
Monday 14th June 1915 GROENEN JAUN	The Battalion went on Bivouac. To Hospital Other Ranks 4. From Hospital Other Ranks 4.	
Tuesday 15th June 1915 GROENEN JAUN	The Battalion went on Bivouac. To Hospital Other Ranks 3. From Hospital Other Ranks 8.	
Wednesday 16th June 1915 GROENEN JAUN	The Battalion went on Bivouac. To Hospital Other Ranks 11. From Hospital Other Ranks 3.	
Thursday 17th June 1915 OOSTHOEK	The Battalion relieved the Cheshire Regt. in the same trenches about OOSTHOEK except as regards No 28 S.P. which were taken over by 6th Bn D.C.L.I. for purposes of this Head was manned by one platoon of No 1 Coy, trs Nos 7, Nos 3 Coy and two platoons of No 4 Coy with the 4th platoon in 27/28 in No 13 in No 28 S.P. in support and one platoon of No 2 Coy and No 2 Coy went to SPOILBANK as also did the other platoons of No 27 Trench, which would otherwise have been in Hospital Other Ranks 6. From Hospital Other Ranks 6.	

Army Form C. 2118.

WAR DIARY
or
INTELLIGENCE SUMMARY.
(Erase heading not required.)

Instructions regarding War Diaries and Intelligence Summaries are contained in F.S. Regs., Part II. and the Staff Manual respectively. Title pages will be prepared in manuscript.

Hour, Date, Place	Summary of Events and Information	Remarks and references to Appendices
Friday 18th June 1915 OOSTHOEK	A quiet day in the trenches except that during the afternoon the enemy did some damage to the parapet of No 21 fire trench occupied by No 3 Coy. by pretty accurate fire. During the evening two platoons of No 1 Coy. under Major N. Kwanson from SPOILBANK relieved two platoons and No 2 Coy H.Qrs. of the Coy. whose was occupying No 21 fire and support trenches and later two other platoons of 1st D.C.L.I. relieved the two remaining platoons of that regiment for the purpose of second in command construction or trench work. The battalion 24 hours 6th D.C.L.I. was also attached to the battalion 24 hours Yh Hospital other Ranks 3, from Hospital other Ranks 5.	Sheet 28 YPRES 1:40,000
Sunday 19th June 1915 OOSTHOEK	A quiet day except for some shelling of No 28 fire trench by the enemy during the afternoon. During the evening two platoons of No 1 Coy. from No 21 fire trench and SPOILBANK respectively relieved the two platoons of 6th D.C.L.I. in trench 2Y fire, after which the latter platoons withdrew with their Coy H.Qrs and the battalion 2nd in Command. The platoon of No 1 Coy. withdrawn from 28 fire trench was not replaced. Subsequently No 2 Coy. relieved the three platoons of No 3 Coy. on 28 fire and the platoon in 28 support and No 3 Coy. withdrew to SPOILBANK. Killed other Ranks 1, Y Hospital Other Ranks 5, from Hospital other Ranks 4.	

WAR DIARY or INTELLIGENCE SUMMARY.

Army Form C. 2118.

(Erase heading not required.)

Instructions regarding War Diaries and Intelligence Summaries are contained in F.S. Regs., Part II. and the Staff Manual respectively. Title pages will be prepared in manuscript.

Hour, Date, Place	Summary of Events and Information	Remarks and references to Appendices
Sunday 20th June 1915 OOSTHOEK	A quiet day on the trench. Killed Other Ranks 2, Wounded Other Ranks 2, to Hospital Other Ranks 4, from Hospital Other Ranks 4.	Sheet 28 YPRES 1:40,000
Monday 21st June 1915 OOSTHOEK	Nothing of incident occurred except that the Battalion in conformity with the other Battalions in the Brigade and the other brigades in the Division et: opened rapid fire for three minutes at 2-30 a.m. with the object of ascertaining whether the enemy had withdrawn troops from the trenches in front. The Battalion was unable to furnish any information on this subject as a result of fusilade. Wounded Other Ranks 3, to Hospital Other Ranks 2, from Hospital Other Ranks 5.	
Tuesday 22nd June 1915 OOSTHOEK	Nothing of note to record. Captain J.M. Llewellyn rejoined 1 Battalion from Hospital Other Ranks 1.	
Wednesday 23rd June 1915 OOSTHOEK	Nothing of note to record. Ten men were detached to form, with similar numbers from the other four Battalions, a Brigade Tunnelling Section. Wounded Other Ranks 3, to Hospital Other Ranks 2, from Hospital Other Ranks 3.	

WAR DIARY
or
INTELLIGENCE SUMMARY.
(Erase heading not required.)

Army Form C. 2118.

Hour, Date, Place	Summary of Events and Information	Remarks and references to Appendices
Thursday 24th June 1915 OOSTHOEK	A quiet day in the trenches. At 6.30pm Brigadier General F.S. Maude C.B. Comdg. 14th Infy. Bde. made a short valedictory address to representatives of the Battalion assembled at SPOIL BANK on the occasion of his approaching elevation to the command of a higher formation. Two Other Ranks died from wounds in 14th Fd. Ambce. Wounded Other Ranks 6, to Hospital Other Ranks 10.	Sheet 28 YPRES 1:40,000
Friday 25th June 1915 OOSTHOEK	Nothing of note to record. Wounded Other Ranks 3 to Hospital Other Ranks 1, from Hospital Other Ranks 2.	
Saturday 26th June 1915 OOSTHOEK	A comparatively quiet day. In the morning the trenches were subject to some shelling on the part of the enemy and during the evening the dugout at SPOILBANK was shelled, possibly as a result of damage done to HOUTHEBEEK Chateau by our own 9.2 inch shells in the forenoon. Wounded Other Ranks 3, from Hospital Other Ranks 1.	
Sunday 27th June 1915 OOSTHOEK	Nothing of note occurred. During the evening No 1 Coy relieved three platoons of No 3 Coy. in 28 Sp. trench and one platoon of No 2 Coy. in 28 Support trench, afterwards withdrawing to the reserve dug-out at SPOILBANK. Wounded Other Ranks 4, to Hospital Other Ranks 10, from Hospital Other Ranks 10.	

WAR DIARY
or
INTELLIGENCE SUMMARY
(Erase heading not required.)

Army Form C. 2118.

Instructions regarding War Diaries and Intelligence Summaries are contained in F. S. Regs., Part II. and the Staff Manual respectively. Title pages will be prepared in manuscript.

Hour, Date, Place	Summary of Events and Information	Remarks and References to Appendices
Monday 28th June 1915 OOSTHOEK	A comparatively quiet day, nothing of note happened. Wounded Other Ranks 1, to Hospital Other Ranks 3, from Hospital Other Ranks 4.	Sheet 28 YPRES. 1: 40,000.
Tuesday 29th June 1915 OOSTHOEK	Nothing of note to be recorded. Major J.H. Ratcliffe D.S.O. proceeded to assume command of 1st Devon Regiment from 29-6-15. Lieut. Hon. J.W. Bampfylde proceeded to BAILLEUL for reasons of indisposition in machine gun work. Wounded Other Ranks 4, to Hospital Other Ranks 4, from Hospital Other Ranks 1.	
Wednesday 30th June 1915 OOSTHOEK	A quiet day. Nothing of note occurred. Wounded Other Ranks 1, to Hospital Other Ranks 4, from Hospital Other Ranks 1.	

E.S.Serum?
Lt.Colonel,
Comdg 1 Devon Regiment

WO 95/1565 pt II

5th Division
14th Infantry Bde
1st Devon Regt.

July to December
1915

(TO 95 BDE   5 DIV)

14th Bde.
5th Div.

1st DEVONSHIRE REGT.

...........JULY...........

1 9 1 5

WAR DIARY or INTELLIGENCE SUMMARY

Army Form C. 2118

Instructions regarding War Diaries and Intelligence Summaries are contained in F.S. Regs., Part II. and the Staff Manual respectively. Title Pages will be prepared in manuscript.

(Erase heading not required.)

Place	Date	Hour	Summary of Events and Information	Remarks and references to Appendices
OOSTHOEK	13th July 1915		A quiet day. During the evening the 1/5 Cheshire Regiment took over trenches etc. in Sector A by 11.45 pm and the Battalion withdrew to bivouac near GROENEN JAUN (DIEPE BUSCH) in H.28.d. YPRES Sheet 28 (1:40000) 9 other Ranks rejoined other Ranks 3, Hospital other Ranks 8.	Sheet 28 YPRES 1:40000. Square H.28.a
GROENEN JAUN	2nd July 1915		The Battalion rested in bivouac. Lieut. R.Y. Hold 3rd Br. Devon Regt and Head Scr. P.V. Williams East 3rd Br. Devon Regt rejoined from leave. Lieut H.E. Clayton 3rd Br. Devon Regt and Lieut Y.H. Joined with 136 other Ranks joined Battalion (32nd Reinforcements) to Hospital other Ranks 21. From Hospital other Ranks 4. 8 other Ranks granted leave to proceed to England.	
GROENEN JAUN	3rd July 1915		The Battalion rested in bivouac. Lieut E.C. Hope Hall 3rd Br. Devon Regt and Lieut H. Hearst 1st Br. Devon Regt granted leave to England. Authority/Division S/103447 dated 3/6/15. Captain D.K. Jeffreys 1st Br. Devon Regt rejoined Battalion from Hospital. other Ranks 3. From Hospital other Ranks 8, to Hospital other Ranks 4.	
GROENEN JAUN	4th July 1915		The Battalion rested in bivouac. 2/Lieut W.F.D. Broster 4th Br. Royal Fusiliers proceeded on leave. 2 other Ranks proceeded to East for duty on lines of Communication. From Hospital other Ranks 4. to Hospital other Ranks 4.	
GROENEN JAUN	5th July 1915		The Battalion rested in bivouac. Lieut. R.Y. Yeed 3rd Br. Devon Regiment, 2/Lieut H.Hellild other Ranks 1 3rd Br. Hospital other Ranks 3 joined Battalion this Ranks 4. Lieut R.H. Cutting 1st Devon Regt proceed to HQ from Hospital. this Ranks 4. 13th Infantry Brigade for duty as Brigade Machine Gun Officer. Lieut J.A. Hillary 3rd Auckland Regiment, New Zealand, post from assumed duties of Machine Gun Officer to the Battalion.	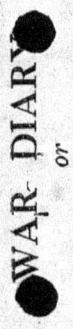

WAR DIARY or INTELLIGENCE SUMMARY

Army Form C. 2118

Instructions regarding War Diaries and Intelligence Summaries are contained in F.S. Regs., Part II. and the Staff Manual respectively. Title Pages will be prepared in manuscript.

(Erase heading not required.)

Place	Date	Hour	Summary of Events and Information	Remarks and references to Appendices
GROENEN JAUN	6th July 1915		The Battalion rested in Bivouac. Wounded Other Ranks 3. 4, From Hospital Other Ranks 1, To Hospital Other Ranks 3.	Sheet 28 YPRES 1:40,000
GROENEN JAUN	7th July 1915		The Battalion rested in Bivouac. Colonel E.H. Williams C.M.G. To Hospital. Lieut E.C. Hope-Hall 3rd Bn. Devon Regt and Capt H. Knight 1st Bn. Devon Regiment reported for duty. From leave. To Hospital Other Ranks 9, From Hospital Other Ranks 6,	
OOSTHOEK	8th July 1915		The Battalion rested in Bivouac until 8.10pm. when it marched to Sector A and started to relieve 1/5 Cheshire Regiment in trenches about OOSTHOEK at 10pm. Relief was completed by 11.55pm. Following distribution was effected. No.1 Coy. and support trenches. No.2 Coy in 28 feet trench 3 platoons of No.1 Coy. and 2 platoons of No.4 Coy. in 28 support trench 1 platoon of No.4 Coy. on 27/28 reserve trench 1 platoon of No.2 Coy. at night mg. at BROCKBANK No.3 Coy. and 1 platoon of No.4 Coy. Hd. Qrs., Batt. Sappers the 50 grenadiers and 16 grenadier class were distributed between 27 and 28 trenches. The machine gun teams distributed throughout the Sector and manned two guns. Major N. Kromer assumed command of the Battalion vice Lieut. Col. E.H. Williams CMG To Hospital. Lieut C.C. Hopper assumed command of No.1 Coy. vice Major N. Kromer. To Hospital Other Ranks 10, From Hospital Other Ranks 4.	
OOSTHOEK	9th July 1915		A quiet day in the trenches. Lieut Hon. L.W. Bampfylde 3rd Bn. Devon Regt rejoined Battalion from Machine Gun Course, BAILLEUL. From Hospital Other Ranks 6, Wounded Other Ranks 1.	
OOSTHOEK	10th July 1915		A quiet day in the trenches. Nothing of note occurred except that the captive balloon two miles by our own front at ST. ELOI at 3.30 a.m. was distinctly perceptible. Lieut C.M. Senger proceeded to BAILLEUL for course of instruction in Machine Gun duties. Lieut E.C. Goth and 4 Other Ranks granted leave to England. Casualties 3/ Corpl. D.J.2587 A. 11/6/15. Wounded Other Ranks 2, To Hospital Other Ranks 3, From Hospital Other Ranks 4.	

WAR DIARY or INTELLIGENCE SUMMARY

Army Form C. 2118

Place	Date	Hour	Summary of Events and Information	Remarks and references to Appendices
OOSTHOEK	11th July 1915		A fairly quiet day except for considerable activity on the part of the German gunners against between 4-30 am and 5 am although little damage was done in the sector occupied by the Battalion. Captain D.R. Jeffreys 1/6th Dron Regt killed and 4 other Ranks wounded. Other Ranks 1 V.O. Wounded. Total of other Ranks 3 wounded viz 1st York Ambce Other Ranks 1, G. Hospital Other Ranks 3, 6 other Ranks rejoining Battalion from leave. Hospital Other Ranks 2, prov. Battalion on duty and account command of No 1 Coy. Captain C.E.R. Prior.	Sheet 28; YPRES 1:40,000
OOSTHOEK	12th July 1915		A fairly quiet day except that between 4-30 am and 6 am the German were active with minenwerfers and that during the afternoon a certain amount of annoyance was caused by their artillery. During the night interference with working parties was caused by German rifle fire. Other Ranks rejoined Battalion 2, G Hospital Other Ranks 3, 2 Other Ranks wounded Other Ranks 2, G Hospital Other Ranks 2.	
OOSTHOEK	13th July 1915		Except for some annoyance by minenwerfer during the early morning the day passed fairly quietly. To Hospital Other Ranks 8, from Hospital Other Ranks 3.	
OOSTHOEK	14th July 1915		A quiet day. The 5th Division was attached to the 5th Corps pending allotment to the 10th Corps. To Hospital Other Ranks 5, from Hospital Other Ranks 5.	

Army Form C. 2118

WAR DIARY or INTELLIGENCE SUMMARY

(Erase heading not required.)

Instructions regarding War Diaries and Intelligence Summaries are contained in F. S. Regs., Part II. and the Staff Manual respectively. Title Pages will be prepared in manuscript.

Place	Date	Hour	Summary of Events and Information	Remarks and references to Appendices
OOSTHOEK	15th July 1915		Nothing of moment happened. Lieut. J. M. Head 10th Bn. Devon Regt attached to the Battalion from 12th to 15th July 1915 for instructional purposes. Wounded Other Ranks 3. To Hospital Other Ranks 5. From Hospital Other Ranks 2.	See 128/FRES 1:40,000 H.28.A.
OOSTHOEK	16th July 1915		A quiet day on the sector occupied by the Battalion. Wounded Other Ranks 2. To Hospital Other Ranks 3.	
OOSTHOEK	17th July 1915		A quiet day in the sector occupied by the Battalion. During the evening the battalion was relieved by the 1/6 Cheshire Regiment and withdrew into bivouac near GROENEN JAGN, DICKEBUSCH. Wounded Other Ranks 1. To Hospital Other Ranks 5.	
GROENEN JAGN Nr DICKEBUSCH	18th July 1915		The battalion rested in bivouac. To Hospital Other Ranks 3. From Hospital Other Ranks 8. Wounded Other Ranks 1.	
GROENEN JAGN Nr DICKEBUSCH	19th July 1915		The battalion rested in bivouac. To Hospital Other Ranks 5. From Hospital Other Ranks 4.	
GROENEN JAGN Nr DICKEBUSCH	28th July 1915		The battalion rested in bivouac but at about 11am and again at about 11am and afterwards, in order to avoid German very long range artillery fire from a direction which could not be ascertained correctly. Wounded Other Ranks 3. To Hospital Other Ranks 1. From Hospital Other Ranks 1. 1 Other Ranks to Base for employment on Lines of Communication.	
GROENEN JAGN Nr DICKEBUSCH	31st July 1915		The battalion rested in bivouac. Lieut. C.G.A. Bennett 4th Battalion Northumberland Fusiliers and 1 Other Ranks rejoined their unit. Captain C.E. William CMG rejoined Battalion from MONT NOIR and leave. To Hospital Other Ranks 4. From Hospital Other Ranks 7.	

1875 Wt. W593/826 1,000,000 4/15 J.B.C. & A. A.D.S.S./Forms/C. 2118.

Army Form C. 2118

WAR DIARY or INTELLIGENCE SUMMARY

(Erase heading not required.)

Place	Date	Hour	Summary of Events and Information	Remarks and references to Appendices
GROENEN JAUN Nr DICKEBUSCH	22nd July 1915		The battalion rested in bivouac. To Hospital other ranks 6, from Hospital other ranks 1.	Sheet 28 YPRES 1/40,000 M.28.A
GROENEN JAUN Nr DICKEBUSCH	23rd July 1915		The battalion rested in bivouac. To Hospital other ranks 9, from Hospital other ranks 2.	
BOESCHEPE	24th July 1915		14th Infy Bde was relieved by 8th Infy Bde and the Bn Highldrs Regt of the latter formation took over the bivouac occupied by the Battalion at GROENEN JAUN near DICKEBUSCH (map 1/40000 YPRES sheet 28 Squared H28a) at 8 pm the battalion marched via RENINGHELST to billets in BOESCHEPE and the farms extending for about one mile along the road running North Eastwards from that village. Billets were reached by about 11.30 pm. 2/Lieut J Wells joined battalion, and 40 other ranks joined battalion. To Hospital other ranks 7, from Hospital other ranks 3.	map 1/10,000 HAZEBROUCK sheet 5A
BOESCHEPE	25th July 1915		The battalion remained in billets about BOESCHEPE until 8 pm when it marched via GODEWAERSVELDE to billets in the farms between one half and one mile in a South-Westerly direction from that town. To Hospital other ranks 1, from Hospital other ranks 2.	
GODEWAERSVELDE	26th July 1915		The battalion remained in its billeting area. From Hospital other ranks 3.	

WAR DIARY or INTELLIGENCE SUMMARY

Army Form C. 2118

Instructions regarding War Diaries and Intelligence Summaries are contained in F. S. Regs., Part II. and the Staff Manual respectively. Title Pages will be prepared in manuscript.

(Erase heading not required.)

Place	Date	Hour	Summary of Events and Information	Remarks and references to Appendices
GODEWAERS- VELDE	27th July 1915		The battalion with remainder of 14th Infy Bde was inspected by Lieutenant-General Sir Herbert C.O. Plumer, K.C.B, Commanding 2nd Army to mark the transfer of the 14th Infy Bde with the remainder of the 5th Division from 2nd Army, 2nd Corps via 5th Corps to 3rd Army, 10th Corps.	
	27th July 1915		In the course of his remarks when addressing the troops the Army Commander said that he had not come there that morning to tell an inspection parade but rather to say a few words to the Brigade before it left to join the new army to which it was being transferred. He was glad to say that the long period during which the men had been engaged in trench warfare had not caused them to forget how to stand still and to handle their arms; their clothing was against them and it would not have pleased those who were used to Aldershot parades, but those who really knew soldiers were able to judge in spite of clothing, and the Brigade had turned out as it ought to have done.

The General went on to say that he need not remind his hearers what they had done in the past for that would be found written few the records which would form the history of the war. They, however, who were acquainted with the facts knew the part which the 5th Division and the 14th Brigade had taken in the early part of the war and they knew that that part had been at least an arduous one.

During the period that the Brigade had been in the sector which it was then leaving it had been occupied with trench warfare rather than with active operations against the enemy with one or two exceptions when although not actually employed as a Brigade two of its battalions — the Devons and the East Surreys — had been very hotly engaged at Hill 60 and by their efforts had contributed very greatly to the retention of that Hill etc. | |

WAR DIARY or INTELLIGENCE SUMMARY

Army Form C. 2118

Place	Date	Hour	Summary of Events and Information	Remarks and references to Appendices
GODEWAERS- VELDE.	27th July 19/5		Since that time the Brigade had continued to be engaged in trench warfare, but trench warfare was not to be rated as the "dull sort" of fighting, that some were prone to think, as Army Commanders knew full well. Comparisons, the General remarked, were odious, but he had no hesitation in saying that so far as the 2nd Army was concerned, and for that matter so far as the expeditionary force was concerned, no Brigade had won so high a reputation for trench warfare as had the 14th Brigade under General Maude. During the operations that had taken place in the Ypres Salient the 14th Brigade had been engaged in fighting which might be characterised as "dull" — from the newspaper point of view, but the General reminded his hearers that unless a Commander can rely on the troops that are holding the line he cannot with draw troops as he otherwise might for fighting elsewhere. Whilst commanding the 5th Corps he knew that the line occupied by the Brigade was absolutely safe, and, he added, it was to the officers, N.C.O, and men whom he was addressing that he ascribed as much credit as he due to those who were engaged in the active fighting. The Army Commander concluded by saying that the Brigade was going to a new Army and to a new corps under General Fergusson and General Moreland respectively, both of whom knew full well the reputation of the Brigade.	

WAR DIARY or INTELLIGENCE SUMMARY

Army Form C. 2118

(Erase heading not required.)

Place	Date	Hour	Summary of Events and Information	Remarks and references to Appendices
GODEWAERS-VELDE	27th July 1915		On those whom he was addressing would devolve the responsibility of living up to the reputation which they had made and of forming the nucleus of the new Army; for they would be the Veterans and the 14th Brigade standard would be the standard which other Brigades would emulate: it must and it would be a high one, and if all the other Brigades reached it both the Army and the Corps Commander would have confidence. The General then expressed his sorrow that the Brigade was parting from the 2nd Corps and the 2nd Army and wished them the best of luck. Lieut G.G. Haynes proceeded to ST OMER to join the R.F.C. as an observer on probation. Lt from Hospital other ranks one.	
GODEWAERS-VELDE	28th July 1915		The Battalion did a practice route march via EECKE, CAESTRE STATION, ST SYLVESTRE CAPPEL, and STEENVOORDE. To Hospital other ranks two.	
GODEWAERS-VELDE	29th July 1915		The battalion did a short practice route march via KRUYSTRAETE and GODEWAERSVELDE during the morning. To hospital other ranks 6	

Army Form C. 2118

WAR DIARY or INTELLIGENCE SUMMARY

(Erase heading not required.)

Place	Date	Hour	Summary of Events and Information	Remarks and references to Appendices
GODEWAERS- VELDE	30th July 1915		The battalion remained in its billeting area. A billeting party under Major A Luxmore, who had been detailed to act as Brigade billeting officer also, entrained for the new Brigade billeting area about RUBEMPRÉ and LA-NEUVILLE five to ten miles East of AMIENS. (MAP 1/80,500 AMIENS Sheet 12) ½ from Hospital other ranks 7	
GODEWAERS- VELDE	31st July 1915		The battalion entrained at GODEWAERSVELDE and left at 2.45 pm for CORBIE. To Hospl other ranks nil, from Hospl other ranks nil	

G Luxmore. Lt Colonel
Comdg. 1st Bn Devon Regt.

14th Bde.
5th Div.

1st DEVONSHIRE REGIMENT

AUGUST

1 9 1 : 5

Army Form C. 2118

WAR DIARY or INTELLIGENCE SUMMARY
(Erase heading not required.)

Instructions regarding War Diaries and Intelligence Summaries are contained in F.S. Regs., Part II. and the Staff Manual respectively. Title Pages will be prepared in manuscript.

Place	Date	Hour	Summary of Events and Information	Remarks and references to Appendices
DAOURS	1st Augt 1915		The Battalion detrained at CORBIE and marched to DAOURS where it was completely billetted by 6.30 P.M. To Hospital other ranks nil, from Hospital other ranks nil.	Ref. Maps 1/80,000 AMIENS Sheet 12.
DAOURS	2nd Augt 1915		The Battalion remained in its billetting area at DAOURS. To Hospital other ranks nil, from Hospital other ranks nil.	
DAOURS	3rd Augt 1915		The Battalion remained in its billetting area at DAOURS. To Hospital other ranks 5, from Hospital other ranks nil.	
DAOURS	4th Augt 1915		At 3 p.m the Battalion with remainder of 14th Infantry Brigade was inspected by the 3rd Army Commander. At 8 p.m the Battalion marched with the remainder of the Brigade via CORBIE and MERICOURT L'ABBE to TREUX where Brigade Headquarters were billetted and thence to its own billetting area in DERNANCOURT. To Hospital other ranks 16. On Battalion rejoined Battalion from M.G. Course ST OMER.	
DERNANCOURT	5th Augt 1915		The Battalion remained in its own billetting area at DERNANCOURT. To Hospital other ranks 2. 10 other ranks joined Brigade Tunnelling Section.	
DERNANCOURT	6th Augt 1915		The battalion remained in its billetting area at DERNANCOURT. From Hospital other ranks 14.	

Army Form C. 2118

WAR DIARY or INTELLIGENCE SUMMARY

(Erase heading not required.)

Instructions regarding War Diaries and Intelligence Summaries are contained in F.S. Regs., Part II. and the Staff Manual respectively. Title Pages will be prepared in manuscript.

Place	Date	Hour	Summary of Events and Information	Remarks and references to Appendices
DERNANCOURT	7th Aug 1915		At 8 p.m. the battalion marched from DERNANCOURT via MEAULTE to BRAY SUR SOMME where it arrived and was billeted by 11.20 p.m. To Hospital other ranks one.	Ref map 1/80,000 AMIENS Sheet 12.
BRAY SUR SOMME	8th Aug 1915		The battalion remained in billets at BRAY SUR SOMME. To Hospital other ranks one.	
MARICOURT	9th Aug 1915		The battalion marched at 12.15 A.M. via SUZANNE to MARICOURT where it proceeded to take over the trenches known as sector A.4 from a battalion of the 99th French Infantry Regiment of the 55th Infantry Brigade. No. 1 Coy occupied the right, No. 2 Coy the left centre, and No. 3 Coy the left, with No. 4 with H.Q. in reserve.	
MARICOURT	10th Aug 1915		Nothing of note to record in sector A.4. Killed other ranks one.	
MARICOURT	11th Aug 1915		Nothing worthy of note occurred in the trenches about MARICOURT. To Hospital other ranks one.	
MARICOURT	12th Aug 1915		Nothing unusual occurred in the sector occupied by the battalion. To Hospital other ranks 4. Wounded other ranks one.	

WAR DIARY
INTELLIGENCE SUMMARY
(Erase heading not required.)

Army Form C. 2118

Place	Date	Hour	Summary of Events and Information	Remarks and references to Appendices
MARICOURT	13th Aug 1915		Nothing unusual happened in Sector occupied by the battalion. To Hospital other ranks 2.	Ref: Map 1/100,000 AMIENS Sheet 12
MARICOURT	14th Aug 1915		Nothing unusual occurred. To Hospital other ranks three.	
MARICOURT	15th Aug 1915		Nothing of importance occurred except that a report was received to the effect that sounds as of German mining had been heard by listeners in a gallery approximately opposite point 361 in the German line. The report was subsequently accepted by the Mining Officers, but in the meantime portions of the second line were continued with additional support and grenades and other materials were sent forward to the portions of the line which was thought to be threatened. To Hospital other ranks 5, from Hospital other ranks one.	
MARICOURT	16th Aug 1915		Nothing calling for report occurred in the Sector occupied by the Battalion. To Hospital other ranks 4, killed other ranks 1, from Hospital other ranks one.	
MARICOURT	17th Aug 1915		Nothing special to record. Major J.T. Radcliff A.S.D. and Major W.H. Goodwyn rejoined Battalion. Wounded other ranks 4.	

Army Form C. 2118

WAR DIARY or INTELLIGENCE SUMMARY

(Erase heading not required.)

Instructions regarding War Diaries and Intelligence Summaries are contained in F.S. Regs., Part II. and the Staff Manual respectively. Title Pages will be prepared in manuscript.

Place	Date	Hour	Summary of Events and Information	Remarks and references to Appendices
MARICOURT	18th Aug 1915		Nothing of note occurred except that at 10-20 AM the enemy fired a few shells at LA FLECHE a projecting portion of our line just east of the FRICOURT–MONTAUBAN railway. To Hospital other ranks 5, from Hospital other ranks 2, wounded other ranks 1.	
MARICOURT	19th Aug 1915		Nothing of note occurred. To Hospital other ranks 2.	
MARICOURT	20th Aug 1915		Nothing of note occurred. To Hospital other ranks 4.	
MARICOURT	21st Aug 1915		Nothing of note occurred. To Hospital other ranks 1, from Hospitals 1 other ranks 2, killed other ranks 1.	
MARICOURT	22nd Aug 1915		Nothing of note occurred. To Hospital other ranks 2, killed other ranks 1.	
MARICOURT	23rd Aug 1915		Nothing of note occurred. Lieut. B.W. Watford and no other tanks proceeded to ST OMER for instruction in M.G. duties. To Hospital other ranks 1, from Hospital other ranks 1.	

Army Form C. 2118

WAR DIARY or INTELLIGENCE SUMMARY

(Erase heading not required.)

Instructions regarding War Diaries and Intelligence Summaries are contained in F.S. Regs., Part II. and the Staff Manual respectively. Title Pages will be prepared in manuscript.

Place	Date	Hour	Summary of Events and Information	Remarks and references to Appendices
MARICOURT	24th Aug 1915		Nothing of note occurred. 2½ Coys relieved by K.O.S.B. and Q.V.R. and withdrew to village MARICOURT for one night and day. To Hospital other ranks 1, from Hospital other ranks 1, wounded other ranks 1.	Ref Map 1/80,000 AMIENS Sheet 12
MARICOURT	25th Aug 1915		2½ Coys relieved D.C.L.I in trenches 28 & 33 inclusive. To Hospital other ranks 3, from Hospital other ranks 4. To Hd Qrs 10 Corps other ranks 1.	
MARICOURT	26th Aug 1915		Nothing of note occurred. To Hospital other ranks 2. from Hospital other ranks 2. Major Won Grauwn proceeded to join 2nd Manchester Regt attachment, 19 other ranks proceeded to join 17th Coy R/E's for attachment	
MARICOURT	27th Aug 1915		Nothing of note occurred. To Hospital other ranks 2, from Hospital other ranks 1.	
MARICOURT	28th Aug 1915		Nothing of note occurred. To Hospital other ranks 7, from Hospital other ranks 1.	

Army Form C. 2118

WAR DIARY or INTELLIGENCE SUMMARY

(Erase heading not required.)

Instructions regarding War Diaries and Intelligence Summaries are contained in F. S. Regs., Part II. and the Staff Manual respectively. Title Pages will be prepared in manuscript.

Place	Date	Hour	Summary of Events and Information	Remarks and references to Appendices
MARICOURT	29th August 1915		Nothing of note occurred. From Hospital other ranks 6, to Hospital other ranks 1,	Ref. map 1/80000 Sheet 12.
MARICOURT	30th August 1915		Nothing of note occurred. To Hospital other ranks 3.	
MARICOURT	31st August 1915		Nothing of note occurred. From Hospital other ranks 3. Wounded other ranks 2, to Base for discharge other ranks 2.	

In the field
3.9.15

Manley
Major,
Comdg 1st Devon Regiment

14th Bde.
5th Div.

1st DEVONSHIRE REGIMENT

September

1 9 1 : 5

Army Form C. 2118

WAR DIARY
or
INTELLIGENCE SUMMARY

(Erase heading not required.)

Instructions regarding War Diaries and Intelligence Summaries are contained in F. S. Regs., Part II. and the Staff Manual respectively. Title Pages will be prepared in manuscript.

Place	Date	Hour	Summary of Events and Information	Remarks and references to Appendices
MARICOURT	1st Sept 1915		In trenches. Battalion was relieved during night by the 1st Bn Bedford Regiment, and marched via (SUZANNE)-BRAY to SAILLY-LORETTE. To Hospital other ranks 2.	Ref map 1-80,000 AMIENS Sheet 12
SAILLY LORETTE	2nd Sept 1915		The battalion rested in billets. Lt Colonel E. G. Williams CMG assumed temporary command of 14th Bde and Major J. J. Radcliffe D.S.O. assumed temporary command of 1st Devon Regiment. To Hospital other ranks 2, from Hospital other ranks 3.	
SAILLY LORETTE	3rd Sept 1915		The battalion rested in billets. Nothing unusual occurred. From hospital other ranks 4.	
SAILLY LORETTE	4th Sept 1915		The battalion rested in billets. Nothing of note occurred.	
SAILLY LORETTE	5th Sept 1915		The battalion rested in billets. Nothing unusual occurred. From Hospital other ranks 3.	

WAR DIARY or INTELLIGENCE SUMMARY

Army Form C. 2118

Place	Date	Hour	Summary of Events and Information	Remarks and references to Appendices
SAILLY-LORETTE	6th Sept 1915		The battalion rested in billets. Nothing of note occurred. To Hospital other ranks 1, from Hospital other ranks 2.	Ref map 1/80,000 AMIENS Sheet 12.
SAILLY-LORETTE	7th Sept 1915		The battalion rested in billets. Nothing to record. From hospital other ranks 1.	
SAILLY-LORETTE	8th Sept 1915		The battalion rested in billets.	
SAILLY-LORETTE	9th Sept 1915		The battalion rested in billets until 6 p.m. when No's 2 & 4 Coys moved forward to billets at MARICOURT. Remainder of battalion followed at 6:30 p.m. and billeted at SUZANNE. Lt E.G. Stope Hall proceeded to 174th Infantry Brigade Tunnelling Section for temporary attachment. To Hospital other ranks 3.	
SUZANNE	10th Sept 1915		No's 2 & 4 Coys remained in billets at MARICOURT. HQ and remainder of battalion in billets at SUZANNE, until the evening when they moved forward to MARICOURT. The battalion then relieved the Bedford Regiment in trenches Sector A 4. Lt Col E.G. Williams CMG assumed command of Battalion. To Hospital other ranks 7. Major W. Luckmore proceeded to 2 Manchester Regt for duty	

Army Form C. 2118

WAR DIARY or INTELLIGENCE SUMMARY
(Erase heading not required.)

Instructions regarding War Diaries and Intelligence Summaries are contained in F.S. Regs., Part II. and the Staff Manual respectively. Title Pages will be prepared in manuscript.

Place	Date	Hour	Summary of Events and Information	Remarks and references to Appendices
MARICOURT	11th Sept 1915		Nothing of note occurred in the sector occupied by the battalion. To hospital other ranks 2, from hospital other ranks 2.	Ref: Map 1-20000 AMIENS Sheet 12
MARICOURT	12th Sept 1915		Nothing to report in sector. A/t. Lieut. & Q.r. Mr J. Downing joined the battalion. To hospital other ranks 1, from hospital other ranks 1.	
MARICOURT	13th Sept 1915		Nothing unusual to record. To hospital other ranks 1.	
MARICOURT	14th Sept 1915		Nothing unusual occurred. "A" & "B" Coys 11th Welsh Regt attached to No.s 1 & 4 Coys respectively for instruction in trench duties. Two officers & 24 other ranks 1st & section were also attached. Wounded other ranks 3, to hospital other ranks 1, from hospital other ranks 1.	
MARICOURT	15th Sept 1915		A quiet day, and nothing to record. From hospital other ranks 6, to hospital other ranks 4.	

Army Form C. 2118

WAR DIARY
or
INTELLIGENCE SUMMARY
(Erase heading not required.)

Instructions regarding War Diaries and Intelligence Summaries are contained in F. S. Regs., Part II. and the Staff Manual respectively. Title Pages will be prepared in manuscript.

Place	Date	Hour	Summary of Events and Information	Remarks and references to Appendices
MARICOURT	15th Sept 1915		Nothing to record. "A" & "B" Coys 11th Welsh Regt and M.G. Section withdrew to SUZANNE during the evening. Wounded other ranks 2, to Hospital other ranks 2, from Hospital other ranks 2.	Ref Map 1/80,000 AMIENS Sheet 12.
MARICOURT	17th Sept 1915		A comparatively quiet day in trenches. Nothing of note occurred. Wounded other ranks 1, to Hospital other ranks 2.	
MARICOURT	18th Sept 1915		A quiet day in trenches. Lt. T.A. Kelsby proceeded to WISQUES for M.G. course. To Hospital other ranks 2, from Hospital other ranks 1.	
MARICOURT	19th Sept 1915		Nothing to record. To Hospital other ranks 3, from Hospital other ranks 3.	
MARICOURT	20th Sept 1915		A quiet day. To Hospital other ranks 3.	
MARICOURT	21st Sept 1915		Nothing unusual occurred in the Sector occupied by the Battalion. To Hospital other ranks 2, from Hospital other ranks 1, killed other ranks 1, wounded other ranks 2.	

WAR DIARY
or
INTELLIGENCE SUMMARY

(Erase heading not required.)

Army Form C. 2118

Place	Date	Hour	Summary of Events and Information	Remarks and references to Appendices
MARICOURT	22 Sept 1915		Nothing to record. Killed other ranks 1, to hospital other ranks 1, to hospital other ranks 2. 2nd Lieut E.C. Hope Hall rejoined Battalion.	Ref map 1/80,000 sheet AMIENS sheet 12.
MARICOURT	23 Sept 1915		During the afternoon enemy's wire entanglements in front of our Centre Company was bombarded by our artillery with good effect. In the evening Battalion was relieved by 1/5th Cheshire Regt and marched to SUZANNE where it was billetted. Killed other ranks 1, wounded other ranks 3, to hospital other ranks 2.	
SUZANNE	24 Sept 1915		The battalion rested in billets.	
SUZANNE	25 Sept 1915		The battalion rested in billets.	
SUZANNE	26 Sept 1915		The battalion rested in billets. 2nd Lieut H Corbett joined battalion for duty. To hospital other ranks 2, from hospital other ranks 2.	

Army Form C. 2118

WAR DIARY
or
INTELLIGENCE SUMMARY
(Erase heading not required.)

Place	Date	Hour	Summary of Events and Information	Remarks and references to Appendices
SUZANNE	27th Sept 1915		The battalion rested in billets 7, from hospital other ranks 4. To hospital other ranks 4.	Ref map 1/40,000 AMIENS
SUZANNE	28th Sept 1915		The battalion rested in billets 3, from hospital other ranks 2. To hospital other ranks	Sheet 12
SUZANNE	29th Sept 1915		The battalion rested in billets. 1 officer & 14 other ranks joined battalion for duty. Captain R.H. Anderson, 2nd Lieut R.J. Kidd and 4 other ranks joined 14 Che Inf Bde West Bomb Thrower Battery. To hospital other ranks 2.	
SUZANNE	30th Sept 1915		The battalion rested in billets. 2nd Lieut C.L.S. Mendl joined battalion for duty. To hospital other ranks 3, from hospital other ranks 2.	

10/15

C.J.Vivian,
Lt Colonel
Comdg 1st Bn Devon Regt.

14th Bde.
5th Div.

1st DEVONSHIRE REGIMENT

OCTOBER
....

1 9 1 5

WAR DIARY or INTELLIGENCE SUMMARY

Army Form C. 2118

(Erase heading not required.)

Instructions regarding War Diaries and Intelligence Summaries are contained in F.S. Regs., Part II. and the Staff Manual respectively. Title Pages will be prepared in manuscript.

Place	Date	Hour	Summary of Events and Information	Remarks and references to Appendices
SUZANNE	1st Oct. 1915.		The Battalion rested in billets. To Hospital, other ranks 5. From Hospital, other ranks 3. To ETINEHAM for duty under Q.P.M. other ranks 1.	Ref: Map 1-80,000 AMIENS Sheet 12.
SUZANNE	2nd Oct. 1915.		The Battalion rested in billets. To Hospital 2/Lieut. C.T.S. Mendl, other ranks 4. From Hospital, other ranks 1.	
SUZANNE	3rd Oct. 1915.		The Battalion rested in billets. To Base for discharge, other ranks 1. To Hospital, other ranks 1. From Hospital, other ranks 4.	
SUZANNE	4th Oct. 1915.		The Battalion rested in billets. To Prison other ranks 1. To Hospital other ranks 8. From Hospital other ranks 1.	
SUZANNE	5th Oct. 1915.		The Battalion rested in billets. To Base for discharge, other ranks 3. To Hospital other ranks 2. From Hospital other ranks 2.	
SUZANNE	6th Oct. 1915.		The Battalion rested in billets. Lieut. F.A. Hellaby rejoined from WISQUES. To Hospital other ranks 3. From Hospital other ranks 4.	
SUZANNE	7th Oct. 1915.		The Battalion rested in billets. During the morning the Battalion was inspected on parade by Brig. Genl. C.W. Compton C.M.G. Commanding 14th Infantry Brigade. To WISQUES for Machine gun Course, other ranks 1. From Hospital, other ranks 3.	

WAR DIARY or INTELLIGENCE SUMMARY

Army Form C. 2118

(Erase heading not required.)

Place	Date	Hour	Summary of Events and Information	Remarks and references to Appendices
SUZANNE	8th Oct. 1915		The Battalion rested in billets until the evening. At 6 p.m. the Battalion left SUZANNE for MARICOURT where it relieved the 1st Battalion D. of Cornwalls L.I. in trenches Sector A.3. 2/Lieut. C.W. Warwood-Smith and 2/Lieut. A.J. St R. Hervy joined Battalion. To Hospital other ranks 7.	Ref: Map. 1/80,000 AMIENS Sheet 12.
MARICOURT	9th Oct. 1915		In trenches. Nothing unusual occurred. Wounded other ranks 1, To Hospital other ranks 1, From Hospital other ranks 1.	Ref: Map. Trench map sheet 62c.N.W.1. 1/10,000.
MARICOURT	10th Oct. 1915		In trenches. Nothing unusual occurred. To Hospital, other ranks 4, From Hospital, other ranks 1.	
MARICOURT	11th Oct. 1915		In trenches. About 4 p.m. the Germans shelled MARICOURT village with eight H.E. shells. No casualties. To England on leave, other ranks 10.	
MARICOURT	12th Oct. 1915		In trenches. A quiet day. To Hospital, other ranks 7. From Hospital, other ranks 4.	
MARICOURT	13th Oct. 1915		In trenches. Nothing of note occurred. Killed, other ranks 1. To Hospital, other ranks 4, From Hospital, other ranks 3.	

Army Form C. 2118

WAR DIARY or INTELLIGENCE SUMMARY

(Erase heading not required.)

Instructions regarding War Diaries and Intelligence Summaries are contained in F. S. Regs., Part II. and the Staff Manual respectively. Title Pages will be prepared in manuscript.

Place	Date	Hour	Summary of Events and Information	Remarks and references to Appendices
MARICOURT	14th Oct 1915.		In trenches. Enemy shelled edge of MARICOURT wood with light high explosives about 30 shells being fired at various times during the day. To England on leave, Major J.H. Radcliffe D.S.O. Major J.H. Bent, other ranks 2. Wounded, other ranks 1. To Hospital, other ranks 1. From Hospital, other ranks 1.	Ref. Map. 1/10,000. Trench map sheet 62c. N.W.1.
MARICOURT	15th Oct 1915.		In trenches. A quiet day. No shelling occurred within Battalion sector. Between 4 p.m. and 6 p.m. Brass Band was heard playing behind German lines in direction of MAUREPAS. From Hospital, other ranks 1.	
MARICOURT	16th Oct 1915.		In trenches. Nothing of note occurred. Killed, other ranks 1. 2/Lieut. Y. Loman, 2/Lieut. B.W.H. Waford, other ranks 8, proceeded to England on leave. To England for discharge, other ranks 1. To Hospital, other ranks 4. From Hospital, other ranks 4.	
MARICOURT	17th Oct 1915.		In trenches. Enemy shelled MARICOURT wood. To Hospital, other ranks 1.	
MARICOURT	18th Oct 1915.		In trenches. About midnight and at various times during the early morning musical instruments were being played in German trenches and songs were being sung. During the morning enemy guns were more active than usual. H.E. and shrapnel shells were burst over 26 trench, Edge of MARICOURT wood and on the Peronne Road. Accidentally killed, other ranks 3. Rejoined Battalion from leave to England, other ranks 10.	

Army Form C. 2118

WAR DIARY
or
INTELLIGENCE SUMMARY
(Erase heading not required.)

Instructions regarding War Diaries and Intelligence Summaries are contained in F. S. Regs., Part II. and the Staff Manual respectively. Title Pages will be prepared in manuscript.

Place	Date	Hour	Summary of Events and Information	Remarks and references to Appendices
MARICOURT.	19th Oct. 1915.		In trenches. A misty day. Nothing of note occurred. To Prison, other ranks 1. To Hospital, other ranks 1. From Hospital, other ranks 1.	Ref: Maps. 1/10,000 Trench Map Sheet. 62.C.N.W.1.
MARICOURT	20th Oct. 1915.		In trenches. A quiet day. Nothing to record. From Hospital, other ranks 1.	
MARICOURT	21st Oct. 1915.		In trenches. A misty day. About 3 p.m. enemy shelled edge of MARICOURT wood. Eight shells came over. Capt. G.M. Llewellyn, 2/Lieut. F. West, other ranks 9, to England on leave. To Hospital, other ranks 2. Major J.H. Radcliffe D.S.O. and Major D.H. Blunt rejoined Battalion from leave.	
MARICOURT	22nd Oct. 1915.		In trenches. About 10 p.m. enemy shelled trenches 24 and 25 and MARICOURT wood with light H.E. About 12 noon slight shelling at corner of BOIS DE MARICOURT. Major J.H. Radcliffe D.S.O. left Battalion to command of 10th Battn. Essex Regiment. To Hospital, other ranks 4. Lieut. B. Walton 1/5th Gordon Highlanders attached to Battalion for instruction. 2 other ranks rejoined from leave.	
MARICOURT	23rd Oct. 1915.		In trenches. A quiet day. Between 10 and 11 a.m. a Brass Band could be heard playing in the direction of MAUREPAS. To Hospital, other ranks 2, From Hospital, other ranks 3. 2/Lieut. J. Roman, 2/Lieut. B.W.H. Wyford, other ranks 8 rejoined from leave.	

Army Form C. 2118

WAR DIARY or INTELLIGENCE SUMMARY

(Erase heading not required.)

Instructions regarding War Diaries and Intelligence Summaries are contained in F.S. Regs, Part II. and the Staff Manual respectively. Title Pages will be prepared in manuscript.

Place	Date	Hour	Summary of Events and Information	Remarks and references to Appendices
MARICOURT	24th Oct. 1915.		In trenches. A misty day. A small white flag was placed by the enemy about 20 yards distant from L.P. trench 24. During the evening this flag was brought in by 2nd Lieut. J.H. Tomlinson. The words ZUTRIT VERBOTEN were written on the cloth. Machine gun fire was opened from T.27 about 11 p.m. in order to find out, if possible, number of rifles in enemy trench. From front practically no fire could be observed but from enemy trenches in Sq. 10.D considerable amount of rifle fire was drawn. Wounded, other ranks 1. To Hospital other ranks 8. To England on leave, other ranks 8. From Hospital, other ranks 2.	Ref: Map. 1/10,000 Trench Map Sheet. 62.C.N.W.1.
MARICOURT	25th Oct. 1915.		In trenches. A quiet day. Wounded other ranks 1. To 9th Bn Devon Regt 2nd Lieut. H. Hearse accompanied by servant. From Hospital, other ranks 1.	
MARICOURT	26th Oct. 1915.		In trenches. During the morning enemy shelled trenches 23, 24, 25 and MARICOURT Wood. About 20 shells came over. Lieut. E.C. Hope Hall, Lieut. Hon. J.W. Bampfylde and 19 other ranks to England on leave. To Hospital, other ranks 4. From Hospital, other ranks 1.	
MARICOURT	27th Oct. 1915.		In trenches. Germans shelled edge of MARICOURT Wood. Killed other ranks 1. To Hospital, other ranks 2.	

Army Form C. 2118

WAR DIARY
or
INTELLIGENCE SUMMARY

(Erase heading not required.)

Instructions regarding War Diaries and Intelligence Summaries are contained in F. S. Regs, Part II. and the Staff Manual respectively. Title Pages will be prepared in manuscript.

Place	Date	Hour	Summary of Events and Information	Remarks and references to Appendices
MARICOURT	28th Oct. 1915.		In trenches. During the morning enemy guns were active. Trench 19 and the PERONNE Road were shelled. About 25 shells were sent over. About 12 noon enemy shelled this vicinity again. Capt. J. M. Llewellyn, 2/Lieut. H. West and 6 other ranks rejoined from leave., from Hospital, other ranks 2.	Ref: Map 1/10,000 Trench map Sheet. 62.c.N.W.1.
MARICOURT	29th Oct. 1915.		In trenches. Enemy shelled our trenches on the PERONNE Road with light H.E. 15 shells came over. To England on leave, other ranks 2., Rejoined from leave, other ranks 3., From Hospital, other ranks 2.	
MARICOURT	30th Oct. 1915.		In trenches. Enemy shelled PERONNE Road with light H.E. Wounded other ranks 1.	
MARICOURT	31st Oct. 1915.		In trenches. Nothing unusual occurred. 2/Lieut. H. E. Clifton, 2/Lieut. J. H. Tomlinson and 14 other ranks to England on leave. From Hospital, other ranks 1.	

1-11-15.

E.S. Turner
Lt. Colonel.
Commanding 1st Bn. Devonshire Regiment.

14th Bde.
5th Div.

1st DEVONSHIRE REGIMENT

NOVEMBER

1 9 1 5

Army Form C. 2118

WAR DIARY
or
INTELLIGENCE SUMMARY
(Erase heading not required.)

Instructions regarding War Diaries and Intelligence Summaries are contained in F. S. Regs., Part II. and the Staff Manual respectively. Title Pages will be prepared in manuscript.

Place	Date	Hour	Summary of Events and Information	Remarks and references to Appendices
MARICOURT	1st Nov. 1915.		In trenches. Germans shelled edge of MARICOURT Wood. During the evening a patrol under 2/Lieut. B.W.H. Wreford went towards German sap head N. of PERONNE road, heard relief of German sentries at 11 p.m. Enemy snipers were very active during the night. Wounded, other ranks 1., To Hospital, other ranks 2., From Hospital, other ranks 1.	Ref: Map. Trench Map. Sheet 62.C. N.W.1. 1/10,000.
MARICOURT	2nd Nov. 1915.		In trenches. About 11.30 a.m. long line of enemy transport or guns could be seen moving Southward from GUILLEMONT. Observation was difficult on account of mist but over eighty horses were counted. Two heavy G.S. waggons brought up the end of the column. The nature of other vehicles could not be discerned. Enemy snipers were less active than on previous day. Lieut. E.C. Hope Hall, Lieut. Hon. H.W. Bampfylde and 19 other ranks rejoined from leave. To Hospital, other ranks 2.	
MARICOURT	3rd Nov. 1915.		In trenches. Observation of enemy trenches showed that earth had fallen in at several points owing to rain. Our trenches were also in a bad state from the rain. Enemy guns were more active during the day. At various times they shelled MARICOURT Wood, Trenches 23 and 24 and PERONNE Road with light H.E. To Hospital, other ranks 3., From Hospital, other ranks 2.	

WAR DIARY or INTELLIGENCE SUMMARY

Army Form C. 2118

(Erase heading not required.)

Place	Date	Hour	Summary of Events and Information	Remarks and references to Appendices
MARICOURT	4th Nov.		In trenches. A misty day. Enemy's Field Guns shelled Trench 24 and edge of MARICOURT WOOD with light H.E. Enemy snipers were a little more active than usual. About 6.30 p.m. the Battalion was relieved by the 2nd Battn. Manchester Regt. After relief Battalion marched to billets at SUZANNE. Wounded, other ranks 1., 2/Lieut. C.A. Fletcher 3rd Bn. Devon. Regt. joined Battalion., From Hospital, other ranks 2.	Ref: Map. Trench map. Sheet. 62.c. N.W.1. 1/10,000.
SUZANNE	5th Nov.		The Battalion rested in billets., 2/Lieut. Sir B.R. Williams Bt. 2/Lieut. J.R.H. Tweed and 2/Lieut. J.R.H. Tweed and 2/Lieut. 27 other ranks to England on leave., To Hospital, other ranks 4., From Hospital, other ranks 1.	Ref: Map. 1/80,000. AMIENS Sheet. 12.
SUZANNE	6th Nov.		The Battalion rested in billets. No 3 Coy working on trenches in Sector O.4. during the day. To Hospital, other ranks 1., From Hospital, other ranks 4.	
SUZANNE	7th Nov.		The Battalion rested in billets. No 4 Coy furnished two platoons in the morning and two platoons in the afternoon for work on trenches in Sector O.4. After work the platoons returned to billets. Divine Service was held in the village at 9.30 and 10.30. a.m. Following recipients of French decorations proceeded to ACHEUX where Army Commander presented decorations to them. Chevalier 5th Class Legion of Honour, Major N. Luxmoore., Medaille Militaire, No 9607 Sgt. A. Whitty., To Hospital, other ranks 1., From Hospital, other ranks 3.	

Army Form C. 2118

WAR DIARY
or
INTELLIGENCE SUMMARY
(Erase heading not required.)

Instructions regarding War Diaries and Intelligence Summaries are contained in F.S. Regs., Part II. and the Staff Manual respectively. Title Pages will be prepared in manuscript.

Place	Date	Hour	Summary of Events and Information	Remarks and references to Appendices
SUZANNE	8th Nov.		The Battalion rested in billets. No 1 Coy furnished two platoons in the morning and two platoons in the afternoon for work on trenches in Sector A.4. After work the platoons returned to billets. 2/Lieut. J.H. Tomlinson, 2/Lieut. H.E. Clifton and 2 other ranks rejoined from leave. To Hospital, other ranks 4.	Ref: Map 1/80,000 AMIENS Sheet 12.
SUZANNE	9th Nov.		The Battalion rested in billets. No 2 Coy furnished 50 men for work on trenches during the evening. After work they returned to billets. To Hospital, other ranks 3. To England on leave, other ranks 7. Rejoined Battn from leave, other ranks 11.	
SUZANNE	10th Nov.		The Battalion rested in billets. No 5501 Cpl. J. Rose and No 11348 Lce Cpl. S.J. Pike were awarded Distinguished Conduct Medals.	
SUZANNE	11th Nov.		The Battalion rested in billets. No's 3 and 4 Coys and 50 men of No 1 Coy were working on communication trenches during the evening afterwards returning to billets. 2/Lieut. R.E.B. Paramore, 2/Lieut. J.H. Tomlinson and 2 other ranks were wounded accidentally during instruction in grenades etc. To England on leave, Capt. G.E.R. Prior, Capt. & Adjt. E.H. Gotto and 26 other ranks. To Hospital, other ranks 1. From Hospital, other ranks 2.	

Army Form C. 2118

WAR DIARY
or
INTELLIGENCE SUMMARY
(Erase heading not required.)

Instructions regarding War Diaries and Intelligence Summaries are contained in F.S. Regs., Part II. and the Staff Manual respectively. Title Pages will be prepared in manuscript.

Place	Date	Hour	Summary of Events and Information	Remarks and references to Appendices
SUZANNE	12th Nov		The Battalion rested in billets. No 2 Coy and 100 men from No 1 Coy were working on shelters just EAST of SUZANNE village from 2. P.M. to 5. P.M. Accommodation was found for 400 men of the Battalion at a concert held during the evening at Bde Headqrs SUZANNE. To Hospital, other ranks 7. From Hospital, other ranks 4.	Ref: Map 1/80,000 AMIENS Sheet 12.
SUZANNE	13th Nov		The Battalion rested in billets. At 10 a.m. the Battalion paraded and formed three sides of a square in Chateau grounds SUZANNE where Brig. Genl. C.W. Compton, C.M.G. Comdg. 14th Infy Brigade presented the D.C.M. to No 5501 Corpl J. Love., 1st Bn. East Surrey Regiment. During the evening Battalion relieved the 1st. Bn. East Surrey Regiment in trenches Sub-Sector A.2. To Hospital, other ranks 7. From Hospital, other ranks 2.	
MARICOURT	14th Nov		In trenches. Wounded, other ranks 3. To Hospital, other ranks 1., 2/Lieut. J. Wells to Third Army School., 2/Lieut. Sir B.R. Williams,Bt., 2/Lieut. J.R.H. Tweed and 24 other ranks rejoined from leave. From Hospital, other ranks 2.	Ref: Map Trench map. Sheet 62.C. N.W.1. 1/10,000.

P.Y.O.

Army Form C. 2118

WAR DIARY
or
INTELLIGENCE SUMMARY
(Erase heading not required.)

Instructions regarding War Diaries and Intelligence Summaries are contained in F. S. Regs., Part II. and the Staff Manual respectively. Title Pages will be prepared in manuscript.

Place	Date	Hour	Summary of Events and Information	Remarks and references to Appendices
MARICOURT	15th Nov		In trenches. Fires were observed burning in enemy line. Trenches 14 and 18 were lightly shelled during the early morning. During the morning and at midday enemy shelling was unusually heavy and vigorous. Trench 16 and 14 street was badly blown in as result of this shelling. At midday when our artillery were shelling Y wood the Germans sent up a green light from their front line trenches. The German artillery then opened fire all along the front of the left Sub-Sector. Killed, other ranks 1, To Hospital, other ranks 3. From Hospital, other ranks 6. Capt. C.O.'S. Bennett, 38th Horse (Indian Cavalry Corps) attached for purpose of learning latest methods of trench warfare.	Ref: Map Trench Map Sheet 62.C. N.W.1. 1/10,000.
MARICOURT	16th Nov.		In trenches. At 4 p.m. a green flag was observed in marsh opposite VERUX. Killed, other ranks 2. Wounded and doing duty, other ranks 1. Wounded, other ranks 3. To England on leave, other ranks 3. To Hospital, other ranks 7. From Hospital, other ranks 6. Rejoined from leave, other ranks 7.	
MARICOURT	14th Nov.		In trenches. Nothing unusual occurred. To Hospital, other ranks 5. From Hospital, other ranks 4.	

1875 Wt. W593/826 1,000,000 4/15 J.B.C. & A. A.D.S.S./Forms/C. 2118.

Army Form C. 2118

WAR DIARY
or
INTELLIGENCE SUMMARY

(Erase heading not required.)

Instructions regarding War Diaries and Intelligence Summaries are contained in F. S. Regs., Part II. and the Staff Manual respectively. Title Pages will be prepared in manuscript.

Place	Date	Hour	Summary of Events and Information	Remarks and references to Appendices
MARICOURT	18th Nov.		In trenches. Thick fog throughout the day. Killed other ranks 1., accidentally wounded other ranks 8. To Hospital, other ranks 4., Lt. Col. E.G. Williams C.M.G., Capt. R.H. Anderson Morshead and 26 other ranks to England on leave., Rejoined from leave Capt. Y.E.R. Prior, Capt. A.J.F.E.H. Gott. and 26 other ranks. From Hospital, other ranks 2.	Ref: Map. Trench Map. Sheet 62.C. N.W.1. 1/10,000.
MARICOURT	19th Nov.		In trenches. At various times a few rifle grenades were fired on trench 16. No damage was done. To Hospital other ranks 7. From Hospital other ranks 1.	
MARICOURT	20th Nov.		In trenches. There was a little more shelling (by enemy) than usual during the morning. Wounded, other ranks 1., Lieut. F.A. Hellaby to England on leave. To Hospital, other ranks 4. From Hospital, other ranks 4.	
MARICOURT	21st Nov.		In trenches. Nothing unusual occurred. To Hospital other ranks 5. From Hospital other ranks 1.	
MARICOURT	22nd Nov.		In trenches. A few Germans were observed on skyline about 300 yards N. of CHAPEAU GENDARME. They were dispersed by rifle fire. About midnight enemy fired several grenades into 15 trench. Our grenadiers retaliated. Lieut. P. Walton and several proceeded to rejoin their own unit. From Hospital, other ranks 7.	

Army Form C. 2118.

WAR DIARY or INTELLIGENCE SUMMARY

(Erase heading not required.)

Place	Date	Hour	Summary of Events and Information	Remarks and references to Appendices
MARICOURT	23rd Nov.		In trenches. A foggy day. A German working party was heard by the QUARRY POST. They were dispersed by rifle fire. To Base for discharge other ranks 1. 2/Lieut. R. Ross and 2/Lieut. B.W. L'E. Malone and 18 other ranks to England on leave. To Hospital, other ranks 5. Rejoined from leave, other ranks 3. From Hospital other ranks 1.	Ref: Map. Trench map. Sheet 62.C. N.W.1. 1/10,000.
MARICOURT	24th Nov.		In trenches. There was more shelling by the enemy than usual, along the whole of the sector. No damage was done. To Hospital other ranks 1. From Hospital other ranks 3.	
MARICOURT	25th Nov.		In trenches. One of our machine guns opened fire on German transport which was observed at 6.45 p.m. At the first burst the transport stopped. It started again however some minutes afterwards and on our firing it started galloping. A German working party was reported in the communication trench leading down to the listening post in the CHATEAU GENDARME. It was dispersed by our machine gun fire. To Hospital, other ranks 4. From Hospital, other ranks 1.	
MARICOURT	26th Nov.		In trenches. A quiet day. Wounded other ranks 1. To England on leave, other ranks 1. Lt. Col. E.G. Williams C.M.G., Capt. R.H. Anderson Morshead and 25 other ranks rejoined from leave. From Hospital other ranks 7.	

Army Form C. 2118

WAR DIARY
or
INTELLIGENCE SUMMARY

(Erase heading not required.)

Instructions regarding War Diaries and Intelligence Summaries are contained in F.S. Regs., Part II and the Staff Manual respectively. Title Pages will be prepared in manuscript.

Place	Date	Hour	Summary of Events and Information	Remarks and references to Appendices
MARICOURT.	27th Nov.		In trenches. Trenches just S. of PERONNE road were slightly shelled. No damage. To Hospital other ranks 1. Rejoined from leave other ranks 1.	Ref: map. French map. Sheet 62.C. N.W.1. 1/10,000.
MARICOURT.	28th Nov.		In trenches. Enemy transport was heard at 5.30 p.m. and going away again at 6.30 p.m. They galloped on being fired at by our machineguns.	
MARICOURT.	29th Nov.		In trenches. Enemy transport was heard at 5.30 p.m. Our artillery fired on them. At 10.p.m. enemy shelled No 18 trench with "whizzbangs". No casualties. To England on leave, other ranks 3. To Hospital, other ranks 20.	
MARICOURT.	30th Nov.		In trenches. Enemy shelled No 18 trench. About 24 shells were fired. 2/Lt A.G.A. Davis, 2/Lt J.J. Norish, 2/Lt L. Pierce and 2/Lt W.F. Adams joined the Battalion.	

2/12/15.

E.S. Vincent,
Lt. Colonel,
Commanding, 1st Bn. Devonshire Regiment.

1st Devon Regiment
Intelligence Report

Observation difficult beyond enemy front line trench. No new work was observed. Enemy is not now working on his trenches with the same vigour of a month ago.

The seven heavy H.E. shells reported yesterday appear to have been something after the nature of trench mortar bombs. The sound of the gun was heard at comparatively short range, the customary whistle did not accompany the flight of the projectile and the hole made in the earth was shallow.

Judging from sound the direction of the gun appeared to be (approx) due east of trench 21.

1 Novr 1915

(Sd) F.N. Hellaby Lt
Intelligence Officer

1st. Devon Regiment
Intelligence Report

Observation difficult. Little new work could be observed in enemy front line trench except at point 17.C.6.

About 11.30 A.M a long line of enemy transport or guns could be seen moving Southward from GUILLEMONT. Observation was difficult on account of mist but over eighty horses were counted. Two heavy G.S. waggons brought up the end of the column. The nature of other vehicles could not be discerned.

Sd. F.A. Hellaby Lt.
Intelligence Officer.

2nd November 1915

1st Devon Regiment

Intelligence Report

Observation of many trenches showed that earth had fallen in at several points owing to the rain.

Little could be observed on ground behind enemy trenches.

About 8.30 A.M. big waggon was observed moving northward along MAUREPAS – GUILLEMONT Road. Nothing else of importance was observed during the day.

Enemy guns have been more active during day. At various times they shelled MARICOURT Wood, Trenches 23, & 24 and Peronne Road with light H.E.

Sd F.N. Hellaby Lt

3rd November 1915   Intelligence Officer

1st Devon Regiment

Intelligence Officer's Report

Little change observed in enemy front line trench.

During day horsemen and single carts observed moving behind enemy lines but general observation difficult on account of mist.

24. Enemy Field Guns shelled Trenches Edge MARICOURT Wood with light H.E.

Sd F.A. Hellaby Lt.
4th November 1915   Intelligence Officer

Intelligence Report

1st Devon Regt

15th Nov-15

Last night one of our wiring parties was fired upon by a German Trench Mortar. No damage was done.

Early this morning a German Patrol was dispersed by the West Bomb Throwers in 13 Trench.

Throughout the day German Artillery has been active especially on the Left Subsector A 2. Smoke apparently from a German Battery was observed in a copse above CURLU, on a bearing of 102° from the Reserve Machine Gun Emplacement in OBSERVATION AVENUE 250ˣ S of BOIS DE L'EPRON. The Shells coming from this Battery pitched about 300ˣ N of VAUX in the Marsh. The Battery was firing between 12 noon & 1 pm.

A Tram was observed approaching HEM at 1.15 pm

Nov. 15th 1915

(Sd) B W L E' Malone
2nd Lt
Intelligence Officer
1st Devons

1st Devon Regiment
Intelligence Report

Nov. 16th 1915

Artillery Activity At midday yesterday when our Artillery were shelling Y WOOD the Germans sent up a green light from their front line trenches. The German's Artillery then opened fire all along the front of the left Sub-Sector. Their fire was slow but continued for a considerable period.

The enemy put several shells into the fire trenches at the MILL this morning at about 10.45 am. Our Artillery replied.

CURLU has been carefully watched and no movement has been seen there in the last two days.

(Sd) B.W. L'Estrange 2nd Lt
Intelligence Officer
1st Devon Regt

Intelligence Report 1st Devons

Nov 17th 1915

Trains A train was seen in HEM at 3.20 P.M. Otherwise nothing to report

(Sd) B to L¹ E Malone
Intelligence Officer
Nov 17th 1915   1st Devons

Intelligence Report
    1st Devons.   Nov 18th 1915

At 7 PM last night a train was heard in the direction of HEM moving W to E.

Owing to the thick fog throughout today nothing could be observed or further information gathered."

(sd) B.W.L E Grahame 2/Lt
            Intelligence Officer
               1st Devons

Intelligence Report. 1st Devons. Nov. 19th

Last night a bluish coloured light was observed in the marshes. The light was seen at intervals during a period of two hours. Another light of the same appearance was observed at the same time in the German lines overlooking the marshes. This was apparently an answering light.

Otherwise nothing to report.

B/Lt L S Malone r.f.
Intelligence Officer
1st Devons

Nov 19th 1915

Intelligence Report. 1/Devons. Nov. 20th

Yesterday evening at about 6.5 p.m. a train was heard in the direction of HEM.

Heavy motor and horse transport was heard in the direction of FERME ROUGE at about 8 p.m. last night.

A working party was heard last night from our listening post in 11 F.T. Fresh chalk and some galvanized iron were observed this morning on the parapet of the german listening post on CHAPEAU ~~Ferdeum~~ ~~ROUE~~ opposite our listening post from 11 F.T.

B.W.L. Malrie Lt.
Intelligence Officer
1/Devons

Nov. 20th 1915.

Intelligence Report — 1st Devons — Nov. 21st

The Centre sub-sector report that noises were heard in the German lines last night, as though a Company Relief was being carried out.

No further work has been heard or observed in German listening post opposite our QUARRY post.

Otherwise nothing to report.

Bluk's Malolo Yr
Intelligence Officer
1st Devon Regt.

Nov. 21st 1915.

Intelligence Report. 1/Devons, Nov. 22nd

A thick fog has prevented any observations.

B.W.L. Malone. Lt.
Intelligence Officer
1/Devon Regt.

Nov. 22nd/15.

Intelligence report – 1st Devons.
Nov 23rd

A German working party was heard by the Quarry post. It was dispersed by rifle fire.

No further work appears to have been done on German listening post in front of Quarry post road

The German transport are now reported to be using a road to the left of Cuplu; that appears to have abandoned the road formerly used, probably owing to the rifle & our machine gun fire now

C.M. Singer 2 Lt.
a/ Intelligence Officer
1st Devon Regt

Nov 23rd – 15

Intelligence Report. Devons. Nov 24th

The Germans appear to have been using a shell of higher calibre against fire Moulin this morning, possibly a 5-9 a.a.

I suggest that the German transport use the road Bouchicourt – Curlu, as far as the cross roads on from Bray to Maricourt; from there I would suggest that material is carried to the Trenches a.a.a.

A man was seen bicycling along the Peronne road from 15 Trench this morning.

Nov 24th 15.

C.M. Singer 2 Lt.
a/ Intelligence officer
1st Devon Regt.

Intelligence report. 1/Devon Regt.
Nov 25th
_____

The Germans have put up an artillery board, which they with vertical stripes I should their trenches at A.29.b.8.0.

No 3 y machine gun fired on the German transport at the crossroads mentioned in yesterday's report at 6.45 p.m. 26 & 25. aaa.

At the first burst the Transport stopped; & when it started again however some minutes afterwards, & on our firing it started galloping. aaa.

A German working party was reported in the communication trench leading down to the watering post of the Chateau Gendarme. aaa.

It was dispersed by No 4 Machine gun. aaa.

I suggest that the Germans were only deepening the trench as

_____

Nov 25th 1915.

C.M. Singer 2Lt.
a/Intelligence Officer
1st Devon Regt.

Intelligence Report
1st Devons
Nov 26th 1915

German Transport reported by Central Sub-Sector at 5-30 p.m on the 25th aaa Nothing was heard by No 3 Machine Gun, but the wind was unfavourable aaa It would appear as if the Germans have changed the time of their transport aaa
Nothing further to report.

Nov 26th 1915.

(Sd) C M Singer 2nd Lt
a/ Intelligence Officer

Intelligence report. 1st Devons. Nov. 27th

Transport was heard in Cuinchy at
5.30 pm of the 26th inst.

Machine gun no 1 fired on communication
trench leading up to Cuinchy between 6
& 9 pm 26th. at first burst shooting
was heard & aa. The bullets were
also heard hitting the tiles of Cuinchy aaa.

A train was heard at 7 pm going
from north to south. aaa

About 9 pm red starshells (4)
were seen going up from the
German listed. opposite the
French trenches. aaa

This was followed by heavy
shelling aaa

Flashes of three guns were
seen slightly east of the
Shrine at the crossroads Peronne
Road, (A 30 b.) aaa

A German was seen on the
Peronne rd near the chapel
at 2 pm 27th inst aaa

An observation balloon was
observed over the hyth end of
Kem wood, between the hours
of 12am & 3 pm. 27th.

27th 1915.
                          C. M. Singer? Lt.
                          & Intelligence officer

Intelligence Report 1st Devons. Nov 28th

It has been observed that the same company of Germans are in front of the Centre subsector as were in front of this trench A.4, when this battalion occupied it, and a German was up. This was recognised by the whistling of one of the Germans.

A German machine gun was enfilading the upper Sayanne Rd, near Maricourt, between 7 & 7.m. of the 27th. The bullets were going high.

Transports was heard in the usual place (at X roads) at 5-30 & going away again at 6.20. They galloped on being fired at by our machine guns.

At 6 p.m. 2 red star shells were observed in German lines, opposite the french; at 5 a.m. 4 red & 1 green, in the same place — on both occasions there was shelling afterwards on us.

Trams were heard several times during the night.

Nov 28th 1915.
C. M. Singer 2 Lt.
a/Intelligence Officer
1st Devon Regt.

Intelligence report. 1/Devons. Nov 29th

German Transport heard at A.30 b.5.8
at 5.30.p.m. Our artillery fired
on them.

More Transport was heard to the
East of Carlin at 9.15 p.m.
at 10 p.m. the Germans opened [fire] from
no 18 Trench; flashes of
their guns were observed
a little to the East of Carlin.
If they fire tonight bearings will
be taken.

Nov 29th 15.   C. M. Singer Lt.
                      a/ Intelligence officer
                      1st Devon Regt.

                      D.

Intelligence report. 1/Devons. Nov 30th

Smoke was seen coming from the North end of ---- wood on the afternoon of the 29th about 3.30 p.m. when the enemy were shelling our french lines. aaa
German Transport was heard towards A.30.b.5.8. at 8 p.m. instead of at 5.30 p.m as usual.
The German battery East of A.30.b.5.8. did not fire last night, hence it was impossible to get a bearing. aaa
A gramophone was being heard at night in ---- Y. wood. aaa
Washing was seen hanging up to dry in ---- this morning. This appeared to be a woman's under linen. aaa.

Nov 30th '15.
C.M. Singer 2 Lt.
a/ Intelligence officer 1/Devon

14th Bde.
5th Div.

1st DEVONSHIRE REGIMENT.

DECEMBER

1 9 1 5

Army Form C. 2118

WAR DIARY
or
INTELLIGENCE SUMMARY

(Erase heading not required.)

Instructions regarding War Diaries and Intelligence Summaries are contained in F.S. Regs., Part II. and the Staff Manual respectively. Title Pages will be prepared in manuscript.

Place	Date	Hour	Summary of Events and Information	Remarks and references to Appendices
MARICOURT	1st. Dec.		In trenches. Patrol under 2/Lieut. P.C. Nash went out from 18 F.T. It was unable to get through the hostile wire as sentries were very alert especially those on PERONNE road. Patrol under 2/Lieut. J.R.H. Sneed encountered hostile work party and covering party which they bombed. Enemy retaliated by firing several rifle grenades into 15 F.T. During the day enemy's artillery was fairly active, their shelling being mostly done with 4.2 howitzers. Accidentally killed other ranks 1, Accidentally wounded other ranks 3, Accidentally wounded and doing duty other ranks 3, To Hospital (sick) 2/Lieut. J. Loman, Draft of 9 other ranks joined, 2/Lieut. R. Ross, 2/Lieut. B.W.L'E. Malone and 14 other ranks rejoined from leave.	Ref: Map Trench Map Sheet 62.C. N.W.1. 1/10,000.
MARICOURT	2nd. Dec.		In trenches. Germans were active with rifle grenades many of which were blinds. Patrol under 2/Lieut. H.C. Clifton proceeded from 18.F.T. towards German wire. It cut the first two rows of wire, then 2/Lt. Clifton and Corpl. Whiting went on to within about 4 yards from German parapet and heard about six Germans walking. Four bombs were thrown among them, six lights were then put up and rifle fire opened. Patrol returned safely. At dusk the battalion was relieved in trenches Sub. Sector A.2. by the 1st Bn. D. Cornwall L.I. After relief the battalion (9 Coys) relieved the 2nd Bn. Manchester Regt. as garrison of MARICOURT defences. Wounded other ranks 2., To Hospital other ranks 4,	

Army Form C. 2118

WAR DIARY or INTELLIGENCE SUMMARY

(Erase heading not required.)

Instructions regarding War Diaries and Intelligence Summaries are contained in F. S. Regs., Part II. and the Staff Manual respectively. Title Pages will be prepared in manuscript.

Place	Date	Hour	Summary of Events and Information	Remarks and references to Appendices
MARICOURT	3rd Dec.		Garrison of MARICOURT defences., To England on leave other ranks 4., To Hospital other ranks 5., Rejoined Battn. from leave other ranks 1., 2/Lieut. S.G. Williams joined from Cadet School., From Hospital other ranks 5.	Ref: Map Trench Map Sheet 62.C. N.W.1. 1/10,000.
MARICOURT	4th Dec.		Garrison of MARICOURT defences., To England on leave other ranks 32., To Hospital other ranks 6., From Hospital other ranks 3.	
MARICOURT	5th Dec.		Garrison of MARICOURT defences., Wounded other ranks 1., From Hospital other ranks 3.	
MARICOURT	6th Dec.		Garrison of MARICOURT defences., Rejoined from leave other ranks 14., Lieut. F.A. Holloby rejoined from leave., From Hospital other ranks 4.	
MARICOURT	7th Dec.		Garrison of MARICOURT defences., 2/Lieut. H.M. Brown and 2/Lieut. B. Morland joined the Battalion., Rejoined from leave other ranks 3., From Hospital other ranks 1., To Hospital other ranks 2.	
MARICOURT	8th Dec.		The Battalion relieved the 2nd Bn. Inniskilling Fusiliers in trenches Sub Sector Q.4., Relief started at 5 p.m. the Inniskillings taking over MARICOURT defences after their relief by Devons. From Hospital other ranks 3., To Hospital 2/Lt. H. Corbett and 5 other ranks.	

Army Form C. 2118

WAR DIARY or INTELLIGENCE SUMMARY

(Erase heading not required.)

Instructions regarding War Diaries and Intelligence Summaries are contained in F.S. Regs., Part II. and the Staff Manual respectively. Title Pages will be prepared in manuscript.

Place	Date	Hour	Summary of Events and Information	Remarks and references to Appendices
MARICOURT	9th Dec.		In trenches. During the night enemy artillery were unusually active. Between 8 and 9 p.m. they heavily shelled MAIN AVENUE with light H.E. and shrapnel. Shells also fell near trenches 30, 31 and their support trenches. At various times during the night rifle grenades were fired at trenches 28, 29 and not the advanced posts in those trenches. In reply to our rifle fire from trench 31 enemy opened heavy rifle fire and machine gun fire on trenches 32 to 28. Wounded other ranks 2. To Hospital other ranks 8. Lt. Col. F. Tristram 13th Bn. (A.P.W.O.) Yorkshire Regiment joined for attachment. From Hospital other ranks 3.	Ref: Map. French map Sheet 62.C. N.W.1. 1/10,000.
MARICOURT	10th Dec		In trenches. About 10 a.m. enemy shelled MARICOURT communication trench. About 1.15 p.m. about 30 shells fell near trenches 33 and 34. 2/Lieut. E.M. Singer, 2/Lieut. G.A. Fletcher and 30 other ranks to England on leave. To Hospital other ranks 3. Rejoined from leave other ranks 7. From Hospital other ranks 1.	
MARICOURT	11th Dec		In trenches. Enemy again shelled MARICOURT Avenue. Died of wounds other ranks 1. Wounded other ranks 1. Rejoined from leave other ranks 29. From Hospital other ranks 4. To Hospital other ranks 4.	

Army Form C. 2118

WAR DIARY or INTELLIGENCE SUMMARY

(Erase heading not required.)

Instructions regarding War Diaries and Intelligence Summaries are contained in F. S. Regs., Part II. and the Staff Manual respectively. Title Pages will be prepared in manuscript.

Place	Date	Hour	Summary of Events and Information	Remarks and references to Appendices
MARICOURT	12th Dec.		In trenches. During the evening the Battalion was relieved by the 1st Bn East Surrey Regt. After relief the Battalion moved to billets vacated by E. Surreys in SUZANNE. Killed other ranks 1. To Hospital other ranks 4. Rejoined from leave other ranks 5. 2/Lieut. J. Wells and 2 other ranks rejoined from 3rd Army School. From Hospital other ranks 3.	Ref: Maps. Trench Maps. Sheet 62.C. N.W.1. 1/10,000.
SUZANNE	13th Dec.		The Battalion rested in billets. Nothing of note occurred. To Hospital other ranks 3. A draft of 4 signallers joined the Battalion from England. From Hospital other ranks 5.	Ref: Maps. 1/80,000 AMIENS Sheet 12.
SUZANNE	14th Dec.		The Battalion rested in billets. In the evening the Battalion relieved the 1st East Surrey Regt in trenches Sector A.4. Capt. E. O'B. Daunt, 38th C.I. Horse proceeded to rejoin own unit. To Hospital other ranks 3. From Hospital other ranks 3.	
MARICOURT	15th Dec.		During the night of 14th/15th a patrol under 2/Lieut. R. Ross bombed the German saps on MONTAUBAN Road. At least six Germans were in the sap and 12 bombs were thrown into it with good effect. Wounded other ranks 1. To England on leave other ranks 26. To Hospital other ranks 6. From Hospital other ranks 3.	Ref: Maps. Trench Maps. Sheet 62.C. N.W.1. 1/10,000.

1875 Wt. W593/826 1,000,000 4/15 J.B.C. & A. A.D.S.S./Forms/C. 2118.

WAR DIARY or INTELLIGENCE SUMMARY

Army Form C. 2118

(Erase heading not required.)

Place	Date	Hour	Summary of Events and Information	Remarks and references to Appendices
MARICOURT	16th Dec		On the night of 15/16th a patrol divided into two parties — 2/Lt. R. Ross 1/Devons, 2/Lt. Grist 15/R. Warwicks and 8 other ranks — 2/Lt. A.J. St.L. Henry 1/Devons and 14 other ranks — bombed the German sap situated at A.10.c.2.6. All carried from 4 to 6 bombs. Having exhausted all the bombs with good effect both parties withdrew. The artillery were called on and their support was excellent both shrapnel and H.E. bursting correctly. During the evening (16/17th) the Battalion was relieved by the 1st East Surrey Regt., after relief Battalion took over the defences of MARICOURT. Missing, other ranks 1. Wounded other ranks 1. To Hospital other ranks 5. From Hospital other ranks 3.	Ref: Map Trenchmap. Sheet 62.C. N.W.1. 1/10,000.
MARICOURT	17th Dec		Garrison of MARICOURT defences. To Hospital other ranks 3. From Hospital other ranks 1. 2/Lieut. G.M. Singer, 2/Lieut. G.A. Fletcher and 30 other ranks rejoined from leave.	
MARICOURT	18th Dec		The Mayor of Exeter visited the Battalion. During the evening Battalion relieved the 1st East Surrey Regt in trenches Sector A.4. To England for discharge other ranks 2. To Hospital other ranks 1. From Hospital other ranks 5.	

Army Form C. 2118

WAR DIARY or INTELLIGENCE SUMMARY

(Erase heading not required.)

Instructions regarding War Diaries and Intelligence Summaries are contained in F.S. Regs., Part II. and the Staff Manual respectively. Title Pages will be prepared in manuscript.

Place	Date	Hour	Summary of Events and Information	Remarks and references to Appendices
MARICOURT	19th Dec		In trenches. Enemy shelling was more than usually active during the day. Between 9 and 10 a.m. enemy heavily shelled MARICOURT avenue. At various times during the day whole sector was shelled with H.E. and shrapnel. About 2 a.m. Germans shouted to Advance Post No 1. (trench 28) "We speak English if you" "don't shoot we won't". After our fire had ceased enemy replied with volleys. Killed other ranks 1. Wounded other ranks 1. Draft of 8 other ranks joined Battalion as signallers. 2/Lt. H. Corbett and 2 other ranks rejoined from hospital.	Ref: Map: Trench Map, Sheet 62.c. N.W.1. 1/10,000.
MARICOURT	20th Dec		In trenches. During night of 19/20th enemy artillery was active. Several salvos of eight H.E. were fired almost hourly over MARICOURT Wood and trenches 29, 30 and 31. Since daybreak there was no enemy artillery fire. In the evening Battalion was relieved by 1st East Surrey Regt. After relief Battalion moved to billets at SUZANNE. Killed other ranks 1. 2/Lieut J. Wells, 2/Lieut D.C. Nash and 26 other ranks to England on leave. From hospital other ranks 1.	
SUZANNE	21st Dec		The Battalion rested in billets. To Hospital other ranks 3. From Hospital other ranks 4.	Ref: Map: 1/80,000 AMIENS Sheet 12.

1875 Wt. W593/826 1,000,000 4/15 J.B.C. & A. A.D.S.S./Forms/C. 2118.

Army Form C. 2118

WAR DIARY or INTELLIGENCE SUMMARY

(Erase heading not required.)

Instructions regarding War Diaries and Intelligence Summaries are contained in F.S. Regs., Part II. and the Staff Manual respectively. Title Pages will be prepared in manuscript.

Place	Date	Hour	Summary of Events and Information	Remarks and references to Appendices
SUZANNE	22nd Dec		The Battalion rested in billets. Nothing of note occurred. From Hospital other ranks 1.	Ref: Map: 1/80,000 AMIENS Sheet 12.
SUZANNE	23rd Dec		The Battalion rested in billets. Nothing of note occurred. Rejoined Battalion from leave 21 other ranks.	
SUZANNE	24th Dec		The Battalion rested in billets. In the evening Battalion relieved the 2nd Bn Manchester Regt in trenches sector A.3. Capt. G.L. Veitch 4th Bn Devon Regt joined 1st Battn for duty. 2/Lt. H. Corbett and 25 other ranks to England on leave. From Hospital other ranks 3.	
			From Hospital other ranks 2.	
MARICOURT	25th Dec		In trenches. A quiet day. From Hospital other ranks 1.	Ref: Map: Trench map. Sheet 62.C. N.W.1. 1/10,000.
MARICOURT	26th Dec		In trenches. In the evening the Battalion was relieved by the 15th Royal Warwick Regt. After relief Battalion took over MARICOURT Defences from 1st D. of Cornwall's L.I. Killed other ranks 1. Lieut. L.A. Heeloby, 2/Lieut. G.M. Slinger and 28 other ranks attached (to form part of) 144th Infty Brigade M.G. Coy. From Hospital other ranks 1.	

1875 Wt. W593/826 1,000,000 4/15 J.B.C. & A. A.D.S.S./Forms/C. 2118.

Army Form C. 2118

WAR DIARY or INTELLIGENCE SUMMARY

(Erase heading not required.)

Instructions regarding War Diaries and Intelligence Summaries are contained in F. S. Regs., Part II. and the Staff Manual respectively. Title Pages will be prepared in manuscript.

Place	Date	Hour	Summary of Events and Information	Remarks and references to Appendices
MARICOURT	24th Dec.		Garrison of MARICOURT Defences. From Hospital other ranks 2.	Ref: Map: Trench Map Sheet 62.C. N.W.1. 1/10,000.
MARICOURT	28th Dec.		Garrison of MARICOURT Defences. In the evening Battalion relieved the 15th Royal Warwicks in trenches Sector A.3., 2/Lieut. J. Wells and 24 other ranks rejoined Battalion from leave. To Hospital other ranks 11.	
MARICOURT	29th Dec.		In trenches. From Hospital other ranks 2.	
MARICOURT	30th Dec.		In trenches. In the evening Battalion was relieved by the 15th Royal Warwicks. After relief Battalion withdrew to billets at SUZANNE. To England on leave 24 other ranks. To Hospital other ranks 4. From Hospital other ranks 3.	
SUZANNE	31st Dec.		The Battalion rested in billets. Nothing of note occurred. Wounded other ranks 1.	Ref: Map 1/80,000 AMIENS. Sheet 12.

1/1/16.

W.W.Vicary

Lt. Colonel,
Comdg.: 1st Bn. Devonshire Regiment.

WO 95/1565/2

WO 95/1565 PT III

5th Division
14th Bde
5th Cheshires

FROM UK

~~July~~ ~~December~~

1915 FEB — 1915 DEC

TO 56 DIV TROOPS (PIONEERS)

14th Bde.
5th Division.

Joined =14th Bde on 19th February 1915
from Army Troops.

5th C H E S H I RXE S.

F E B R U A R Y
....

1 9 1 5

Army Form C. 2118.

WAR DIARY or INTELLIGENCE SUMMARY.

5th Bat. Cheshire Regt.

(Erase heading not required.)

Place	Date	Hour	Summary of Events and Information	Remarks and references to Appendices
Cambridge	14/2/15	5.0 am to 9.30 am	Left Cambridge – arrived Southampton – left from 3.0 pm – Lieut.Col. T.E.G. Groves T.D. in command	117
Southampton	14/2/15	7.0 to 7.30 pm	Left by S.S. Oxonian, Manchester Importer, & Glenearn Head – arrived HAVRE 7.30 am 15/2/15.	117
HAVRE	15/2/15		Rest Camp –	117
"	17/2/15	4.30 pm	Entrained –	117
BAILLEUL	16/2/15	7.30 pm	Arrived – Buetzel – 30 Officers. 1000 N.C.Os. & men	117
"	19/2/15	2.0 pm	Marched to NEUVE EGLISE via DRANOUTRE arriving 5.30 pm. Attached to 14th Inf. Bde.	117
NEUVE EGLISE	20/2/15		2/Lieut M. CHURDY wounded – Suttery bomb throwers. Y Division.	117
NEUVE EGLISE	22/2/15 to 25/2/15		Detachments of officers & N.C.Os sent to trenches for instruction.	117
"			4 men wounded by shell in NEUVE EGLISE	117
"	1/3/15		D Co proceeded to trenches for 24 hours –	117
"	2/3/15		A Co proceeded to trenches for 24 hours	117
"			2 men wounded by rifle fire while employed on fatigue duty in rear of trenches	117
"	3/3/15		B Co proceeded to trenches for 24 hours –	117
"			1 man died of wounds from shell fire in the trenches – 1 man wounded by rifle fire in the trenches –	117
"	4/3/15		C Co proceeded to trenches for 24 hours –	117
"			1 man wounded by rifle fire in the trenches	117
"	5/3/15		A Co proceeded to trenches for 24 hours.	117
"			1 man killed + 2 wounded by shell fire in NEUVE EGLISE.	117

14th Bde.
5th Division.

5th C H E S H I R E S.

March

1 9 1 5

WAR DIARY
INTELLIGENCE SUMMARY.

5th Batt. Cheshire Regt.

Army Form C. 2118.

Place	Date	Hour	Summary of Events and Information	Remarks and references to Appendices
NEUVE EGLISE	6.3.15		1 man killed in trenches —	11A
"	8.3.15		1 man wounded by rifle fire in trenches —	11A
"	9.3.15		Lieut. L.G.M. CRICK admitted to hospital —	11A
"	10.3.15		1 man wounded by shell fire in trenches —	11A
"	11.3.15		2 men wounded by shell fire in trenches — LIEUT. L. EVANS admitted to hospital —	11A
"	13.3.15		Captain C.A.PRICE admitted to hospital —	11A
"	15.3.15		1 man wounded by rifle fire in trenches —	11A
"	16.3.15		1 man wounded by rifle fire in trenches —	11A
"	18.3.15		1 Officer 2/Lieut. C. JOHNSON wounded by shell fire in trenches [2 men wounded by shell fire in trenches —] died of wounds in hospital [2 men wounded by shell fire in trenches —]	11A
"	19.3.15		1 man wounded by rifle fire in trenches & died of wounds in hospital —	11A
"	20.3.15		1 man wounded by accidental discharge of rifle in NEUVE EGLISE — 2 men wounded by rifle fire in trenches —	11A
KEMMEL	23.3.15	7.30 pm	Battalion left NEUVE EGLISE 7.30 pm and marched to KEMMEL. "C" & "D" Co's relieved ROYAL IRISH RIFLES in trenches H4. J1, J2, J3, J10. HQ at ESTAMINET ROSSIGNOL – "A" & "B" Co's billeted in KEMMEL.	11A
LOCRE	24.3.15	6.30 pm	"A" & "B" Co's left KEMMEL 6.30 pm and marched to LOCRE and billeted there —	11A
KEMMEL	25.3.15		1 man killed & 8 wounded by rifle fire in trenches —	11A
"	"		2 men wounded by rifle fire in trenches — Captain F.A.FREETH returned to ENGLAND to resume civil employment by order of W.O.	11A
"	26.3.15		1 man killed & 3 wounded by rifle fire in trenches —	11A
"	27.3.15		"A" & "B" Co's relieved "C" & "D" Co's in trenches — "C" & "D" Co's marched to billets in LOCRE — 1 man wounded by rifle fire in trenches & died of wounds in hospital [4 men killed, 2 men wounded by rifle fire in trenches —]	11A

Army Form C. 2118.

WAR DIARY
— or —
INTELLIGENCE SUMMARY.   5th Batt. Cheshire Regt.
(Erase heading not required.)

Instructions regarding War Diaries and Intelligence Summaries are contained in F. S. Regs., Part II. and the Staff Manual respectively. Title pages will be prepared in manuscript.

Place	Date	Hour	Summary of Events and Information	Remarks and references to Appendices
KEMMEL	26.3.15		1 man wounded by rifle fire in trenches	11A
"	29.3.15		4 men wounded by rifle fire in trenches — 1 man died of wounds from rifle fire in trenches —	11A
"	31.3.15		1 man killed in trenches, 1 man wounded in trenches by shattered periscope — "C" & "D" Co.s relieved "A" & "B" Co.s in trenches — "A" & "B" Co.s marched to billets at LOCRE —	11A
"	1.4.15		1 man killed & 6 wounded by rifle fire in trenches — 2/Lieut. A.H. JOLLIFFE joined from 2/5th CHESHIRE REGT. Strength — 25 officers, 869 N.C.O.s + men — 8 casualties from shell fire, 4 from rifle.	11A

"A" Form.   Army Form C. 2121.

MESSAGES AND SIGNALS.   No. of Message..........

Prefix........ Code........ m.	Words	Charge	This message is on a/c of:	Recd. at........ m.
Office of Origin and Service Instructions	66			Date........
	Sent		.... Service.	From........
	At........ m.			
	To........		(Signature of "Franking Officer.")	By........
	By........			

TO { 4th Infantry Bde.

Sender's Number.	Day of Month.	In reply to Number	AAA
* D.112			
Herewith	a	by	to	hand
you	plan	&	fragments	of
still aaa	This	plan	was	drawn
by	one	of	our	subalterns
yesterday	when	J10	was	killed.
&	is	forwarded	in	the
hope	that	it	may	be
useful	to	the	artillery	aaa

From   Clyshwis
Place   9.55 p.m.
Time

The above may be forwarded as now corrected.   (Z) S. H. Smith, asst adjt
                                    Censor.   Signature of Addressor or person authorised to telegraph in his name.
                                               * This line should be erased if not required.

To The Adjutant.
  5th Cheshire Regt.

Notes on Observation of Enemy's Artillery Fire on March 30th 1915.

<u>1</u>. Time enemy's artillery fired 3·50 to 4·30 p.m.

<u>2</u>. i. From observation of slow travel & circular crater I concluded the shells came from a <u>Howitzer</u>.

ii. Sketch below gives direction from which shells arrived.

iii. With the exception of one air burst, all the bursts were graze.

iv. Size of craters = In hard macadam road 2'-6" dia:
        In fairly hard earth 4'-0" dia:

[Sketch map showing:
- "From Kemmel" road with trenches J11, J3, J2, J10, J1, BH4
- "Artillery Observation. Flag at end of J10 Trench ⌗ is the point from which bearing was taken."
- "air·b·" marking
- "Ruined Cottage"
- areas labelled a, b, c, d
- "shows approx: position of craters"
- "Approx: direction of enemy's artillery fire. Magnetic bearing = 95°"
- "To Wytschaete"
- "24"]

Along with this report I send two fragments of shell with explanatory notes attached. marked A + B.

In the Field
31.3.15.

A. Hayton Cowap Lt.
  M.G. Section
    5th Ches: Regt

14th Bde.
5th Division.

5th CHESHIRES.

April

1915

Army Form C. 2118.

WAR DIARY or INTELLIGENCE SUMMARY.

(Erase heading not required.)

5th Battalion, Ps. Chishire Regiment.

Instructions regarding War Diaries and Intelligence Summaries are contained in F.S. Regs., Part II. and the Staff Manual respectively. Title pages will be prepared in manuscript.

Place	Date	Hour	Summary of Events and Information	Remarks and references to Appendices
KEMMEL	3.4.15		2/Lieuts B.H. Grigg, H.R. Pugh, E.B Morgan joined from 2/5th Battalion at KEMMEL 2, + half Battalion in billets at LOCRE.	S.H.S.
"	4.4.15		1 man killed and 2 wounded in trenches at KEMMEL. Half Battalion in trenches	S.H.S.
"	5.4.15		Battalion moved from LOCRE 9.30 a.m. and marched to billets between DICKEBUSCH and OUDERDOM. Trenches H4, J1, J2, J3 + J10 handed over to 2/Royal Scots.	S.H.S.
DICKEBUSCH	7.4.15		Battalion marched to YPRES and took over trenches 27 + 27R from 1st Bn Cheshire Regt. Half Battalion Barracks YPRES. Brigade Headquarters at WOODCOTE HOUSE, Battalion Headquarters at SPOILBANK. Half Battalion billets way 4 days	S.H.S.
YPRES	8.4.15		1 man killed in trenches near YPRES.	S.H.S.
"	9.4.15		1 " and 3 wounded in trenches near YPRES.	S.H.S.
"	10.4.15		3 men killed and 2 " " " "	S.H.S.
"	11.4.15		" " " " "	S.H.S.
"	14.4.15		" " " " "	S.H.S.
"	15.4.15		Lieut. S.M. Dixon and 7 men wounded in trenches near YPRES. Half Battalion moved to Black Works + Trenches at Abri near YPRES	S.H.S.
"	16.4.15		Major H Watts admitted to hospital sick, and 3 men wounded in trenches near YPRES.	S.H.S.
"	17.4.15		1 man killed and two men wounded in trenches near YPRES. Attack on Hill 60 at 7 P.M. cooperated in by opening rifle and machine gun fire.	S.H.S.
"	18.4.15		Bombardment of YPRES, which continued without intermission till 30th.	S.H.S.
"	19.4.15		14 Inf Bde to assist 13th Bde on Hill 60. Having 1/2 5th Cheshires as safe reserve for 14 Inf Bde. "East Surreys" and 1/Devons moved from 2/Lieut A.G. Hall Joined from 2/5th Battalion	S.H.S.
"	20.4.15		1 man killed and 2 wounded in trenches, + 1 man wounded in Brigade near YPRES	S.H.S.
"	21.4.15		2 men wounded in Brigade near YPRES	S.H.S.
"	22.4.15		1 man killed in trenches near YPRES. Half Battalion moved to new bivouac at KRUISSTRAAT, near YPRES	S.H.S.
KRUISSTRAAT	23.4.15		1 " wounded " " " " " and on " " wounded in Bivouac near YPRES	S.H.S.
"	24.4.15		Captain L Bruyngh arrived from 3/Cheshire Regt and assumed duties of adjutant. 1 man killed + 9 men wounded (3 slightly)	S.H.S.
"	25.4.15		3 men wounded in trenches near YPRES	S.H.S.
"	26.4.15		2 " " " " " 3 men wounded in YPRES, 3 men wounded at KRUISTRAAT.	S.H.S.
"	27.4.15		2/Lieut A.H. Jolliffe wounded, one man killed at KRUISTRAAT. Capt. J.H Davies assumed command of "A" Company and 10 men wounded in trenches near YPRES	S.H.S.

1577 Wt. W10791/1773 500,000 1/15 D.D. & L. A.D.S.S./Forms/C. 2118.

Army Form C. 2118.

WAR DIARY or INTELLIGENCE SUMMARY.

(Erase heading not required.)

5th Battalion, Th, Chishire Regiment

Place	Date	Hour	Summary of Events and Information	Remarks and references to Appendices
KRUISSTRAAT near YPRES.	28.4.'15		2 men killed, 13 men wounded & 7 men shaken by shell fire in trenches near YPRES. 4 men wounded in transport lines at KRUISSTRAAT. Trench 27.S, a new support trench, garrisoned for first time, & trench 28R garrisoned for one night by H.E. Coys.	S.H.S.
	29.4.15		2 men killed, 7 men wounded & 3 slightly wounded in trenches near YPRES. 1 man died of wounds received 28.4.15.	S.H.S.
	30.4.15→		One man company moved up to mine dug-outs at SPOILBANK, leaving one company only at KRUISSTRAAT. 2/Lieuts V M Drummond Fraser & H W Glendenning joined from 2/5th Battalion. [1 man wounded in trenches near YPRES. STRENGTH — 28 Officers, 752 other ranks.	S.H.S.

14th Bde.
5th Division.

5th CHESHIRES.

May.

1915

WAR DIARY or INTELLIGENCE SUMMARY.

Army Form C. 2118.

(Erase heading not required.)

Instructions regarding War Diaries and Intelligence Summaries are contained in F.S. Regs., Part II. and the Staff Manual respectively. Title pages will be prepared in manuscript.

Place	Date	Hour	Summary of Events and Information	Remarks and references to Appendices
YPRES	1.5.15		1 man wounded on working party near YPRES	QB
	2.5.15		Interpreter De Maeyer joined. Belgian. 1 man killed in trenches near YPRES	QB
	3.5.15		Major T.L.Fennell admitted to hospital sick 1 man wounded in trenches near YPRES	QB
	4.5.15		2nd Lt [P.B. Bax] joined from 2/1st Bn Ches Regt 1 man wounded in trenches near YPRES	QB
	5.5.15		2 men wounded in trenches near YPRES	QB
	6.5.15		1 man killed	QB
	7.5.15		1 man wounded	QB
	8.5.15		2 men wounded	QB
	9.5.15		Draft of 30 men arrived from 2/5 Ches Regt. No 2 F.F.9 S.S., 2 S.R. 1 man wounded. 1 man taken for general hospital No 2764 Sergt. Major Kimmett J wounded at dressing station during truce near YPRES 2nd Lt B.S. Walbox killed in trenches near YPRES 1 man killed in trenches near YPRES 2 men wounded	QB
	10.5.15		Capt W Rogers. R.A.M.C. Medical Officer wounded Lt C.N.Halmoton wounded in trenches near YPRES 1 man wounded 2nd Lt [B.Wayman] joined from 2/5 th Bn Ches Regt Lt R.E.Lee R.A.M.C. attached as Medical Officer from 14th Field Ambulance	QB

Army Form C. 2118.

WAR DIARY
or
INTELLIGENCE SUMMARY.
(Erase heading not required.)

Instructions regarding War Diaries and Intelligence Summaries are contained in F. S. Regs., Part II. and the Staff Manual respectively. Title pages will be prepared in manuscript.

Place	Date	Hour	Summary of Events and Information	Remarks and references to Appendices
YPRES	11.5.15		2nd Lt G Gledhill wounded in trenches near YPRES.	QR
"	12.5.15		3 men " " " "	QR
"	13.5.15		Battalion relieved from duty in trenches and went to bivouac in H22b.	QR
"	14.5.15		1 man killed in storm during relief in trenches near YPRES	QR
"	19.5.15		1 man wounded on working party near YPRES.	QR
"			Captain T Dutton admitted to hospital sick.	
"	20.5.15		80 men admitted to convalescent depot at BOESCHEPE with abnormal temperatures	QR
"	21.5.15		7 men sent to L. nes of Communication	QR
"	22.5.15		1 man wounded on working party near YPRES	QR
"	23.5.15		1 man " " " "	QR
"			Battalion marched to BOESCHEPE. Left bivouac in H22b at 8.30 p.m arrived BOESCHEPE at 1 a.m. 24.5.15	QR
BOESCHEPE	24.5.15		Battalion billeted in barns at BOESCHEPE	QR
"	26.5.15		2 men wounded by accidental discharge of a rifle in billet at BOESCHEPE	QR
"	28.5.15		Capt. A.E. Hodgkin admitted to hospital sick	QR
"			Capt. J.H. Coldicott admitted to hospital sick	
"			1 man wounded by accidental discharge of a rifle in stores at BOESCHEPE	
"			1 man transferred to R.E.	
"	31.5.15		Battalion marched from BOESCHEPE to bivouac in H28a near DICKEBUSCH	QR
"			Left BOESCHEPE at 2 p.m arrived bivouac H28a at 9 p.m	

14th Bde.
5th Division.

5th CHESHIRES

June

1915

Army Form C. 2118.

WAR DIARY
of
INTELLIGENCE SUMMARY.
(Erase heading not required.)

Instructions regarding War Diaries and Intelligence Summaries are contained in F.S. Regs., Part II. and the Staff Manual respectively. Title pages will be prepared in manuscript.

Place	Date	Hour	Summary of Events and Information	Remarks and references to Appendices
YPRES	1.6.15		Battalion took over trenches 27, 27R, 27S, 28, 28R 28S from 1st Devon Regt	O.R.
"	2.6.15		1 man killed and 1 man wounded in trenches. Battalion left by Grade 9M at 4 p.m. for	O.R.
"	3.6.15		2/Lt V. O. Drummond French died of wounds received in action. 1 man wounded in trenches.	O.R.
"	5.6.15		1 man died of wounds received in action in trenches near YPRES	O.R.
"	6.6.15		1 man killed in trenches near YPRES	O.R.
"	7.6.15		1 man killed 1 man died of wounds received in action 4 men wounded in trenches	O.R.
"	8.6.15		Capt W.O.V. Robinson admitted to hospital sick	O.R.
"			1 man killed 3 men wounded in trenches near YPRES	O.R.
"	9.6.15		1 man wounded in trenches near YPRES	O.R.
"	10.6.15		2 men wounded in trenches	O.R.
"	11.6.15		1 killed 1 dead of wounds and 2 wounded in action. 2 10 men wounded in trenches near YPRES.	O.R.
"	12.6.15		7 men wounded in trenches near YPRES	O.R.
"	13.6.15		3 men wounded in trenches near YPRES	O.R.
"	14.6.15		4 men wounded in trenches near YPRES	O.R.
"	15.6.15		Belgian Interpreter A. Brown and attached to 42nd coy R.E.	O.R.
"	16.6.15		1 man wounded in trenches near YPRES	O.R.
"	17.6.15		1 man killed by accidental discharge of a rifle 2 men died of wounds and 1	
"			man wounded in trenches near YPRES	O.R.
"			Battalion relieved in trenches by 1st Devon Regt & marched to bivouac in H.28.a.	
"	18.6.15		1 man killed and 1 man wounded whilst on fatigue near H.30.9.0	O.R.
"	20.6.15		1 man wounded on enemy's artillery	3
"	21.6.15		1 man wounded on enemy's artillery	3
			2nd Lt B. Wayman rejoined Battalion having recovered from his wound whilst on covering party.	O.R.

1577 Wt.W10791/7773 500,000 1/15 D. D. & L.   A.D.S.S./Forms/C. 2118.

Army Form C. 2118.

WAR DIARY
INTELLIGENCE SUMMARY.
(Erase heading not required.)

Instructions regarding War Diaries and Intelligence Summaries are contained in F. S. Regs., Part II. and the Staff Manual respectively. Title pages will be prepared in manuscript.

Place	Date	Hour	Summary of Events and Information	Remarks and references to Appendices
YPRES.	24.6.15		2nd Lt R. Wiseman admitted to hospital sick	Q.R.
"	26.6.15		2nd Lt H.R. Clough admitted to hospital sick	Q.R.
"	27.6.15		2nd Lt Heald S. L. admitted to hospital sick. 1 man wounded whilst on working party near HILL 60. Major Leonard J. Stranack D.S.O. assumed the battalion on relinquishing command of the brigade	Q.R.
"	28.6.15		1 man wounded on working party near HILL 60.	

1577 Wt.W10791/1773 500,000 1/15 D. D. & L. A.D.S.S./Forms/C. 2118.

14th Bde.
5th Division.

5th. CHESHIRES

July

1915

Army Form C. 2118.

WAR DIARY
or ~~INTELLIGENCE SUMMARY~~ 43.
(Erase heading not required.)

Instructions regarding War Diaries and Intelligence Summaries are contained in F.S. Regs., Part II. and the Staff Manual respectively. Title pages will be prepared in manuscript.

Place	Date	Hour	Summary of Events and Information	Remarks and references to Appendices
YPRES	1.7.1915		Battalion took over Trenches 27, 27 S. and 27 R. and 28, 28 S. and 28 R. from 1st Devon Regt. One man wounded by stray bullet near YPRES.	43.
YPRES	2.7.1915		2/Lieut. E.B. MORGAN wounded in face by Mill. One man slightly wounded near YPRES.	43.
YPRES	3.7.1915		2/Lieut. M.F. DAVIES killed in action, 1 man wounded and 1 man accidentally wounded near YPRES.	43.
YPRES	4.7.1915		1 man wounded and 1 man accidentally wounded near YPRES.	43.
YPRES	5.7.1915		1 man accidentally wounded near YPRES.	43.
YPRES	6.7.1915		1 man died of wounds.	43.
YPRES	8.7.1915		Battalion was relieved in Trenches by 1st Devon Regt. and proceeded to Bivouacs in H.28.A. One man wounded by stray bullet.	43.
YPRES	9.7.1915		1 man wounded whilst on working party near YPRES.	43.
YPRES	10.7.1915		1 man wounded whilst on working party near YPRES.	43.
YPRES	11.7.1915		1 man killed and 2 men wounded whilst on working party near YPRES.	43.
YPRES	12.7.1915		No. 2288 L/Sgt. F. BISHOP gazetted as 2nd Lieutenant from 26th June 1915.	43.
YPRES	13.7.1915		2 men wounded whilst on working party near YPRES.	43.
YPRES	17.7.1915		Battalion took over Trenches 27, 27 S. and 27 R. and 28, 28 S. and 28 R. from 1st Devon Regt.	43.
YPRES	19.7.1915		2/Lieut. J.G. McGOWAN admitted to Hospital with sprained ankle. Capt. A.E. HODGKIN wounded in back. Two men killed in action. Two men died of wounds received in action. Three men were wounded. Lieut. R.E. LEE R.A.M.C. was withdrawn from the Battalion. Capt. J.M.A. COSTELLO R.A.M.C. (T.) joined Battalion from 7th Welsh Regt.	43.
YPRES	21.7.1915		Following joined the Battalion from 3/5 Bn. Cheshire Regt. : 2/Lieuts W.E. DAVIES, E.S. HERON, O.K.S. LAUGHARNE, H.E. RATCLIFFE.	43.
YPRES	24.7.1915		One man wounded. Battalion relieved in Trenches by 2nd Suffolk Regt. and proceeded to Woodhen Huts in RENINGHELST.	43.
RENINGHELST	25.7.1915		4th Battalion left RENINGHELST at 6.0 p.m. and marched to EECKE.	43.
EECKE	26.7.1915		Battalion arrived at EECKE at 2.0 a.m. Following joined the Battalion from 3/5 Bn. Cheshire Regt. : 2/Lieut. T.J.S. DAVIES, A.J. ALLMAND, F.T. VERNON, J.D. SALMON.	43.
EECKE	27.7.1915		14th Infantry Brigade inspected and addressed by Lieut. General Sir HERBERT C.O. PLUMER K.C.B. Commanding 2nd Army.	43.
EECKE	28.7.1915		2/Interpreter R.E. TROCMÉ reported for duty.	43.

14th Bde.
5th Division.

5th CHESHIRES

August

1915

WAR DIARY or INTELLIGENCE SUMMARY

Army Form C. 2118.

(Erase heading not required.)

Instructions regarding War Diaries and Intelligence Summaries are contained in F.S. Regs., Part II. and the Staff Manual respectively. Title pages will be prepared in manuscript.

Place	Date	Hour	Summary of Events and Information	Remarks and references to Appendices
DAOURS	4-8-1915		14th Infantry Brigade was inspected by General Sir C.C. MONRO K.C.B. Comdg. 3rd Army. The Battalion left DAOURS (VECQUEMONT) at 8.0 p.m. and arrived at TREUX via CORBIE.	43
TREUX	5-8-1915		Battalion arrived at TREUX and VILLE SUR ANCRE at 1.0 a.m. Battalion Headquarters and two Companies billetted at TREUX and remainder billetted at VILLE SUR ANCRE.	43
TREUX	6-8-1915		Draft consisting of :- Capt. G. HATT-COOK, 2/Lieut. J.H. ROWLANDS and three other ranks joined. 2/Lieut. G. McGOWAN joined from Hospital.	43
TREUX	7-8-1915		No. 1547 R/Sergeant R.E. TROOME left Battalion. No. 1882 (Cpl) R/Sergeant F.C. BONNEFOI joined Battalion. One man accidentally wounded in left arm by cartridge exploding in fire.	43
TREUX	8-8-1915		Captain W. VERNON and Captain E.S. BOURNE joined Battalion. Battalion left TREUX at 9.45 p.m. and marched to SUZANNE via MORLANCOURT and BRAY SUR SOMME.	43
SUZANNE	9-8-1915		Battalion arrived at SUZANNE at 1.50 a.m.	43
SUZANNE	10-8-1915		2/Lieut. A.H. COWAP and 4 machine guns attached to 8/Somerseys from this date.	43
SUZANNE	10-8-1915		Relief of 2/4 Oxf & Bucks Regiment by the Battalion commenced at 5.0 a.m. From E. Entrenchment extended from the River SOMME to FARGNY MILL (exclusive). Trenches 1 to 9. Later A. Company took over right position at ROYAL DRAGONS wood, B. Company "BOIS DE VAUX", C. Company VAUX village, D. Company in Reserve at SUZANNE. Battalion Headquarters at SUZANNE. Relief of 2/4th French Regiment completed at 4.25 a.m. 2/Lieut. F. STOTT joined Battalion. Lieut. A.H. COWAP admitted to Hospital.	43
SUZANNE	13-8-1915		One man wounded.	43
SUZANNE	18-8-1915		One man died of wounds.	43
SUZANNE	20-8-1915		One Officer and four Indian soldiers attached to the Company in VAUX village.	43
SUZANNE	21-8-1915		Two more Indian soldiers attached to the Company in VAUX village. One man wounded.	43
SUZANNE	22-8-1915		One man died of wounds.	43
SUZANNE	23-8-1915		Draft of 2 Sergeants, 2 Corporals, above Corporals and 52 men arrived from 2/5 R. Cheshire Regt.	43
SUZANNE	24-8-1915		2/Lieut. T.L.C. HEALD admitted to Hospital. One man slightly wounded.	43

Army Form C. 2118.

WAR DIARY
INTELLIGENCE SUMMARY.

(Erase heading not required.)

Instructions regarding War Diaries and Intelligence Summaries are contained in F. S. Regs., Part II. and the Staff Manual respectively. Title pages will be prepared in manuscript.

Place	Date	Hour	Summary of Events and Information	Remarks and references to Appendices
SUZANNE	25.8.1915		Draft of 1 Sergeant, 3 Corporals, 4 Lance Corporals and 72 men arrived from 2/5th Cheshire Regt. One man killed and one man wounded etc. now attached to Brigade Travelling Kitchen ourselves.	43.
SUZANNE	26.8.1915		One Machine Gunner wounded in East Airways Trenches.	43.
SUZANNE	27.8.1915		Two men wounded by accidental discharge of another mans rifle. NSSSN	43.
SUZANNE	28.8.1915		2/Lieut. T.L.C. HEALD rejoined from Hospital.	43.
SUZANNE	29.8.1915		2/Lieut. A.J. ALLMAND accompanied by his servant left the Battalion to join Headquarters 3rd Army as Assistant Chemical Advisor.	46.
SUZANNE-VAUX	30.8.1915		At about 7:30 P.M. a hostile patrol consisting of four men approached one of our listening Posts which was situated in the marsh East of VAUX village. The listening post opened fire and wounded one of the enemy. The remainder of the enemy withdrew to a wood and opened fire in turn. Killing 2/Lieut. F.T. VERNON and one man who had moved up with reinforcements. The ground in front of the listening post was then searched and the wounded German secured. The prisoner was sent to 14th Brigade Headquarters. The works on his tunic, this was "Bau. F.R. 12 Coy 479" Battalion Headquarters moved from SUZANNE to VAUX village, the move being completed at 11:10 P.M.	48. 43.
VAUX	31.8.1915		Strength of Battalion 32 Officers and 856 other ranks.	43.

1577 Wt.W10791/1773 500,000 1/15 D. D. & L. A.D.S.S./Forms/C. 2118.

14th Bde.
5th Division.

5th CHESHIRES

September

1915

1/5• Bn. Cheshire Regt.

Army Form C. 2118.

WAR DIARY
or INTELLIGENCE SUMMARY.

(Erase heading not required.)

Instructions regarding War Diaries and Intelligence Summaries are contained in F. S. Regs., Part II. and the Staff Manual respectively. Title pages will be prepared in manuscript.

Place	Date	Hour	Summary of Events and Information	Remarks and references to Appendices
SUZANNE	2.9.1915		Battalion was relieved in trenches by 6th Battn. Liverpool Regt. Relief completed 10.45 p.m. Battalion Bivouacked & billeted in SUZANNE.	43.
SUZANNE	3.9.1915		Strength of Battalion 33 Officers 891 other ranks.	43.
Trenches	9.9.1915		Battalion relieved 6th Bn. The Liverpool Regiment in outpost A1 extending from river SOMME near ECLUSIER to MOULIN DE FARGNY inclusive. Relief completed 8.30 p.m. Battalion Headquarters at VAUX village.	43.
do.	10.9.1915		Strength of Battalion 30 Officers 889 other ranks.	43.
do.	14.9.1915		Captain N. VERNON appointed Claims Officer 5th Division.	43.
do.	17.9.1915		Strength of Battalion 32 Officers 882 other ranks.	43.
do.	19.9.1915		Capt. I. A. S. JONES and 6 Indian soldiers of the 36th Sikhs House arrived to be attached to the Battalion. French Battalion on our right at FRISE was relieved by the 3rd Battn. King's Own Rifle Corps of 2nd Army Korps. Captain F.C. BONNEFOI (Ch. Lepanley) of the French 54th Regt of Infantry of 81st Regt of Infantry. Brigade at 2.30 a.m. attached to the Battalion.	43.
do.	22.9.1915		Battalion was relieved in trenches by 6th Bn. the Liverpool Regiment. Relief completed 8.45 p.m. Battalion Bivouacked & billeted in SUZANNE.	43.
do.	23.9.1915		Battalion relieved 1st Devon Regt. in outposts A4. Relief completed 9.30 p.m. Lieutenant Colonel LONG 2/Lieut. S. WYMAN admitted to Hospital. 34 and 35 Battalion Headquarters at MARICOURT.	43.
do.	24.9.1915		Strength of Battalion 31 Officers 853 other ranks.	43.
do.	25.9.1915		In the early morning a German working party was seen in front of Outpost Post No. 1. It was dispersed by rifle fire from Post Bombing guard was sent from Trench 35 out into the open and opened fire on gap in German trench and obtained two rounds by our Artillery. The Machine gun was immediately silenced by the Germans. Its position was changed but it was again shelled. The gun and Gun Detachment, No. 1263 Sgt. T. LOCKLEY was in charge of the gun and his name was forwarded to 14 S. Brigade Headquarters for good work.	43.

Army Form C. 2118.

1/5" Bn, Cheshire Regt.

WAR DIARY
—OF 43—
INTELLIGENCE SUMMARY. 43.

(Erase heading not required.)

Instructions regarding War Diaries and Intelligence Summaries are contained in F. S. Regs., Part II. and the Staff Manual respectively. Title pages will be prepared in manuscript.

Place	Date	Hour	Summary of Events and Information	Remarks and references to Appendices
Trenches	25.9.1915 Cont.		The following Operations were carried out: At 4:45 p.m. the whole of the Artillery of the Division fired our round gunfire. At the same time the Battalion showed its bayonets over the Trenches and cheered. As many men as possible were put into the front Trenches in order to induce the enemy to believe that the line was strongly held. At 4:30 p.m. the Artillery of the Division fired two minutes gun fire. The Germans did not retaliate. One man slightly wounded.	43.
Trenches	26.9.1915		2/Lieut. T.B.WYMAN discharged from Hospital. One man died of wounds. At 9.25 a.m. the enemy was very annoying with Rifle Grenades directed at Advanced Post No.2, Advanced Post No.3 and Trench 30. Two H.E. shells from our Artillery stopped the annoyance.	43.
Trenches	27.9.1915		During the night 26/27. The enemy were very persistent in attempting to put wire in position. Several working parties were fired on but they continued the attempt until they were finally stopped by two H.E. shells.	43.
Trenches	28.9.1915		Capt. E.S.BOURNE and 2/Lieut. B.WYMAN admitted to Hospital. At 11:30 p.m. an enemy working party was dispersed by Rifle fire.	43.
Trenches	29.9.1915		At 12 noon enemy fired 10 field gun shells at Trenches 29 and 30. No damage was done.	43.
Trenches	30.9.1915		At 6.30 p.m. a loud explosion was heard on the left of the Battalion in the direction of Trench 36. One man wounded. Strength: 31 Officers 860 other ranks. The Officers and N.C.Os. of letter A Company 11 Worcesters attached to the Battalion for Instruction in Trench duties.	43.

14th Bde.
5th Div.

5th CHESHIRES

October

1915

Army Form C. 2118.

WAR DIARY
INTELLIGENCE SUMMARY

1/5th Bn. Cheshire Regiment.

(Erase heading not required.)

Instructions regarding War Diaries and Intelligence Summaries are contained in F. S. Regs., Part II. and the Staff Manual respectively. Title pages will be prepared in manuscript.

Place	Date	Hour	Summary of Events and Information	Remarks and references to Appendices
MARICOURT	1.10.1915		2/Lieut. H.R.LEIGH admitted to Hospital. Strength: 31 Officers 860 Other ranks. Letter A. Company 1/1st Worcesters attached to the Battalion for Instruction in Trench Warfare. Lieut. Col. BARKER 2nd in Command 2/1st Worcesters attached to Bn. Hdqrs.	
do.	2.10.1915		A copy of the Continental Edition of the Daily Mail dated 30th October 1915 was placed on a stick close to a german listening post in front of A.P.3 at 11.30 p.m. The Daily Mail mentioned above was collected by the Germans at 5.30 p.m. One man wounded.	43. 43.
do.	3.10.1915		Letter A. Company 1/1st Worcesters took over Trenches 30, 31 and 32 from B. Coy. 1/5 Ches.R. The latter Company remained in support. Four men wounded.	43.
do.	4.10.1915		2/Lieut. B. WYMAN discharged from Hospital.	43.
do.	6.10.1915		One man wounded. 2/Lieut. H.R. LEIGH discharged from Hospital. Letter A. Company 1/1st Worcesters ceased to be attached to the Battalion and was replaced by C. Company from the same Battalion.	43.
do.	7.10.1915		C. Company 1/1st Worcesters took over Trenches 30, 31 and 32 from B. Coy. 1/5 Ches.R. The latter Company remained in support. 2 Lt. in Command of 1/1st Worcesters also ceased to be attached to the Battalion and withdrew to SUZANNE at 6.30 p.m. Lt.Col. BARKER in Command of F.CESMAT joined Battalion from French Field Artillery. One man killed.	43.
do.	8.10.1915		Strength 31 Officers 846 Other Ranks.	43.
do.	10.10.1915		2/Lieut. J.D. SALMON wounded in both hands and admitted to Hospital. Capt. E.S. BOURNE discharged from Hospital. Enemy fired twenty eight shells fifty yards in rear of 29.7th Trench. Our Artillery retaliated.	43.
do.	11.10.1915		At 7.30 p.m. a German Searchlight was observed playing on the sky; magnetic bearing of Searchlight from junction of CENTRE Avenue and 32 Support Trench was 30 degrees; distance considerable.	43.
do.	12.10.1915		One man wounded.	43.
do.	13.10.1915		One man wounded.	43.
do.	14.10.1915		At 4.35 p.m. enemy fired two large Trench Mortar Bombs at AP.1. One man wounded. Some John of Aircraft passed over our Trenches at 2.40 a.m. heading due North.	43.
do.	15.10.1915		Strength: 30 Officers 840 Other Ranks. Two men wounded. At 7.10 p.m. enemy fired ten trench shells at 31 Trench. No damage.	43.

WAR DIARY

1/5 Bn. Cheshire Regt.

INTELLIGENCE SUMMARY

(Erase heading not required.)

Army Form C. 2118.

Instructions regarding War Diaries and Intelligence Summaries are contained in F.S. Regs., Part II and the Staff Manual respectively. Title pages will be prepared in manuscript.

Place	Date	Hour	Summary of Events and Information	Remarks and references to Appendices
MARICOURT	18.10.1915		One man wounded. At 4.30 p.m. enemy shelled 29 Fire Trench with small H.E. Our Artillery replied vigorously however.	23.
do.	19.10.1915		One man killed. Heavy and continuous hostile rifle fire was kept on us west and north of MONTAUBAN from 6.30 a.m. until 6.30 a.m. Hostile sniping caused delay but time was more kindly sparing than usual.	23.
do.	20.10.1915		One man died of wounds and two men were wounded. 2nd Lieut. G. McGOWAN 1st Battn. on attachment to R.F.C. Wireless Station, Maricourt Park. At 5.00 p.m. enemy fired eight light shells at 28 Fire Trench. Our Artillery replied effectively.	23.
do.	21.10.1915		One man wounded.	23.
do.	22.10.1915		Strength: 29 Officers. 635 Other Ranks.	23.
do.	23.10.1915		At 4.30 p.m. enemy fired six Trench Mortar Bombs at Q.P.1 and 28 Fire Trench. Enemy also fired four H.E. shells near Headquarters of D Company. Our Artillery replied effectively. Enemy appear to have given up use of rifle fire. Two men killed and seven wounded as result of 8 shells. One of our own Grenades in own 8" Grenadier Shells (2nd Lt. F. HARRISON killed).	23.
do.	24.10.1915		3rd Platoon of "C" Coy took over Trenches. Enemy very friendly and talkative and frequently expressed intention of coming over to our trenches.	23.
do.	25.10.1915		Enemy seemed to be very nervous during the night 25/26th. They sent up a great many VERY lights. At 7.50 a.m. a movement Tactical of "B" and "C" Coy's. D.C.L.I. Relief was completed at 6.30 a.m. Lieut. A. The Battalion was relieved in trenches by A4 by the D.C.L.I. Relief was completed at 6.30 a.m. and the Battalion took over the MARICOURT	23.
do.	26.10.1915		Company proceeded to SUZANNE and the remainder of the Battalion took over the MARICOURT from the MANCHESTERS, this relief being completed at 9.30 p.m.	23.
do.	29.10.1915		Strength: 29 Officers. 822 Other Ranks.	23.

14th Bde.
5th Div.

Became Pioneers 5th Division 29th November '15.

5th
~~8th~~ CHESHIRES

November

1915

WAR DIARY
INTELLIGENCE SUMMARY.

Army Form C. 2118.

Instructions regarding War Diaries and Intelligence Summaries are contained in F. S. Regs., Part II. and the Staff Manual respectively. Title pages will be prepared in manuscript.

(Erase heading not required.)

Place	Date	Hour	Summary of Events and Information	Remarks and references to Appendices
MARICOURT	1.11.1915		Capt. E.S. BOURNE admitted to Hospital.	43.
"	5.11.1915		Strength of Battalion 26 Officers and 808 other ranks.	43.
"	9.11.1915		Lieut. J. LANG attached to Battalion.	43.
"	13.11.1915		Capt. E.S. BOURNE discharged from Hospital. Strength 28 Officers and 805 other ranks. Battalion was relieved in MARICOURT defences by 1/Bedf. Regt. Relief complete 9.0 p.m. Battalion then went into Billets in SUZANNE where Mrs. A. Company already was.	43.
SUZANNE	15.11.1915		Letter A. Company relieved one Company of 5/Liverpools in ROYAL DRAGONS wood in Sub-sector A1.	43.
"	16.11.1915		B. Company relieved one Company of 5/Liverpools in VAUX wood in Sub-sector A1. One 3 inch gun relieved one gun of 5/Liverpools in Sub-sector A1 and three machine guns relieved three guns of 5/Liverpools in Sub-sector A2. Remainder of Battalion remained in SUZANNE.	43.
"	17.11.1915		Battalion Headquarters and C.+D. Companies relieved Headquarters and two companies of 5/Liverpools in VAUX wood. Relief complete 6.29 p.m.	43.
"	18.11.1915		The Battalion Formation was broken up and relieved two Companies.	43.
	20.11.1915		Strength 28 Officers and 805 other ranks.	43.
VAUX	21.11.1915		Lieut. T.L.C. HEALD attached as instructor to the 3rd Divisional Grenade School at CHIGNOLLY. Lieut. J. LANG R.A.M.C. attached to 13 F. Field Ambulance. Lieut. SPIKEMAN joined Battalion and left D Company.	43. 43.
"	23.11.1915		Capt. N.B. ELLINGTON proceeded to England for duty with machine gun Cops at GRANTHAM. 2nd Lt. S.P. GAMON assumed command of D Company vice Capt. E. ELLINGTON.	43.
"	24.11.1915		Polygnion L. CESMAT left Battalion.	43.
"	27.11.1915		Strength 24 Officers and 800 other ranks.	43.
"	29.11.1915		The Battalion less the scouts, signals and D. Company, left instructor A1 on relief by 1/Liverpools Royal Regt. The four machine guns were dismounted throughout sector A. The Battalion in relation to billets in BRAY. Relief complete at 9.0 a.m. Battalion then became s/Divisional Reserve Battalion.	43.
BRAY	30.11.1915		D. Company moved from VAUX to SUZANNE.	43.

S/Abrahams
Field Report
Nov 1915

Army Form C. 2118.

WAR DIARY
or
INTELLIGENCE SUMMARY.

(Erase heading not required.)

Place	Date	Hour	Summary of Events and Information	Remarks and references to Appendices
VAUX	17.11.15 18.11.15		Nil. Owing to thick Fog.	
		4.P.M.		

Place	Date	Hour	Summary of Events and Information	Remarks and references to Appendices
VAUX	17/11/15 18.11.15		Patrol under 2/Lt Wigram left Dug Post at 9.30 am and proceeded towards CURLU. A short distance E. of FARGNY Crossway they found an empty ford van and a German jack knife cut from down the leg as if it had been removed from a wounded man as the hole thereon was sewn. They were off the side of the path and appear to have been there some time. The Patrol heard trains b/w E. & CURLU, and a good deal of hammering in the village. Patrol returned 12.30 P.M. No shew observations possible owing to mist.	ALBERT 1-40,000

19/11/15
A.P.M.

Army Form C. 2118.

WAR DIARY
or
INTELLIGENCE SUMMARY.
(Erase heading not required.)

Instructions regarding War Diaries and Intelligence Summaries are contained in F. S. Regs., Part II. and the Staff Manual respectively. Title pages will be prepared in manuscript.

Place	Date	Hour	Summary of Events and Information	Remarks and references to Appendices
VAUX	19.4.15 20.4.15	12.10 p.m. 12.30 p.m.	Small working party seen near Railway Embankment H.3.D and H.9.B. Ivans seen travelling N to S in same area. New trench has been dug from opp. 49 CHAPEAU (A.29 B.48) towards listening post and steps added half way down the trench to MOULIN DE FARGNY. Patches of white chalk seen at intervals on line running S.15 N on West of CLERY SUR SOMME.	ALBERT 1-40,000

20/4/15
4 P.M.

[signature]
S. Cheshire Rgt.

WAR DIARY
or
INTELLIGENCE SUMMARY

Army Form C. 2118.

Hour, Date, Place	Summary of Events and Information	Remarks and references to Appendices
VAUX. 20-11-15. 21-11-15.	New work appears to have been done close to German front line trenches. Traverses have been dug close to German front line with our trenches. Some with posts. Connecting saps leading to trench at foot of CHAPEAU. Observation difficult owing to mist and twilight. Patrol on march during night, reported no signs of enemy.	

21/11/15
4 P.m.

[signature]
O.C. Che Rifts

Army Form C. 2118.

WAR DIARY
or
INTELLIGENCE SUMMARY
(Erase heading not required.)

Instructions regarding War Diaries and Intelligence Summaries are contained in F. S. Regs, Part II. and the Staff Manual respectively. Title pages will be prepared in manuscript.

Hour, Date, Place	Summary of Events and Information	Remarks and references to Appendices
VAUX. 21-11-15 22-11-15	10 P.M. Patrol proceeded on marsh towards FARGNY CAUSEWAY. No sign of enemy. 9. A.M. Patrol proceeded on marsh towards FARGNY CAUSEWAY and beyond. No sign of enemy. Noise of machinery heard in CURLU. No other observation possible owing to Fog.	

(Sgd.) Prujean
5. Cheshire
22/11/15
4 P.M.

Army Form C. 2118.

WAR DIARY
or
INTELLIGENCE SUMMARY

(Erase heading not required.)

Instructions regarding War Diaries and Intelligence Summaries are contained in F. S. Regs., Part II. and the Staff Manual respectively. Title pages will be prepared in manuscript.

Hour, Date, Place	Summary of Events and Information	Remarks and references to Appendices
VAUX. 22.11.15	6.45 p.m. Patrol worked via marsh towards FRISE nothing seen or heard except unusual lowing of cattle towards CURLU.	
23.11.15.	10.30 a.m. Patrol under 2/Lt Bishop proceeded via marsh to FRISE. Officer reported to French Officer who was informed him that the Sentries had noticed unusual lowing of cattle last night, and that strong enemy patrols had been reported on French right last night. on left. French consider German relief takes place on Mondays. Nothing seen or heard of enemy.	

23/11/15
H.T.W.

Army Form C. 2118.

WAR DIARY
or
INTELLIGENCE SUMMARY
(Erase heading not required.)

Hour, Date, Place	Summary of Events and Information	Remarks and references to Appendices
VAUX 23.11.15.	Patrols went out at 8.15 p.m. towards FRISE and CURLU, no signs of Enemy seen. The derelict cart on Enemy Island was visited and found to contain nothing of importance. Noise as if wounded heard, whistle CURLU from 9.55 p.m. – 10.15 p.m.	
24.11.15.	9.15 a.m. Shells from German aeroplanes, burst near — H.3. 9.33 a.m. do do do do do — 1.21.B. 2.57 p.m. Shells from German machine gun S.E. Friards CLERY SUR SOMME Seen [H.12.6] Wire had been put up in front of present trench on West side MONTAUBAN. A working party has been seen in Railway Embankment in H.2.B. at 10.40 a.m. Train arrived at 7 a.m. presently towards CURLU at 7 a.m. in H.1. c/P.	

24/11/15.
4 p.m.

1247 W 3299 200,000 (E) 8/14 J.B.C. & A. Forms/C. 2118/11.

Army Form C. 2118.

WAR DIARY
or
INTELLIGENCE SUMMARY
(Erase heading not required.)

Hour, Date, Place	Summary of Events and Information	Remarks and references to Appendices
VAUX. 24.11.15.	At 5 P.M. Officers Patrol proceeded [route] to front [MOULIN DE FARGNY?] reaching [Vaux?] at 6.15 p.m. they headed [out?] to DEVON's winning hands.	ALBERT 1/40,000
	9 P.M. Patrol left Vaux. No marsh [and proceeded?] towards CURLU.	
	No Sign [Enemy?]	
25.11.15.	9.15 a.m. Smoke of train seen moving N. towards CLERY SUR SOMME	
	10.5 a.m. " " " " " " S. from "	
	11.0 a.m. Enemy aeroplane flew S to N along river SOMME passing over marsh.	
	11.30 a.m. Punt with 2 men started on river close to LA GRENOUILLERE	
	12.55 p.m. Enemy transport wagon drawn by 2 horses left HEM by road going E towards CLERY SUR SOMME	
	1.55 p.m. One mounted man entered HEM by road from East.	

[signature]
Major
5: [?]

[signature]
4 pm
25/11/15.

WAR DIARY or INTELLIGENCE SUMMARY

Army Form C. 2118.

Hour, Date, Place		Summary of Events and Information	Remarks and references to Appendices
VAUX.	25-11.15. 2.15 p.m.	2/Lt Bishop and one N.C.O left Duck Post and Explored Ground & river towards FRISE. Way completed. Landing place as were found but were all old.	ALBERT. 1-40.000.
	10.p.m.	2/Lt Bishop and large patrol proceeded to CAUSEWAY at MOULIN. No Signs of enemy.	
	26.11.15. 7.20 A.M.	Working party on railway embankment N.W. of CLERY SUR SOMME seen.	
	7.40 A.M.	Party of Germans seen entering HEM from East.	
	8.15 A.M.	Smoke from same seen travelling S. through I.14.D	
	9.10 A.M.	do	
	9.45 A.M.	2/Lt Bishop and N.C.O examined waterways between VAUX and FARGNY. No new tracks found. A punt was drowned near FARGNY. It had apparently been used by troops at MOULIN, it was brought to Posts to-day.	
	10 A.M.	Patrol visited FARGNY Causeway and for enable along line of Esplanes. No signs of enemy. I Curlu a telegraph wire insulator was found & brought to H.Q. while horse went & drove to Church.	
	10.57 A.M.	Three German Aeroplanes flying E over Posts for some time.	
	1.20 p.m.	German on cycle entered CURLU Road from ME wearing dark blue uniform.	

26/4/15

Army Form C. 2118.

WAR DIARY
INTELLIGENCE SUMMARY.
(Erase heading not required.)

Instructions regarding War Diaries and Intelligence Summaries are contained in F.S. Regs., Part II. and the Staff Manual respectively. Title pages will be prepared in manuscript.

Place	Date	Hour	Summary of Events and Information	Remarks and references to Appendices
VAUX	25/11/15	9.5 AM	2 Allied Aeroplanes flew over Bois deVaux flying East.	
		9.20 AM	Officers Patrol proceeded in marsh to FARGNY Causeway, they then advanced towards CURLU Observation Northmoor revealed no landing places in front. Among poplars forked sticks were found upping rifle rests of German construction. No enemy seen.	
		1.0 pm	Heavy shelling on both sides S. of FRISE	

Isar Finkigan
S. Rutler Rgt

4 pm.
25/11/15.

WAR DIARY

INTELLIGENCE SUMMARY.

(Erase heading not required.)

Army Form C. 2118.

Place	Date	Hour	Summary of Events and Information	Remarks and references to Appendices
VAUX.	27: Nov.	9.50 a.m.	Patrol proceeded via marsh towards CURLU. No sign of enemy. Much noise coming from CURLU including driving of Stakes & village also sounds of children playing.	ALBERT 1-40.000
		10.15 a.m.	German Aeroplane passed over Eastern edge of Bois DEVAUX flying north.	
		2.20 p.m.	Enemy Saussiche Balloon up behind SE edge of Bois de METEROCOURT.	

27/11/15. A.p.m.

L. V. Rush
Major
1st Rif. Rif.

5th Div. Pioneers

5th CHESHIRES

December

1915

Army Form C. 2118

WAR DIARY
1/5th Bn. Cheshire Regiment.
INTELLIGENCE SUMMARY
(Erase heading not required.)

Instructions regarding War Diaries and Intelligence Summaries are contained in F.S. Regs, Part II. and the Staff Manual respectively. Title Pages will be prepared in manuscript.

Place	Date	Hour	Summary of Events and Information	Remarks references Appendices
BRAY	3.12.1915		The Battalion Sappers rejoined the Battalion at BRAY from BOIS DE VAUX.	48.
BRAY	16.12.1915		One man wounded by rifle fire whilst on working party behind No. 22 Fire Trench (near MARICOURT).	48.
BRAY	18.12.1915		Captain W. VERNON (claims Brien 5th Division) admitted to Hospital.	48.
BRAY	23.12.1915		One man wounded by shrapnel whilst on working party near BRAY.	48
BRAY	28.12.1915		One N.C.O. killed on the MARICOURT - SUZANNE road by Rifle fire.	48.
BRAY	29.12.1915		One man wounded on the SUZANNE - MARICOURT by Rifle fire. Twenty-nine Yorkshire Garment rejoined the Battalion at BRAY from SUZANNE when they were attached to the 14th Infantry Brigade.	48.
BRAY	31.12.1915		During the month of December the Battalion was employed building Shelters for the 5th Division Battle Headquarters and also for a Battalion. They were also employed repairing the following Avenues; In Sector B. the CARNOY and PERONNE Avenues. In Sector C. the LUCKNOW and SUFFOLK Avenues. Work was also done on the BRAY - CORBIE and the BRAY - CAPPY roads which were repaired in many places. D. Company, which still remained at SUZANNE, was employed in digging a new Fire Trench in front of No. 31 Fire Trench in Sector A, sub-sector A4. All four companies assisted in erecting steel shelters in and behind the Fire Trenches along the Divisional Front.	48

L Bengough Capt. Adjutant
1/5 Bn. Cheshire Regt.

1/1/15

www.ingramcontent.com/pod-product-compliance
Lightning Source LLC
Chambersburg PA
CBHW080848230426
43662CB00013B/2053